Lecture Notes in Computer

Commenced Publication in 1973
Founding and Former Series Editors:
Gerhard Goos, Juris Hartmanis, and Jan van Leeuwen

Boris Bellalta   Alexey Vinel   Magnus Jonsson
Jaume Barcelo   Roman Maslennikov
Periklis Chatzimisios   David Malone (Eds.)

Multiple Access Communications

5th International Workshop, MACOM 2012
Maynooth, Ireland, November 19-20, 2012
Proceedings

 Springer

Volume Editors

Boris Bellalta
Universitat Pompeu Fabra, Barcelona, Spain
E-mail: boris.bellalta@upf.edu

Alexey Vinel
Tampere University of Technology, Finland
E-mail: alexey.vinel@tut.fi

Magnus Jonsson
Halmstad University, Sweden
E-mail: magnus.jonsson@hh.se

Jaume Barcelo
Universitat Pompeu Fabra, Barcelona, Spain
E-mail: jaume.barcelo@upf.edu

Roman Maslennikov
University of Nizhny Novgorod, Russia
E-mail: roman.maslennikov@wcc.unn.ru

Periklis Chatzimisios
Alexander Technological Educational Institute of Thessaloniki
Sindos, Greece
E-mail: peris@it.teithe.gr

David Malone
National University of Ireland, Maynooth, Ireland
E-mail: david.malone@nuim.ie

ISSN 0302-9743   e-ISSN 1611-3349
ISBN 978-3-642-34975-1   e-ISBN 978-3-642-34976-8
DOI 10.1007/978-3-642-34976-8
Springer Heidelberg Dordrecht London New York

Library of Congress Control Number: 2012951532

CR Subject Classification (1998): C.2, H.4, K.6.5, D.4.6, C.2.4, H.3, D.2

LNCS Sublibrary: SL 5 – Computer Communication Networks and Telecommunications

Typesetting: Camera-ready by author, data conversion by Scientific Publishing Services, Chennai, India

Printed on acid-free paper

Springer is part of Springer Science+Business Media (www.springer.com)

Preface

It is our great pleasure to present the proceedings of the 5th International Workshop on Multiple Access Communications (MACOM) that was held in Maynooth during November 19–20, 2012.

Our gratitude goes to the Technical Program Committee and external reviewers for their efforts in selecting 18 high-quality contributions to be presented and discussed in the workshop. A total of 13 full papers were accepted for oral presentation and five contributions were presented in the demo&posters session. The demos represent a novelty in the MACOM program and are a great opportunity for interaction and experimentation with hands-on research.

The contributions gathered in these proceedings describe the latest advancements in the field of multiple access communications, with an emphasis of network coding, interference, location, and medium access control, as well as different aspects of wireless access networks.

Finally, we would like to take this opportunity to express our gratitude to all the participants, together with the local organizers, who helped to make MACOM 2012 a very successful event.

November 2012

Boris Bellalta
Alexey Vinel
Magnus Jonsson
Jaume Barcelo
Roman Maslennikov
Periklis Chatzimisios
David Malone

Organization

MACOM 2012 was organized by the Hamilton Institute from NUIM (National University of Ireland, Maynooth), Ireland.

Executive Committee

General Chairs

Alexey Vinel	TUT, Finland
Boris Bellalta	UPF, Spain
Magnus Jonsson	HH, Sweden

TPC Chairs

Jaume Barcelo	UPF, Spain
Roman Maslennikov	Wireless Competence Center of Lobachevsky State University of Nizhny Novgorod, Russia
Periklis Chatzimisios	ATEITHE, Greece

Local Chair

David Malone   Hamilton Institute, Ireland

Publication Chair

Cristina Cano   Hamilton Institute, Ireland

Technical Programme Committee

Sergey Andreev	Tampere University of Technology, Finland
Konstantin Avrachenkov	INRIA Sophia Antipolis, France
Abdelmalik Bachir	Imperial College London, UK
Jaume Barcelo	Universitat Pompeu Fabra, Spain
Boris Bellalta	Universitat Pompeu Fabra, Spain
Torsten Braun	University of Bern, Switzerland
Raffaele Bruno	IIT-CNR, Italy
Peter Buchholz	TU Dortmund, Germany
Cristina Cano	Hamilton Institute, Ireland
Andrea Cattoni	Aalborg University, Denmark
Eduardo Cerqueira	Federal University of Para, Brazil
Periklis Chatzimisios	Alexander Technological Educational Institute of Thessaloniki, Greece
Tugrul Dayar	Bilkent University, Turkey

Javier Del Ser	TECNALIA, Spain
Desislava Dimitrova	University of Bern, Switzerland
Alexander Dudin	Belarusian State University, Belarus
Alexey Dudkov	NRPL Group, Finland
Marc Emmelmann	Fraunhofer FOKUS, Germany
Azadeh Faridi	Universitat Pompeu Fabra, Spain
Olga Galinina	Tampere University of Technology, Finland
Gaoning He	Huawei Technologies, P.R. China
Geert Heijenk	University of Twente, The Netherlands
Andras Horvath	University of Turin, Italy
Gang Uk Hwang	KAIST, Korea
Magnus Jonsson	Halmstad University, Sweden
Eduard Jorswieck	Dresden University of Technology, Germany
Vinay Kolar	IBM Research Labs, India
Jonathan Loo	Middlesex University, UK
David Malone	NUI Maynooth, Ireland
Vincenzo Mancuso	Institute IMDEA Networks, Spain
Ninoslav Marina	Princeton University, USA
Roman Maslennikov	The University of Nizhny Novgorod, Russia
Dmitri Moltchanov	Tampere University of Technology, Finland
David Morales	Universitat Pompeu Fabra, Spain
Dmitry Osipov	IITP RAS, Russia
Edison Pignaton de Freitas	University of Brasilia, Brazil
Vicent Pla	Universitat Politecnica de Valencia, Spain
Claudio Sacchi	University of Trento, Italy
Zsolt Saffer	Budapest University of Technology and Economics, Hungary
Alexander Safonov	IITP RAS, Russia
Christian Schlegel	University of Alberta, Canada
Pablo Serrano	Universidad Carlos III de Madrid, Spain
Susanna Spinsante	Universitá Politecnica delle Marche, Italy
Dirk Staehle	Docomo Euro-Labs, Germany
Andrea Tonello	University of Udine, Italy
M. Angeles Vázquez-Castro	Universidad Autónoma de Barcelona, Spain
Alexey Vinel	Tampere University of Technology, Finland
Yan Zhang	Simula Research Laboratory and University of Oslo, Norway

Referees

Sergey Andreev	Raffaele Bruno	Periklis Chatzimisios
Konstantin Avrachenkov	Peter Buchholz	Javier Del Ser
Abdelmalik Bachir	Cristina Cano	Desislava Dimitrova
Jaume Barcelo	Andrea Cattoni	Alexey Dudkov
Boris Bellalta	Eduardo Cerqueira	Olga Galinina

Radhika Gowaikar
Hiroshi Harada
Magnus Jonsson
Eduard Jorswieck
Vinay Kolar
Ruizhi Liao
Jonathan Loo
David Malone
Ninoslav Marina

Roman Maslennikov
Jelena Mirkovic
R. Morelos-Zaragoza
Dong Nguyen
Vicent Pla
Denis Rosário
Zsolt Saffer
Alexander Safonov
Pablo Salvador

Luis Sanabria-Russo
Christian Schlegel
Pablo Serrano
Susanna Spinsante
Dirk Staehle
M.A. Vázquez-Castro
Alexey Vinel

Acknowledgements

- WIreless NEtworking for Moving Objects (WINEMO). IC0906 COST action
- Federated, Autonomic Management of End-to-end communication services (FAME): Science Foundation Ireland grant 08/SRC/I1403
- FLexible Architecture for Virtualizable future wireless Internet Access (FLAVIA) European Commission FP7-257263
- Spanish Ministry of Science and Innovation (TEC2008-06055/TEC)
- Foundations and Methodologies for Future Communication and Sensor Networks (COMONSENS). CONSOLIDER-INGENIO 2010

Table of Contents

Wireless Access Networks

Medium Access Control

Network Coding as a WiMAX Link Reliability Mechanism

Surat Teerapittayanon[1], Kerim Fouli[1], Muriel Médard[1],
Marie-José Montpetit[1], Xiaomeng Shi[1], Ivan Seskar[2],
and Abhimanyu Gosain[3],*

[1] Research Laboratory of Electronics (RLE), Massachusetts Institute of Technology
(MIT), Cambridge, MA 02139, USA
{steerapi,fouli,medard,mariejo,xshi}@mit.edu
[2] WINLAB, Rutgers University, Piscataway, NJ 08854, USA
seskar@winlab.rutgers.edu
[3] Raytheon BBN Technologies, Cambridge, MA 02138, USA
agosain@bbn.com

Abstract. We design and implement a network-coding-enabled reliability architecture for next generation wireless networks. Our network
coding (NC) architecture uses a flexible thread-based design, with each
encoder-decoder instance applying systematic intra-session random linear network coding as a packet erasure code at the IP layer. Using GENI
WiMAX platforms, a series of point-to-point transmission experiments
were conducted to compare the performance of the NC architecture
to that of the Automatic Repeated reQuest (ARQ) and Hybrid ARQ
(HARQ) mechanisms. In our scenarios, the proposed architecture is able
to decrease packet loss from around 11-32% to nearly 0%; compared to
HARQ and joint HARQ/ARQ mechanisms, the NC architecture offers
up to 5.9 times gain in throughput and 5.5 times reduction in end-to-
end file transfer delay. By establishing NC as a potential substitute for
HARQ/ARQ, our experiments offer important insights into cross-layer
designs of next generation wireless networks.

Keywords: ARQ, GENI, HARQ, Network Coding, WiMAX.

1 Introduction

Network Coding (NC) enables nodes to combine or separate transient bits, packets, or flows through coding and decoding operations, in addition to storing and
forwarding [1]. In a wireless setting, NC adapts to the dynamics of the network
topology. Numerous studies have shown that NC in Wireless Local Area Networks (WLANs) can significantly enhance throughput, robustness, and security.
Notably, 3-4x throughput gains were demonstrated in a WiFi context through

---

* The authors would like to thank Mr. H.E. Mussman (Raytheon BBN Tech.), Prof.
Giovanni Pau (UCLA), Drs. Danail Traskov, Ali ParandehGheibi, MinJi Kim, and
Jason Cloud for their invaluable support.

B. Bellalta et al. (Eds.): MACOM 2012, LNCS 7642, pp. 1–12, 2012.

the use of simple binary network codes [2]. Random Linear Network Coding (RLNC) [3], where the NC coefficients are selected randomly over a given Galois field, has proven effective in optimizing network resource consumption in WLANs [4]. Despite the demonstrated effectiveness of NC in WLANs, NC for Wireless Metropolitan Area Networks (WMANs) such as Worldwide Interoperability for Microwave Access (WiMAX) has gained attention only recently.

In this work, we design and implement an NC-enabled reliability architecture in a WiMAX platform provided by the Global Environment for Network Innovations (GENI) project. To alleviate the impact of wireless errors on performance, WiMAX adopts two retransmission mechanisms: Automatic Repeated reQuest (ARQ) at the upper MAC layer, and Hybrid ARQ (HARQ) at the lower MAC and PHY layers. In the proposed NC architecture, instead of using either or both of these mechanisms, we apply systematic intra-session RLNC as a packet erasure code at the IP layer. In particular, we consider a flexible thread-based design, where parallel encoding-decoding instances are put in place to ensure reliability is achieved without incurring significant delay. A series of point-to-point transmission experiments are conducted to compare the performance of our architecture to that of the HARQ and ARQ mechanisms. Since the GENI WiMAX base stations (BSs) only support chase combining (CC) HARQ, only CC-HARQ is considered in our study. At the application layer, *Iperf* and UDP-based File Transfer Protocol (*UFTP*) are used to measure throughput, packet loss, and file transfer delay. In our scenarios, the proposed architecture substantially decreases packet loss from around 11-32% to nearly 0%. Compared to the HARQ and HARQ-ARQ mechanisms, the NC architecture offers up to 5.9 times gain in throughput and 5.5 times reduction in end-to-end file transfer delay. Our experimental setups were limited by our ability to access and configure the GENI WiMAX platform. Nonetheless, our assessment of the NC reliability architecture illustrates its potential advantages over the HARQ/ARQ scheme, and offers exciting opportunities for further investigation.

The remainder of this article is organized as follows. Section 2 is an overview of NC-based HARQ/ARQ alternatives and enhancements. Section 3 describes the NC-based reliability architecture. Section 4 considers the experimental setup and introduces the performance metrics. Section 5 illustrates and discusses the main results. Finally, Section 6 concludes the paper.

2   Related Work

WiMAX uses two independent retransmission mechanisms for reliability: ARQ at the upper MAC layer and HARQ at the lower MAC and PHY layers. In ARQ, block retransmissions are processed independently; in HARQ, Forward Error Correction (FEC) and ARQ are combined, where subsequent retransmissions of a given information block are jointly processed. Retransmissions under HARQ and/or ARQ require the reception of positive (ACK) or negative (NACK) acknowledgment messages for each block, hence compounding overhead.

NC is initially studied as a capacity-achieving coding scheme for multicast in wired networks [1]. RLNC [3] is then proposed to make NC a practical scheme. A number of analytical works consider NC as an information-theoretic technique to improve throughput in wireless networks [5,6]. Packet retransmission using NC as a reliability mechanism, a scheme we call *retransmission coding*, has been widely studied. Some studies combine retransmission coding with HARQ (NC-HARQ), using XOR retransmission coding in conjunction with FEC, thus combining network and channel coding. In [7], we provide more detailed discussions of these prior works.

In this paper, we are interested in the use of NC in a WiMAX setting. Most of the past work in this area has been based on the MAC RLNC (MRNC) scheme [8], where data blocks are segmented and coded together at the MAC layer. MRNC has been shown to offer a 10% gain in throughput over HARQ in single-hop transmissions. The adaptive extension of MRNC [9] outperforms regular MRNC by 28.4% and HARQ by 57.7% in terms of throughput. Adaptive MRNC uses the channel state information feedback to adjust dynamically packet size according to current channel conditions. It is also possible to restrict the number of retransmissions in MRNC to an upper bound [10], a constraint important for delay sensitive applications. N-in-1 NC [11] extends MRNC by coding over more than one block for retransmissions, and offers a throughput gain of up to 106% over conventional CC-HARQ. Despite the large number of studies covering NC as an alternative or enhancement to HARQ and ARQ mechanisms, they are limited to analysis and simulation, and none are supported by experimentation. To our knowledge, our work provides a first experimental implementation of NC as a throughput efficiency and reliability mechanism in a single-hop link.

3   NC-Enhanced Architecture

Our NC-enabled reliability architecture is implemented in user-space as an NC module at the IP layer, as shown in Fig. 1. It acts as an encoder at the base station (BS) and as a decoder at the subscriber station (SS). At the BS, the source application sends outgoing IP packets to the Operating System (OS) where the transport and IP layers are run. A Linux packet filtering framework (*netfilter*) [12] 1. intercepts those packets and 2. sends them to the encoder NC module in user-space; 3. the encoder returns to the OS coded IP packets, which traverse the WiMAX stack. At the SS, netfilter intercepts the incoming coded IP packets handed from WiMAX to the OS and delivers them to the NC decoder. Decoded packets are sent back to the OS, where they are forwarded to the destination application. In the NC-enhanced architecture, ARQ and HARQ, run at the upper and lower MAC sublayer respectively, are switched off. Table 1 lists the key design parameters for the proposed NC module, and variables derived from these parameters. Exact definitions of these will be provided below.

The NC module uses a flexible thread-based design, where parallel encoding-decoding instances process packets concurrently. Systematic intra-session RLNC is applied. The encoder and decoder processes each have a master thread and N_p

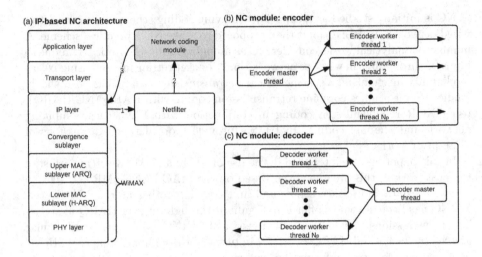

Fig. 1. (a) IP-based NC architecture, with (b) Encoder, and (c) Decoder modules

Table 1. Design parameters and variables for the NC Module

	Parameter Description		Variable Description
N_p	concurrent encoder-decoder thread pairs	L_s	calculated segment length
L_t	buffer list length threshold	N_s	calculated number of segments
T_i	buffer list processing time threshold	L_o	length of outgoing IP packet
L_m	maximum length of segments	L_b	coding block length
N_r	preferred number of segments	L_p	length of the current IP packet
N_k	rounds of redundancy transmission		(temporary)
N_m	redundancy packets per round		
T_r	time interval between each round		

worker threads, as shown in Fig. 1 (b) and (c). Each encoder-decoder thread pair operates independently from other pairs and is identified by a unique Thread ID (TID). The encoder master thread load-balances encoder worker threads by distributing incoming packets in a round-robin fashion. The decoder master thread dispatches incoming coded IP packets from encoder worker threads to the corresponding decoder worker threads according to their TID.

Encoding Mechanism. Fig. 2 illustrates the encoding mechanism.

(1) Incoming IP packets are first buffered at the master thread, and stored successively as a *buffer list*. Alg. 1 is used to determine when the buffer list is handed to the next worker thread. A timeout mechanism is combined with a maximum size trigger for buffer list concatenation, which occurs before time interval T_i or buffer length threshold L_t are reached.

(2) At a worker thread, the block is concatenated into a block.

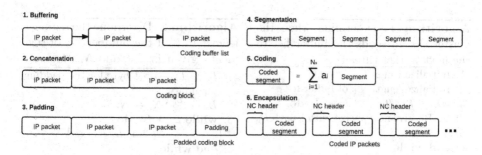

Fig. 2. Encoder process

(3) Byte padding is applied so that the padded block is a multiple of the number of segments N_s. N_s and segment length L_s are calculated according to Alg. 2.

(4) The padded block is divided into *segments*, the basic unit of operation for the NC module.

(5) Segments are coded according to Alg. 3 with *systematic* RLNC: N_s uncoded *systematic* segments are first generated, followed by *nonsystematic* segments generated with random coefficients. Up to N_k rounds of N_m nonsystematic segments are transmitted. There is an inter-round pause of duration T_r to allow other threads to process their blocks. Note that, although a received ACK terminates the encoding process, the encoder does not require ACKs to operate. Encoding may be terminated when N_k rounds are completed, thus protecting against inefficiencies due to ACK errors or losses. RLNC if performed in a Galois Field of size 2^8 [3], thus each coefficient is expressed as a byte. To reduce overhead, we include in the coded packet the seed for the pseudo-random number generator, rather than coding coefficients.

(6) Each coded segment is encapsulated with a NC header to generated a coded IP packet. The NC header contains the IP header, Thread ID (TID), Block ID (BID), Segment ID (SID), number N_s of segments, and coding coefficients. Hence, although segment size is constant for each block, it varies among blocks depending on traffic intensity. Detailed description of the NC header is provided in [7].

The Code Rate (CR) of the presented design is defined as the ratio of the number N_s of segments, to the sum of N_s and the redundancy segments:

$$CR \equiv \frac{N_s}{N_s + N_k \times N_m},\tag{1}$$

where N_k is the number of redundancy rounds, and N_m is the number of redundancy segments transmitted per round. Note that this is an upper bound on the effective code rate, as an ACK may interrupt transmission before the N_k rounds of N_m redundancy segments is completed. More detailed discussions of design considerations are provided in [7].

Algorithm 1. Determine when the master thread sends the buffer list to the next worker thread

1: Initialize timer T
2: Initialize length L_b of buffer list
3: **while** $T < T_i$ **and** $L_b < L_t$ **do**
4:     Receive new packet with length L_p
5:     $L_b \leftarrow L_b + L_p$
6: **end while**
7: Transfer buffer list to next worker thread

Algorithm 2. Determine the segment length L_s and the number N_s of segments, given L_b, L_m, and N_r

1: $L_b \leftarrow L_b + 1 \triangleright 1$ byte for the padding boundary.
2: $L_s \leftarrow \frac{L_b}{N_r}$, $N_s \leftarrow N_r$
3: **while** $L_s > L_m$ **do**
4:     $N_s \leftarrow N_s + 1$, $L_s \leftarrow \lceil \frac{L_b}{N_s} \rceil$
5: **end while**

Algorithm 3. Encode. Terminate immediately if an ACK for the same coding block is received.

1: **for** $x = 1 \rightarrow N_s$ **do**
2:     generate an uncoded segment.
3: **end for**
4: **while** ACK has not yet been received. **do**
5:     **for** $y = 1 \rightarrow N_k$ **do**
6:         **for** $z = 1 \rightarrow N_m$ **do**
7:             generate a coded segment.
8:         **end for**
9:         wait for duration T_r
10:     **end for**
11: **end while**

Algorithm 4. Block decode. **M** is the coefficient matrix of incoming coded packets (pkts). $\mathbf{M}[r + 1]$ is the r+1-th row of **M**.

1: $r \leftarrow 0$, $\mathbf{M}_{N_s \times (N_s + L_s)} \leftarrow \mathbf{0}$
2: **for** each incoming coded IP pkt N_p **do**
3:     Gauss-Jordan elimination on $(r + 1) \times (N_s + L_s)$ of **M**
4:     **if** $rank(\mathbf{M}) = r + 1$ **then**
5:         $r \leftarrow r + 1$
6:         **if** $r = N_s$ **then**
7:             done decoding
8:         **end if**
9:     **end if**
10: **end for**

Decoder and Feedback Mechanisms. At a decoder worker thread, operations described in Fig. 2 are reversed in order to recover the original IP packets. First, decapsulation strips off the NC header. For each reassembled coded block, received coded IP packets are decoded progressively using Gauss-Jordan elimination based on Alg. 4. Once a block is decoded, the decoder worker thread sends an ACK packet, which contains the IP header, TID and BID.

4   Experimental Setup and Performance Metrics

The proposed architecture is implemented over a WiMAX IEEE-802.16 downlink (DL) available through the GENI collaborative research framework [13]. Four fixed DL modulation and coding schemes (MCSs) and transmission power levels are available at the BS. For each of those PHY layer settings, 11 reliability configurations are run. For each of the reliability configurations, two transmission trials are conducted through Iperf and UFTP, respectively. At the GENI WiMAX stations, the default HARQ and ARQ settings are used [7].

Table 2. Available Downlink and Uplink PHY Settings

Downlink					Uplink
MCS	Tx. Power	PHY Rate	CINR	RSSI	MCS
64 QAM CTC 1/2	13 dBm	15.120 Mbps	13 dB	-76 dBm	QPSK, 1/2
64 QAM CTC 2/3	17 dBm	20.160 Mbps	17 dB	-76 dBm	Tx. Power
64 QAM CTC 3/4	18 dBm	22.680 Mbps	18 dB	-75 dBm	-63 dBm
64 QAM CTC 5/6	20 dBm	25.200 Mbps	18 dB	-73 dBm	Rate: 1.344 Mbps

Table 3. Reliability Configurations with Code Rate

Table 4. NC parameters

Config	ARQ	HARQ	NC	CR
Raw	OFF	OFF	OFF	1
HARQ	OFF	ON	OFF	variable
HARQ-ARQ	ON	ON	OFF	variable
NC-10	OFF	OFF	ON, $N_m = 10$	12/13 = 0.92
NC-15	OFF	OFF	ON, $N_m = 15$	8/9 = 0.89
NC-20	OFF	OFF	ON, $N_m = 20$	6/7 = 0.86
NC-24	OFF	OFF	ON, $N_m = 24$	5/6 = 0.83
NC-30	OFF	OFF	ON, $N_m = 30$	4/5 = 0.80
NC-40	OFF	OFF	ON, $N_m = 40$	3/4 = 0.75
NC-60	OFF	OFF	ON, $N_m = 60$	2/3 = 0.67
NC-120	OFF	OFF	ON, $N_m = 120$	1/2 = 0.50

Param	Value
N_p	1
N_k	1
T_r	0 ns
T_i	1 s
L_t	22400 bytes
L_m	1400 bytes
N_r	120
N_m	Follows NC config index

PHY/MAC Settings, Reliability Configurations, and Transmission Trials. At the physical layer, four fixed DL MCSs and BS transmission power levels are available, with increasing PHY code rates and power levels. These are listed in Table 2, along with Carrier to Interference plus Noise Ratio (CINR), Received Signal Strength Indication (RSSI) and Average Tx Power, measured at the SS. Owing to a fixed 10 Mhz channel bandwidth, the corresponding [14] PHY data rates are also shown. For each PHY setting, we run a number of reliability configurations with different NC, HARQ, and ARQ settings. In particular, for HARQ, PDU SN extended sub-header reordering is enabled and the maximum number of retransmissions is set to 4. For detailed PHY-layer parameters, see [7].

For each PHY setting, the 11 tested reliability configurations are shown in Table 3, where N_m is the number of redundancy packets per round in NC. Table 3 also lists the code rate of each NC configuration. We set NC parameters to the configurations summarized in Table 4. Note that a single thread ($N_p = 1$) is implemented, and a single redundancy round ($N_k = 1$) of N_m packets is transmitted immediately ($T_r = 0$) after the block.

For each PHY setting and reliability configuration, two transmission trials are conducted. First, Iperf [15] is used to measure throughput and loss, then UFTP [16] is employed to measure file transfer delay. Both application-layer tools deploy UDP as the underlying transport protocol, offering a load of 6Mbps at a fixed 1400-byte packet-size. The offered load is thus well below the effective DL PHY data rates of Table 2. Each individual Iperf trial is terminated after a fixed duration of 60 s, whereas the UFTP transmissions are run until a 50MByte file is successfully transferred. Note that measured losses are observed at the application layer (through Iperf), as lower-layer statistics are not accessible.

Performance Metrics. We report the following performance metrics for each reliability configuration.

DL Iperf loss percentage is the percentage of packets lost over the total number of packets over the duration of the experiment.

DL Iperf throughput, loss and redundancy bandwidth: The throughput is the number of packets successfully received by Iperf over the duration of the experiment. The bandwidth loss is calculated by subtracting the throughput from the offered load. The redundancy bandwidth is the additional bandwidth used beyond the offered load for the propose of redundancy (i.e., in the raw case, it is 0). For HARQ and HARQ-ARQ, since performance measurements are not available, we assume a best-case scenario where redundancy bandwidth is 0. For NC, we simply approximate the redundancy bandwidth as

$$\frac{N_m}{N_r} \times o, \qquad (2)$$

where N_m and N_r are defined in Table 1 and o is the offered load. Note that for exact calculations, the computed number of segments N_s should replace N_r, and the actual redundancy bandwidth should include the NC header overhead.

DL Iperf Throughput to Loss plus Redundancy Ratio (TLR): A measure of link efficiency. Given the throughput T, the lost bandwidth L and the redundancy bandwidth R, TLR is calculated as

$$TLR \equiv \frac{T}{L + R}. \qquad (3)$$

DL UFTP file transfer delay is the total duration required for successful delivery of a file at the SS. Since UFTP includes its own application-layer NACK-based reliability process [16], the file transfer is completed when the transmitter receives no NACKs from the receiver.

5   Results and Discussion

We compare the results of the raw, HARQ and HARQ-ARQ configurations with the best NC configuration, which we term *NC-Best*. This is the NC scheme that yields the highest performance for any given measured metric. Full details of the experimental results can be found in [17], and a case-study is provided in [7] for the case of 64 QAM CTC 5/6 at 20dBm.

Fig. 3(a) shows the average DL loss. Observe that, as CR increases, the raw loss increases. However, losses for HARQ and HARQ-ARQ are higher for lower

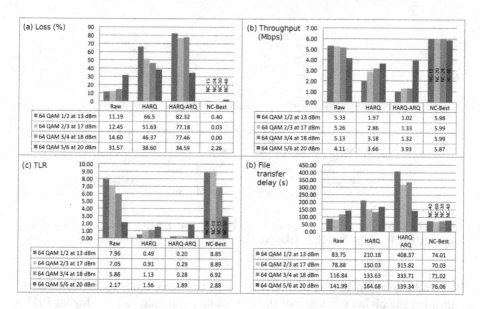

Fig. 3. Comparisons under an offer load of 6Mbps. (a) Average downlink (DL) loss (Iperf, 60s). (b) DL throughput (Iperf, 60s). (c) Throughput to loss plus redundancy ratio (TLR)(Iperf, 60s). (d) Downlink file transfer delay (UFTP, 50MB file).

CRs. The use of ARQ, in particular, increases losses significantly (15%–25%) under the three PHY settings with the lower rates. In contrast, the best NC configuration keeps losses close to 0% for all PHY settings.

Fig. 3(b) shows the average DL throughput. Note that the raw throughput refers to unreliable throughput, whereas HARQ and ARQ throughput represent reliable in-order packet flows. As expected from the loss results, when PHY CR increases, raw throughput decreases, whereas HARQ and HARQ-ARQ throughputs increase. The inefficiency of HARQ/ARQ at low PHY CRs may be due to the lower data rate available for DL retransmissions (see Table.3). The best NC configuration keeps throughput close to the full offered load of 6Mbps. Therefore, in addition to introducing a high level of reliability, NC is capable of multiplying the raw throughput by up to 1.4 times. More significantly, it multiplies the throughput of HARQ and HARQ-ARQ by up to 3.0 and 5.9, respectively.

Fig. 3(c) depicts the TLR. As CR increases, losses grow, leading to decreasing raw TLR levels. The NC configurations exhibit a similar decreasing profile. Although NC removes losses seen in the raw configuration almost entirely through redundancy, it remains more efficient than raw for all PHY settings. As for losses, TLR levels increase with higher PHY CRs for HARQ and HARQ-ARQ. Despite our ignoring any potential redundancy bandwidth in HARQ and HARQ-ARQ, they remain less efficient than NC.

Fig. 3(d) shows the DL file transfer delay. Observe that as PHY CR increases, raw delay tends to increase. Also, the delay figures here apply to best effort

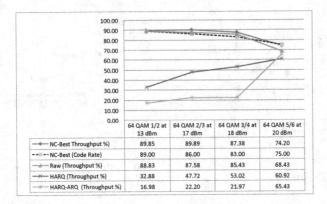

	64 QAM 1/2 at 13 dBm	64 QAM 2/3 at 17 dBm	64 QAM 3/4 at 18 dBm	64 QAM 5/6 at 20 dBm
NC-Best Throughput %)	89.85	89.89	87.38	74.20
NC-Best (Code Rate)	89.00	86.00	83.00	75.00
Raw (Throughput %)	88.83	87.58	85.43	68.43
HARQ (Throughput %)	32.88	47.72	53.02	60.92
HARQ-ARQ (Throughput %)	16.98	22.20	21.97	65.43

Fig. 4. The throughput percentage of Raw, HARQ and HARQ-ARQ, NC-Best compared to the CR of the NC-Best (the NC configuration with the highest throughput)

(BE) traffic flows. In HARQ and HARQ-ARQ, the delay tends to decrease, thus confirming the higher efficiency of those reliability configurations at higher PHY CRs and CINR levels. Owing to its lower packet losses, NC maintains the lowest transfer delay of all the tested configurations, with a delay around 70s. NC reduces the file transfer delay by 1.9 times compared to raw, 2.8 times compared to HARQ and 5.5 times compared to HARQ-ARQ.

Discussion.   The trend across different PHY settings is consistent: NC configurations use the redundancy bandwidth to increase throughput and reduce losses significantly. In contrast, HARQ and HARQ-ARQ reduce throughput and increase losses, particularly at lower PHY code rates. The loss percentage graph of Fig. 3(a) shows that NC works well as a packet erasure code.

The amount of loss reduction and throughput gains of NC configurations depend on the number N_m of redundancy packets per round. Although not shown explicitly in this paper, under each PHY setting, it can be observe that a large N_m may not be necessary, while a small N_m may not be sufficient [17,7]. When N_m is too small, most coded blocks cannot be recovered, incurring additional loss, reducing throughput and increasing file transfer delay. When N_m is too large, redundant packets become overheads, leading to possible buffer overflows. Intuitively, the optimal N_m should be at a level that makes the resulting NC CR match the raw throughput percentage, i.e., by sending an appropriate amount of redundancy a priori with the NC scheme, the raw unreliable throughput is fully utilized while reliability is achieved. Indeed, Fig. 4 shows that the raw throughput percentage closely matches the CRs of NC-Best (dashed line). Also observe that the throughput percentages of HARQ and HARQ-ARQ show large gaps when compared to the best NC schemes, particularly at low PHY CRs.

At a load of 6 Mbps, HARQ and ARQ do not perform well. Compared to raw, HARQ and HARQ-ARQ show additional losses, reduced throughput and increased delays. Their performances improve as PHY CRs increase, although they do not outperform NC in our experiments. The low performance of HARQ and ARQ may be due to faulty implementation or non-optimal default parameters (e.g., delay timeouts, maximum number of retransmissions), which we were not able to verify due to limited access to the WiMAX platform.

Our experimental results suggest that NC has a potential to replace HARQ and ARQ in future wireless network design. One way of interpreting the potential advantages of the proposed NC architecture over HARQ/ARQ is to view the latter as an a posteriori repetition code adaptation mechanism, with rates determined by the number of reactive retransmissions for each unit of data. Since retransmissions are packet-specific, the rate granularity is low, and the maximum rate is small. By comparison, NC formulates unique packets into equivalent degrees of freedom (dofs), offering three advantages as a code adaptation scheme. First, coded packets can be sent a priori, in expectation of losses, thus reducing the effect of large round trip times in ARQ. Second, each newly received dof can make up for any previously lost packet, thus leading to rate adaptation in steps of 1/block-size, where a block is the group of data packets coded together. Third, HARQ/ARQ rely heavily on the acknowledgment process, thus is prone to ACK/NACK errors, delays, and losses, which in turn can result in inefficient retransmission of correctly received packets. NC is less sensitive, since each transmitted coded packet is a new dof that can be useful in decoding. The combination of proactive transmissions, rate adaptation with a finer granularity, and robustness to ACK losses makes NC an efficient alternative reliability mechanism with low overhead. It is also more in-line with the ever increasing speed and performance of a priori adaptative modulation and coding at PHY.

6   Conclusions

This work proposes and demonstrates a network-coding (NC) enabled reliability architecture for next generation wireless networks. In our design, NC is used as a packet erasure code providing resilience against errors below the IP layer. We validate our design through an experimental case study at a GENI WiMAX site. We compare our NC architecture to default HARQ and ARQ in terms of packet loss, throughput and file transfer delay. We demonstrate that NC is potentially superior as a packet erasure code. Compared to HARQ and ARQ, NC potentially offers a gain of 5.9 times in throughput and a reduction of 5.5 times in file transfer delay. Our experimental setups were limited by our ability to access and configure the GENI WiMAX platform. Owing to its flexibility and simplicity, the proposed NC architecture may become crucial in providing more efficient next generation wireless network services through low-cost upgrades.

This initial architectural design opens up a number of new and exciting venues for future investigation. Apart from varying the parameters of the proposed NC schemes and investigating the performance sensitivity under different offered loads, wider access to the wireless communication equipment (i.e., WiMAX BS and SS, in our case) would enable a more complete study, encompassing features such as signal-to-noise ratio (SNR) and power control, HARQ and ARQ fine-tuning, operation under adaptive modulation and coding (AMC), and mobility.

In addition, the joint optimization of rate and power control under NC would be a valuable next step. The optimization of the decoding time is also an interesting direction to pursue. Different decoding algorithms such as the Jacobi iterative method for finite field matrix inversion may be considered.

Acknowledgment. The authors are grateful to Mr. Harry E. Mussman (Raytheon BBN Technologies) and Pr. Giovanni Pau (UCLA) for their support. They also thank Drs. Danail Traskov, Ali ParandehGheibi, MinJi Kim and Mr. Jason Cloud for their assistance. The authors thank NEC Corporation for making a state of the art IEEE 802.16e WiMAX base station available to the GENI project.

References

1. Ahlswede, R., Cai, N., Li, S.Y.R., Yeung, R.W.: Network information flow. IEEE Trans. Inf. Theory 46(4), 1204–1216 (2002)
2. Katti, S., Rahul, H., Hu, W., Katabi, D., Médard, M., Crowcroft, J.: Xors in the air: practical wireless network coding. ACM SIGCOMM Computer Comm. Rev. 36, 243–254 (2006)
3. Ho, T., Médard, M., Koetter, R., Karger, D.R., Effros, M., Shi, J., Leong, B.: A random linear network coding approach to multicast. IEEE Trans. Inf. Theory 52(10), 4413–4430 (2006)
4. Jakubczak, S., Rahul, H., Katabi, D.: One-size-fits-all wireless video. ACM SIG-COMM HotNets (2009)
5. Lun, D., Médard, M., Koetter, R., Effros, M.: On coding for reliable communication over packet networks. Physical Communication 1(1), 3–20 (2008)
6. Dana, A., Gowaikar, R., Palanki, R., Hassibi, B., Effros, M.: Capacity of wireless erasure networks. IEEE Trans. Inf. Theory 52(3), 789–804 (2006)
7. Teerapittayanon, S., Fouli, K., Médard, M., Montpetit, M.J., Shi, X., Seskar, I., Gosain, A.: Network coding as a WiMAX link reliability mechanism. Arxiv (2012)
8. Jin, J., Li, B., Kong, T.: Is random network coding helpful in WiMAX? In: INFO-COM 2008, pp. 2162–2170 (2008)
9. Jin, J., Li, B.: Adaptive random network coding in WiMAX. In: ICC 2008, pp. 2576–2580 (2008)
10. Yazdi, A., Sorour, S., Valaee, S., Kim, R.: Optimum network coding for delay sensitive applications in WiMAX unicast. In: INFOCOM 2009, pp. 2576–2580 (2009)
11. Li, Z., Luo, Q., Featherstone, W.: N-in-1 retransmission with network coding. IEEE Trans. Wireless Commun. 9(9), 2689–2694 (2010)
12. The netfilter.org project, http://www.netfilter.org
13. Global Environment for Network Innovations (GENI), http://www.geni.org
14. Andrews, J., Ghosh, A., Muhamed, R.: Fundamentals of WiMAX: understanding broadband wireless networking. Prentice Hall (2007)
15. Iperf, http://sourceforge.net/projects/iperf/
16. Bush, D.: UFTP, http://www.tcnj.edu/~bush/uftp.html
17. Teerapittayanon, S.: Performance enhancements in next generation wireless networks using network coding: A case study in WiMAX. Master's thesis, MIT (2012)

Initialization Procedure of Wireless Network Coding with Hierarchical Decode and Forward Strategy in Random Connectivity Networks

Tomas Hynek and Jan Sykora

Faculty of Electrical Engineering, Czech Technical University in Prague,
Technicka 2, 166 27 Prague, Czech Republic
{hynektom,Jan.Sykora}@fel.cvut.cz

Abstract. A Wireless Network Coding (WNC) a.k.a. a Physical Layer
Network Coding in multi-source multi-node scenarios has shown its potential to increase network throughput compared to a communication
based on an orthogonal separation of individual transmissions. In this
paper we analyse necessary steps that have to be done to initialize the
WNC communication including mainly establishing of relay operations.
In our set-up a core network (we named it *a cloud*), that provides the
WNC capabilities of reliable source – destination communication, starts
its operation with no system state (connectivity) knowledge. Our goal is
to design an algorithm that is capable to gain this information directly
from the received constellation that is formed by the superposition of unknown number of transmitting sources with random channel realization
and provide it to any cloud node. The algorithm has to be designed to
work with the minimum demands on source node cooperation, the most
of the functionality is laid upon the cloud.

Keywords: Physical Layer, Wireless Network Coding, Automatic Modulation Classification.

1 Introduction and Related Work

Multi-source multi-node networks have attracted an interest of research community in recent years. For wired networks it was shown that the routing with
orthogonally (in time, frequency, orthogonal code, hopping sequence, etc. or any
of their combination) separated users is suboptimal in the terms of achievable capacity. Improvement of the network throughput can be achieved by a technique
called a Network Coding (NC) [1], when the intermediate network nodes are
capable to provide defined operations upon the incoming data instead of simple
storing and forwarding. The NC was developed for wired network thus it assumes
dedicated communication channels among the network nodes. The extension to
the wireless environment is not a simple procedure. It introduces novel issues
far different from the wired networks, especially natural broadcast behaviour,
inherent superposition of the signals, unavoidable channel parametrization etc.

B. Bellalta et al. (Eds.): MACOM 2012, LNCS 7642, pp. 13–24, 2012.
© Springer-Verlag Berlin Heidelberg 2012

In recent years many authors try to develop techniques for the extension of the NC principle to the wireless networks. We call this extension a Wireless Network Coding (WNC) it is also known as a Physical Layer Network Coding (PLNC). Various signal processing schemes performed by the network nodes on the data were proposed. Strategies basically differ in the fact whether the intermediate nodes make or do not make a decision about some function of data. This leads to a variety of Decode/Compute/Amplify/Compress & Forward techniques [2,3,4]. Throughout this article we will consider one particular strategy named a Hierarchical Decode & Forward (HDF) [4] in unknown stochastic wireless connectivity scenario.

To the best of our knowledge any paper that deals with the initialization of the WNC procedure in stochastic unknown connectivity network is not known. All previous works assume a priori given network topology that is known to all network nodes, especially to the relays, that are able to utilize it when defining proper WNC operations. In a real world situation the source nodes are expected to be able to access the communication in an ad-hoc manner. The cloud is thus uncertain about the state of the network, e.g. the number of communicating nodes, the node connectivity and channel states are unknown. During the initialisation every inter-cloud node has to obtain the information mainly about the number of the sources in the neighbourhood together with their channel parametrization to be able to design its WNC operations properly. In the case of the WNC/HDF this mainly means establishing of proper relay input-output relation named a HDF map. Note that some kind of initialization (recovery of the unknown environment) in random connectivity networks is necessary for any other Decode/Compute/Amplify/Compress & Forward WNC technique.

A classical solution for ad-hoc networks is based on a dedication of individual source specific identification keys (addresses, pilot signals, training sequences etc.). This approach has a lot of drawbacks – the number of the sources is limited by the finite number of available resources that has to be distributed a priori to all source nodes. This needs a huge amount of the network coordination. The solution proposed in this paper tries to recover the necessary information with minimum source – cloud cooperation. Due to this the source can access the network, communicate and disconnect from the network selfishly, totally ignorant to any source in its neighbourhood. This property is very well suited to ad-hoc networks. Source identification sequences are also used but they are generated randomly and independently by the sources. These sequences do not need to be known at the receiving relay and serves only to recover uncertain network state. An Automatic Modulation Classification (AMC) is performed at the PHY layer over *the superimposed constellation that is random due to the random network topology and the random channel parametrization* to obtain the network state information. This solution can be seen as a non-coherent approach since no projection or match filtering of training sequences or pilot signals is performed. The very similar, but coherent, non-coordinated method is to dedicate the orthogonal identifications to the sources in a random way. Each cloud node performs a projection to the space of identifications in a step by step manner to recover what sources are included within the transmission and thus recover the necessary information to establish WNC/HDF mapping operation. The other possible solution is to design a network topology tolerant scheme based on random channel classes [5] that inherently deals with uncertain node connectivity at the cost of increased demands in the following communication steps.

It is important to note that the initialization procedure only provides necessary information to establish WNC/HDF communication – particularly the relay HDF maps has to be designed. No useful data payload is transmitted during this step. The useful data are transmitted in the consecutive stages with possibly far different modulation and coding schemes. The initialization procedure has to be repeated from time to time as the network state changes.

The rest if the paper is organised as follows. Section 2 provides the definitions and the model of the network. In section 3 the initialization of the cloud is formally described, this section also explain the necessity of the cloud initialization. K-means clustering and its application in the initialization process is described in section 4. Section 5 discuss the channel estimation abilities. The numerical results are presented in section 6 and the paper is concluded in section 7.

2   System Model and Background

Our wireless communication system consist of three elements – a set of N_S sources $\mathcal{S} = \{S_1, \cdots, S_i, \cdots, S_{N_S}\}$, a set of destinations $\mathcal{D}$ and of a wireless distributed self-organized entity named a cloud. The cloud is formed by N_R nodes $\mathcal{R} = \{R_1, \cdots, R_j, \cdots, R_{N_R}\}$ that are neither sources nor destinations. The key functionality of the cloud is to establish the reliable wireless connection between the sources and the destinations. See Fig.1.

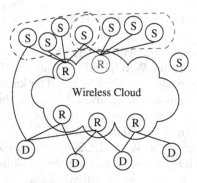

Fig. 1. Network topology

The cloud operations in our case are based on the Wireless Network Coding with the Hierarchical Decode & Forward strategy (WNC/HDF), HDF details are beyond the scope of this paper, [4] provides detailed formal description. This signal processing is a decode & forward type thus the relay makes the decision about the received signal. When the HDF strategy is applied the relay decided about the whole received superposition which jointly represents all of incoming transmissions. This forms a virtual hierarchical alphabet made of so called hierarchical symbols. But the concrete form of the hierarchical alphabet depends on the way how the signals are superposed, i.e. on the channel parametrization, individual source alphabets, number of the sources, etc.

For simplicity let us assume two sources communicating over the shared relay. Each source independently produces symbols c_A, c_B. The relay estimates the hierarchical symbol $\hat{c}_{AB}$ from the received superposition of the transmitted signals based on the extreme (e.g. max for simplicity) of some metric μ over all possible hierarchical symbols

$$\hat{c}_{AB} = \arg\max_{c_{AB}} \mu(c_{AB}) = \arg\max_{c_{AB}} \mu \left(\bigcup_{c_A, c_B : \mathcal{X}(c_A, c_B) = c_{AB}} \{c_A, c_B\} \right) . \qquad (1)$$

Note that another possible relay strategy a Joint Decode & Forward (JDF) tries to estimate both individual sources from the received observation

$$[\hat{c}_A, \hat{c}_B] = \arg\max_{c_A, c_B} \mu(c_A, c_B) . \qquad (2)$$

Hierarchical symbol is a joint representation of both individual data streams. If the hierarchical symbols are properly defined at the relay the destinations are able to recover the intended data by the help of the other observations. For simple one relay network the invertibility is formally given by an exclusive law [3,4]. For multi-relay networks the exclusive law is generalized in [6].

3   Cloud Initialization Procedure

During a Cloud Initialization Procedure (CIP) the cloud has to obtain all necessary information to start its WNC/HDF operations. The number of active users has to be known to design the HDF maps. The knowledge of the states of the individual wireless channels can be utilised to avoid the MAC phase failures caused by the channel parametrization or the MAC phase can be based on a parameter invariant design of modulations [3,7,8].

At the early beginning of the WNC/HDF operation the cloud nodes are assumed to use the full HDF maps [4] to ease the establishing of the source – destination communication. The map cardinalities can be significantly reduced later as long as the condition of the WNC invertibility is met at the destinations.

When the full HDF map is used the cardinality of the relay output is given by the product of the incoming transmission signal cardinalities and corresponds to classical Multi-user PHY communications (e.g. 2-user MAC channel). Due to the practical reasons the maximum output cardinality is limited to low powers of two. Hence the number of the source nodes operated by one relay has to be limited too. This becomes very important for complex networks with multiple relay layers (when the outgoing relay transmission is processed by other relay(s)).

By $\mathcal{S}_j \subseteq \mathcal{S}$ we denote the set of sources operated by the j-th relay R_j. Number of sources operated by this relay is denoted $|\mathcal{S}_j| = L_j$. Because of the full HDF maps used in the initial phases of the WNC/HDF operation we limit the maximum number of sources per one relay to $L_{MAX} = 4$.

An example of two sets of the operated sources of two relays is depicted in Fig.1. It is important to note that two distinct sets $\mathcal{S}_i$ and $\mathcal{S}_j$ can have non empty intersection $\mathcal{S}_i \cap \mathcal{S}_j \neq \emptyset$ in fact to utilize all of the benefits of the WNC/HDF it is necessary that the source transmission passes through the cloud along several different paths.

Our aim is to design a tractable algorithm for the CIP that provides to the cloud all necessary information about the sources to start the WNC/HDF operations. The goal is to make this algorithm as blind as possible. We want to avoid any orthogonal solution, any solution that needs complex cooperation among the nodes and/or a solution guided by any form of a genie.

The proposed algorithm is based on the Automatic Modulation Classification (AMC). We try to recover required parameters directly from the received constellation that is formed by the superposition of unknown number of transmitting sources with random channel realization. An exhaustive overview of the single source AMC techniques can be found in [9]. To the best of the authors' knowledge any publication dealing with the multi-source AMC is not known.

The proposed CIP algorithm is based on a blind clustering of the received constellation by simple k-means algorithm [10]. The only a priori assumptions are the perfect time synchronization of the sources and the cloud and given limit of the number of the operated sources L_{MAX} (4 in our case).

Since the sources transmit within the same time, frequency and code subspace each relay $R_j \in \mathcal{R}$ receives the superposition of the transmissions

$$y_j(t) = \sum_{i:S_i \in \mathcal{S}_j}^{L_j} h_{ij} s_i(t) + w_j(t) \tag{3}$$

where $h_{ij} \in \mathbb{C}$ is the channel state between the source S_i and the relay R_j, $s_i(t)$ is the signal transmitted by the source S_i, $w_j(t)$ is the additive white Gaussian noise at the relay R_j with variance σ_w^2, L_j is the number of the sources operated by the relay R_j and the notation $i : S_i \in \mathcal{S}_j$ means such sources S_i that are operated by the relay R_j.

Throughout this paper we will assume a balance among the amplitudes of the channel states. $|h_{ij}| \ \forall i, j$ is a random variable with the uniform distribution on the closed interval $[0.5, 1]$. The channel phases $\angle h_{ij} \ \forall i, j$ are random variables with the uniform distribution on the closed interval $[0, 2\pi]$.

Constellation space model is

$$y_j[k] = \sum_{i:S_i \in \mathcal{S}_j}^{L_j} h_{ij} q_i[k] + w_j[k] \tag{4}$$

where k is used to index over the transmitted symbols and q_i are the channel symbols transmitted by the source S_i.

We define a signal to noise ratio (SNR) at the relay R_j by $\gamma_j = E[\|Q_j\|]^2/\sigma_w^2$, where $E[\|Q_j\|]^2$ is the energy of the superposition constellation which is a function of the number of the sources L_j, set of channel realizations $\{h_{ij}\}_{i:S_i \in \mathcal{S}_j}$ and the individual source channel alphabets $Q_i = \{q_i\} \; \forall i : S_i \in \mathcal{S}_j$. Operator $E[\cdot]$ denotes the expectation.

The CIP clustering algorithm works over the superposition constellation $Q_j(L_j, \{h_{ij}\}, Q_i) = \{q_j\} \; \forall i : S_i \in \mathcal{S}_j$ and tries to estimate the number of operated source L_j and the channel states $\{h_{ij}\}_{i:S_i \in \mathcal{S}_j}$ from it. To make the Q_j as simple as possible to ease the initialization the sources are assumed to utilize an On-Off Keying (OOK) modulation, i.e. $Q_i = \{0, 1\} \; \forall S_i \in \mathcal{S}$. Note again that during the CIP no useful data are transmitted, it serves only to resolve the uncertain network state.

After the reception of defined signalization (e.g. defined preamble) which serves only for timing synchronization from the cloud all synchronized sources start to simultaneously transmit the sequences of the OOK symbols. Due to the assumption of algorithm blindness the generated sequences are randomly and mutually independently drawn from the uniform distribution and thus no cooperation between the sources is needed. The relay R_j is expected to observe all 2^{L_j} constellation points of Q_j which is required by the clustering algorithm. This is guaranteed by the sufficient length of the transmission of the random sequence.

Define an event E meaning that the relay observes each constellation point of Q_j at least once. We want to find such a length of the sequence n_0 that guarantees $\Pr\{E\} \to 1$. This probability can be evaluated analytically by an inclusion-exclusion principle. Probability of the event E for various sequence length and various number of operated sources is plotted in Fig.2. One can see that the sequence length $n_0 = 150$ is sufficient for $\Pr\{E\} \to 1$ up to 4 (our L_{MAX}) operated users. For 4 sources and $n_0 = 150$ we have $\Pr\{E\} = 0.999$.

4   K-means Clustering

After the reception of n_0 length superimposed OOK sequences the relay R_j starts the clustering algorithm to estimate the number of operated users L_j and to estimate the set of the channel states $\{h_{ij}\}_{i:S_i \in \mathcal{S}_j}$. The algorithm is based on simple k-means algorithm [10] that proceeds in the following way:

Algorithm 1. k-means

    Place l points (initial centroids) randomly into the space of all received symbols $y_j[k]$
    while stop condition is not met **do**
        Assign each received point $y_j[k]$ to the closest centroid
        New centroids $\leftarrow$ points that minimize sum of squared inter-cluster distances
    end while

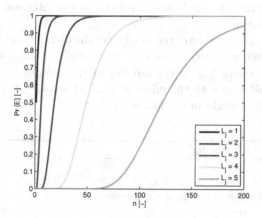

Fig. 2. Probability of the event E

The algorithm returns the position of the l centroids $\{c^{(1)}, \cdots, c^{(l)}\}$ and the identification to which cluster each received point belongs to. In the case of the signal space the used metric is the Euclidean distance. Although the k-means algorithm guarantees the termination the optimal solution is not guaranteed at all. The algorithm may converge to local optimum [10].

The correct number of clusters l is not known a priori since it is a function of the unknown number of the operated sources as well as the channel parametrization, i.e. $l(L_j, \{h_{ij}\}_{i:S_i \in \mathcal{S}_j})$. Thus we start k-means with different number of the clusters l from 1 to $2^{L_{MAX}}$. For some particular channel states some points in Q_j can fall close to or even upon each other and thus will be grouped into the same cluster. We choose the number of clusters l_{best} that fits best to the received constellation. The criterion is the minimum distance to all centroids, i.e. the total sum of the squared Euclidean distances among the centroids and the points corresponding to their clusters

$$d_{sum}(l) = \sum_{a=1}^{l} \sum_{b:y[b] \in c^{(a)}} |y[b] - c^{(a)}|^2 \tag{5}$$

where $b : y[b] \in c^{(a)}$ denotes received signal space points $y[b]$ that belong to the cluster with the centroid $c^{(a)}$.

The maximum possible number of distinct constellation points of Q_j is given by 2^{L_j}. The minimum number depends on concrete channel parametrizations, obviously the minimum is achieved when the channel gains h_{ij} are collinear and their amplitudes are constant $|h_{ij}| = $ const. For example two operated sources can produce up to four points – $Q_j = \{0, h_{1j}, h_{2j}, h_{1j} + h_{2j}\}$, see Fig.3a. Three distinct points can also happen – $Q_j = \{0, h_{1j}, h_{1j}, 2h_{1j}\}$ if $h_{1j} = h_{2j}$ or $Q_j = \{0, h_{1j}, -h_{1j}, 0\}$ if $h_{1j} = -h_{2j}$, see Fig.3b. It is important to note that the minimum number of the points cannot be arbitrary low, e.g. constellation with only two points for two operated sources is not possible. Remind that we do not allow $|h_{ij}|$ to go to zero.

Since the significant decrease of the number of the distinct constellation points of Q_j happens rarely we decide to estimate the number of operated sources by $\hat{L}_j = \lceil \log_2(l_{best}) \rceil$, where l_{best} is the number of the clusters that approximate the received constellation with the minimal $d_{sum}(l)$ among all possible l.

The CIP algorithm works in the following way:

Algorithm 2. CIP Clustering

Receive $y_j[k]$ $k \in \{1, \cdots, n_0\}$
Set the threshold d_{th} based on the SNR γ_j
Set the number of the repetitions of the k-means r_{MAX}
for $l = 1 \rightarrow 2^{L_{MAX}}$ **do**
    for $r = 1 \rightarrow r_{MAX}$ **do**
        perform the k-means over $y_j[k]$ $\forall k$ with l clusters
    end for
    remember the clustering with the minimal $d_{sum}(l)$
end for
$l_{best} \leftarrow$ Find the first l with $d_{sum}(l) \leq d_{th}$
if $d_{sum}(l) > d_{th}$ $\forall l$ **then**
    $l_{best} = 2^{L_{MAX}}$
end if
return $\hat{L}_j = \lceil \log_2(l_{best}) \rceil$
return $\{c\}_{best} = \left\{ c_{best}^{(1)}, \cdots c_{best}^{(l_{best})} \right\}$

The threshold value d_{th} depends on the SNR of received constellation γ_j as well as on the desired probability of correct detection. Fig.5 shows the probability of the correct detection of the number of the operated sources for various values of d_{th} as a function of the SNR. These curves can be used for adaptive choice of the d_{th} value based on the actual SNR to achieve the desired probability of the correct detection.

The application of the threshold value to obtain the best clustering is necessary due to the obvious property of the k-means algorithm – generally the higher the number of the clusters l the lower the $d_{sum}(l)$ can be. Evidently the best possible clustering (in terms of the minimal $d_{sum}(l)$) is the one when each cluster contains exactly one data point that coincides with the centroid of its cluster, i.e. $c^{(i)} = y[i]$ $\forall i$, this leads to $d_{sum} = 0$. Having the threshold value (according to the SNR and the desired probability of the correct detection) we choose the first solution with $d_{sum}(l) \leq d_{th}$ so as not to "over-cluster" the received data.

5   Channel Estimation Capabilities

From the estimation of the best position of the centroids $\{c\}_{best}$ the relay is able to estimate the channel states. Received superposition constellation Q_j

is formed by all possible binary linear combinations of the channel states, see Eq.(4). Estimation of the channel states can be described by the simple matrix equation

$$\mathbb{A}\mathbf{h}_j = \mathbf{b} \tag{6}$$

where $\mathbb{A}$ is a $(2^{\hat{L}_j} - 1) \times \hat{L}_j$ matrix of all possible non-zero binary $\hat{L}_j$-tuples, $\mathbf{h}_j = [h_{1j}, \cdots, h_{\hat{L}_j j}]^T$ is a vector of unknown channel states from $\hat{L}_j$ operated sources and the right-hand side vector $\mathbf{b}$ is an unknown ordering (possibly with repetitions of some elements) of the centroid positions $\{c\}_{best}$.

The goal is to find an appropriate ordering of the right-hand side vector $\mathbf{b}$. We illustrate this on a simple $L_j = 2$ example, see Fig.3a. By application of Algorithm 2 we obtain the correct estimate of the number of the operated source $\hat{L}_j = L_j = 2$ because the best clustering is the one with $l = 4$. We also obtain the positions of the centroids $\{c^{(1)}, c^{(2)}, c^{(3)}, c^{(4)}\}$ (red crosses in Fig.3a). One of them, let us say $c^{(4)}$, corresponds to the transmission of the zero OOK symbols and bears no information about the channel state.

In this example the particular form of Eq.(6) is

$$\begin{pmatrix} 1 & 1 \\ 1 & 0 \\ 0 & 1 \end{pmatrix} \begin{pmatrix} h_{1j} \\ h_{2j} \end{pmatrix} = \begin{pmatrix} c^{(u)} \\ c^{(v)} \\ c^{(w)} \end{pmatrix} . \tag{7}$$

The goal is to find a proper assignment between the estimated cluster centroids $\{c^{(1)}, c^{(2)}, c^{(3)}\}$ and its ordering $\{c^{(u)}, c^{(v)}, c^{(w)}\}$. From Eq.(7) it is obvious that we seek a pair of centroids that summed together gives the third one. If the solution is for example $c^{(1)} + c^{(2)} = c^{(3)}$ then $c^{(1)}$ and $c^{(2)}$ equals to h_{1j} and h_{2j}. Note that there is an ambiguity because we are not able to distinguish which channel parametrization belongs to which source. But this ambiguity can be neglected for symmetric HDF maps.

Similar procedure can be extended to more than two operated sources. But the assumption of the symmetric HDF maps is very strict and the channel estimation capabilities have to be deeply investigated.

6   Numerical Results

We have implemented the proposed Algorithm 2 in MATLAB and numerically evaluate its properties in various scenarios (number of operated sources, random channels, impact of the threshold level, etc.). The simulations mainly test the abilities of the CIP to correctly estimate the number of the communicating sources under random channel parametrizations. All simulations were performed with the following parameters: the random OOK sequence length $n_0 = 150$, the number of the repetitions of the k-means algorithm $r_{MAX} = 5$ and the maximum number of the operated sources $L_{MAX} = 4$. Figs.3a, 3b and 4 show the example results after the clustering of the received superposition of the randomly generated 150 symbols long OOK sequences with two respectively three sources for random channel parametrizations. Fig.3a shows the correct clustering in the case of two sources. The incorrect clustering is depicted in Fig.3b. Here the channel parametrizations cause two points of Q_j to fall close to each other and thus to be clustered within one cluster. It is important to note that the number of the operated sources is correctly estimated in this situation due to $\hat{L}_j = \lceil \log_2(l_{best}) \rceil$. On the other hand the incorrect clustering will complicate the channel estimation procedure and also the estimation error will increase. Fig.4 shows the correct clustering of the signal from three operated sources.

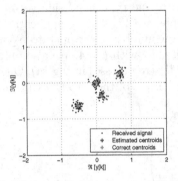 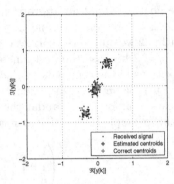

(a) Successful clustering $\gamma_j = 15$dB.   (b) Unsuccessful clustering $\gamma_j = 15$dB.

Fig. 3. Two source clustering

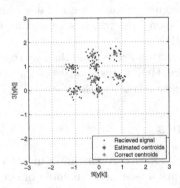

Fig. 4. Three sources - successful clustering $\gamma_j = 15$ dB

The performance of the CIP algorithm is significantly determined by the choice of the threshold value d_{th}. Fig.5 shows the probability of the correct estimation of the number of the operated sources parametrized by the threshold value, i.e. $\Pr\{L_j = \hat{L}_j | d_{th}\}$. The proposed algorithm achieves approximately 97% probability of the correct detection of the number of the operated sources at the high SNR regime. The optimal d_{th} is close to 3. At the lower SNRs the high probability of correct estimation can be achieved by adaptive selection of the threshold value according to the actual SNR.

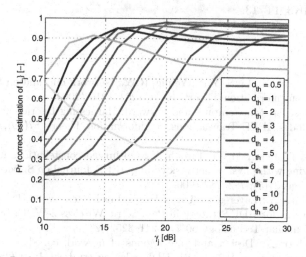

Fig. 5. Probability of the correct estimation of the number of the sources

7   Conclusions

In this paper we design a simple blind non-coherent algorithm that provides the estimation of the number of the operated sources to every cloud relay node. This knowledge is necessary for the proper design of the WNC/HDF operation at each relay. The proposed algorithm works in the distributed way and needs no cooperation between the sources. The only a priori assumption is the perfect time synchronization of the cloud that is revealed to the sources. The received superposition of known alphabets (but the number of the sources and the channel parametrization are unknown) is processed by the clustering algorithm based on the k-means. From the results of this clustering the number of operated sources is estimated and the position of the resulting centroids can serve for the channel estimation.

The algorithm is tested in scenarios that take into account the practical aspects of the wireless cloud entity. The numerical simulations show that the high probability (at about 97%) of the correct detection can be achieved at the high SNR regime in the AWGN channel with the properly set threshold value. At the lower SNR regime the threshold value can be adaptively optimized based on the measurement of SNR to maximize the probability of the correct detection.

Acknowledgement. Work in this paper was supported by the European Science Foundation through FP7-ICT SAPHYRE project the Grant Agency of the Czech Republic, grant 102/09/1624, the Ministry of education, youth and sports of the Czech Republic grant LD12062 and by the Grant Agency of the Czech Technical University in Prague, Grants no. SGS10/287/OHK3/3T/13 and SGS12/076/OHK3/1T/13.

References

1. Ahlswede, R., Cai, N., Li, S.-Y.R., Yeung, R.W.: Network information flow. IEEE Transactions on Information Theory 46(4), 1204–1216 (2000)
2. Nazer, B., Gastpar, M.: Compute-and-Forward: Harnessing Interference Through Structured Codes. IEEE Transactions on Information Theory 57(10), 6463–6486 (2011)
3. Koike-Akino, T., Popovski, P., Tarokh, V.: Optimized constellations for two-way wireless relaying with physical network coding. IEEE Journal on Selected Areas in Communications 27(5), 773–787 (2009)
4. Sykora, J., Burr, A.: Layered Design of Hierarchical Exclusive Codebook and Its Capacity Regions for HDF Strategy in Parametric Wireless 2-WRC. IEEE Transactions on Vehicular Technology 60(7), 3241–3252 (2011)
5. Sykora, J., Burr, A.: Design and rate regions of network coded modulation for random channel class in WNC with HDF relaying strategy. In: COST IC1004, Lyon, France, pp. 1–6 (2012)
6. Sykora, J., Burr, A.: Cooperative wireless network coding for uplink transmission on hierarchical wireless networks. In: COST IC1004, Barcelona, Spain, pp. 1–8 (2012)
7. Uricar, T., Sykora, J.: Non-Uniform 2-Slot Constellations for Bidirectional Relaying in Fading Channels. IEEE Communications Letters 15(8), 795–797 (2011)
8. Uricar, T., Sykora, J.: Design criteria for hierarchical exclusive code with parameter invariant decision regions for wireless 2-way relay channel. EURASIP J. Wireless Comm. and Networking (2010)
9. Dobre, O.A., Abdi, A., Bar-Ness, Y., Su, W.: Survey of automatic modulation classification techniques: classical approaches and new trends. IET Communications 1(2), 137–156 (2007)
10. MacQueen, J.B.: Some methods for classification and analysis of multivariate observations. In: Proc. of the Fifth Berkeley Symposium on Mathematical Statistics and Probability, pp. 281–297. University of California Press (1967)

Broadcasting XORs: On the Application of Network Coding in Access Point-to-Multipoint Networks

Kerim Fouli[1], Jérôme Casse[2], Ivan Sergeev[1],
Muriel Médard[1], and Martin Maier[3]

[1] Research Laboratory of Electronics (RLE), Massachusetts Institute of Technology
(MIT), Cambridge, MA 02139, USA
{fouli,vsergeev,medard}@mit.edu
[2] Department of Methematics and Applications,
École Normale Supérieure (ENS), Paris, France 75005
jerome.casse@ens.fr
[3] Optical Zeitgeist Laboratory, INRS, Montréal, Canada H5A 1K6
maier@emt.inrs.ca

Abstract. We investigate network coding (NC) in access point-to-multipoint (PMP) broadcast networks. Characterized by a shared unicast upstream channel and a time-shared broadcast downstream channel, PMP networks are widely deployed in optical and wireless access networks. We develop a queuing-theoretic model of NC at the medium access control (MAC) sublayer and analyze the impact of NC on packet delay. Our analysis is validated through discrete-event simulation and demonstrates significant delay advantages for NC under high loads and localized traffic.

Keywords: Access Networks, Network Coding, Packet Delay, Point-to-Multipoint, Polling.

1 Introduction

Network coding (NC) is an innovative technology that has been shown to improve throughput, simplify routing, and provide robustness against transmission errors and failures in various packet networks [1,2]. In addition to their traditional forwarding and routing functions, NC-enabled nodes may combine or separate transient bits, packets, or flows through coding and decoding operations without loss of information. A growing number of promising NC applications have been proposed in diverse areas such as wireless mobile networks, video transmission, peer-to-peer networks, security, monitoring, and sensor networks [1,3,4]. In a recent study, significant throughput gains were demonstrated experimentally in NC-enabled WiFi-based mesh networks [5].

In this work, we focus on the application of NC within a particular class of point-to-multipoint (PMP) broadcast networks. Figs. 1 (a) and (b) depict their fundamental characteristics. These are centralized networks with a number of user nodes (U) communicating exclusively through a central access point (AP)

B. Bellalta et al. (Eds.): MACOM 2012, LNCS 7642, pp. 25–36, 2012.
© Springer-Verlag Berlin Heidelberg 2012

as follows. The uplink from any user towards the AP is a point-to-point link while the downlink from the AP back to the users is a broadcast PMP link. Although the uplink and downlink may use more than one frequency channel or transmission medium (e.g., separate fibers, wireless spatial diversity), we restrict our study to the use of one separate channel in each of the upstream and downstream directions. The AP arbitrates the transmissions of the terminals over the uplink channel dynamically, whereas the downlink uses time-division multiplexing (TDM).

In such PMP architectures, NC can exploit the underlying broadcast architecture to convert unicast transmissions into more efficient broadcast transmissions, as depicted in Figs. 1 (c) and (d). In this illustrative scenario, two packets are exchanged between two users, U_1 and U_2. Without NC, such an exchange may be performed in four separate packet transmissions, with the hub receiving and then broadcasting each packet individually, as shown in Fig. 1 (c). With NC, the hub may code the received packets into a single packet using a simple bitwise exclusive-OR (XOR) operation, denoted by $\oplus$ (see Fig. 1 (d)). Upon receiving the coded packet, the terminals decode the packets destined to them using a copy of their previously transmitted packets. NC hence achieves the packet exchange in only three packet transmissions, using 50% less downstream bandwidth.

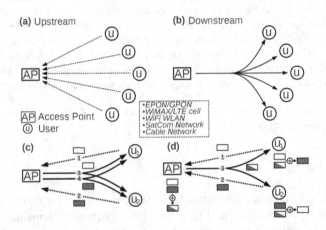

Fig. 1. Network coding in Point-to-Multipoint (PMP) networks

The example of Figs. 1 (c) and (d) is a particular case of NC where the receiver nodes (U_1 and U_2) use copies of their own previously transmitted packets to decode received packets. The concept has been explored in the context of wireless communications, where it is denoted reverse carpooling [6], piggybacking, or pairwise XOR coding.

The centralized form of reverse carpooling illustrated in Fig. 1 is applicable not only to PONs, but to a number of access-metro network architectures such as wireless local area networks (e.g., infrastructure-mode WiFi), cellular access networks (e.g., long term evolution (LTE) and WiMAX), broadband satellite networks, and cable networks (e.g., DOCSIS). The study of localized traffic in PMP networks is motivated by the tremendous growth of traffic generated by applications that stand to benefit from local packet exchanges, including user-generated high-definition video, peer-to-peer, video gaming, as well as voice and video conferencing [10]. Furthermore, content caching at user nodes may open up further opportunities for local exchanges.

The application of NC in a centralized PMP setting for local traffic was recently studied in the context of passive optical networks (PONs) through simulation [8,7,9]. However, previous studies of NC in PONs offer limited analyses of performance gains. Our work differs from previous performance analyses of NC in PONs [7] in the following ways. First, we do not consider normally distributed traffic rates. Second, we focus on the use of NC at the MAC sublayer. Most importantly, we are concerned with the queueing effects on delay within a switch, particularly at high loads.

In this article, we present a generic queuing-theoretic framework of a PMP network. To simplify the analysis, we ignore upstream channel arbitration and focus on queuing delay at the AP. We derive expressions for the average throughput and queuing delay under local traffic when NC is applied at the MAC sublayer. Our analytical results are then validated through OPNET [11] discrete-event simulations. In our discussion, we emphasize the high-load regime, where NC gains are visible.

The remainder of this article is organized as follows. In Section 2, we describe our analytical model and assumptions. In Section 3, we show analytically the potential advantages of the use of NC in PMP networks through deriving or bounding the average throughput, queue size, and queuing delay at the AP. In Section 4, we verify the conducted analysis and further investigate NC through simulation. Finally, we conclude in Section 5.

2   Network Model

Let the PMP network have n users exchanging traffic locally, as depicted in Fig. 2. As mentioned in Section 1, since we focus on queuing delay at the AP, we assume a contention-free upstream channel where packets transmitted by users arrive instantaneously at the AP.

At the AP, two queuing configurations are studied. In the first, incoming packets are simply stored in an infinite first-in-first-out (FIFO) queue, as shown in Fig. 2 (a), with a fixed service time T. In the second, incoming packets are stored in a two-dimensional buffer matrix according to their source-destination pair, as depicted in Fig. 2 (b). In this configuration, $Q_{i \to j}$ denotes the queue from user i to user j, where i and j are distinct indices in $(1..n)$. The buffer matrix has $N = n(n-1)$ infinite queues. This queuing configuration was proposed in [7] to allow the NC-enabled server (NC server) to process source-destination queue pairs jointly, thus eliminating any required search for coding opportunities. Since the coding consists of low-complexity XOR operations, we assume that coding delays are negligible compared to queueing delays.

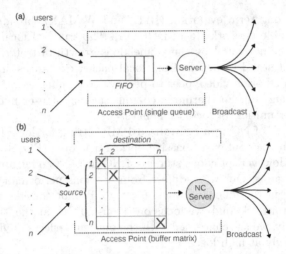

Fig. 2. PMP network model with (a) a single first-in-first-out (FIFO) queue or (b) a two-dimensional buffer matrix. NC's bidirectional relaying implies that the symmetrical entries of the upper and lower triangulars are visited simultaneously by the NC server.

Each user is modeled as the source of a stream of packets with arrivals that are independent and identically distributed (i.i.d.) over a period $\frac{N}{2}T$. Furthermore, each packet is destined to one of the remaining $(n-1)$ users in an i.i.d. fashion.

A NC-enhanced AP uses exclusively the buffer matrix configuration of Fig. 2 (b). For any distinct indices i and j in $(1..n)$, the NC server is capable of processing the pair of queues $Q_{i \to j}$ and $Q_{j \to i}$, denoted $(i \to j, j \to i)$, simultaneously. Alg. 1 gives a formal description of NC server operation. The NC server iterates through all queue pairs following a round-robin discipline, allocating a fixed time-slot T to each queue pair irrespective of the queue contents. This allows it to code packets opportunistically [5]. Queuing delay in such a strict TDM scheme constitutes an upperbound for the dynamic case where the NC server does not wait when no packets are present in $(i \to j, j \to i)$.

Algorithm 1. NC server

---
for $i = 1 \to (n-1)$ **do**
    for $j = (i+1) \to n$ **do**
        Process $(i \to j, j \to i)$ in time T
        1. Queues non-empty $\Rightarrow$ transmit one coded packet
        2. One queue empty $\Rightarrow$ transmit one uncoded packet
        3. Both queues empty $\Rightarrow$ wait T *(only TDM scheme)*
    end for
end for

---

3   Analysis

In this section, we derive an expression for the average delay in the system for the two configurations of Fig. 2 under Poisson user-traffic arrivals. We hence assume that packet arrivals are Poisson with parameter λ, where λ is the rate of arrival of packets originating from user i and destined to user j.

3.1   No Coding: The Single-Queue Configuration

Under aggregate Poisson arrivals, the configuration of Fig. 2 (a) satisfies the Markov property [12], and is therefore a classical $M/D/1$ Markov chain where the fixed service time is T and the total packet arrival rate is $N\lambda$.

The condition for stability is $N\lambda < \frac{1}{T}$. Therefore, the maximum system throughput satisfies

$$\mathcal{T}_{\max} < \frac{1}{T} \tag{1}$$

We use the Pollaczek-Khinchine (P-K) mean-value formula [12] to derive the average number of packets in the queue

$$N_Q = \frac{(N\lambda)^2 \mathcal{E}\left(T^2\right)}{2\{1 - (N\lambda)\mathcal{E}\left(T\right)\}} = \frac{(N\lambda)^2 T^2}{2\{1 - (N\lambda)T\}}, \tag{2}$$

and the average queuing delay

$$W = \frac{N\lambda T^2}{2\{1 - (N\lambda)T\}}. \tag{3}$$

3.2   NC: The Buffer Matrix Configuration

Definitions. In the architecture of Fig. 2 (b), the time between any two visits from the NC server to any $Q_{i \to j}$ is $\frac{N}{2}T$. We define the following variables:

- $\mathcal{N}_{t,i \to j}$: number of packets arriving in $Q_{i \to j}$ over the time interval $[0, t[$.
- p_k: probability of k arrivals in an interval $[t, t + \frac{N}{2}T[$, or

$$p_k = \mathcal{P}\left(\mathcal{N}_{t + \frac{N}{2}T, i \to j} - \mathcal{N}_{t,i \to j} = k\right), \tag{4}$$

where $i \neq j$. Our assumptions on incoming traffic ensure that p_k is independent from t, i, and j. Under Poisson arrivals, p_k is given by

$$p_k = e^{-\lambda \frac{N}{2}T} \frac{(\lambda \frac{N}{2}T)^k}{k!}, \tag{5}$$

where λ is the packet arrival rate into any queue $Q_{i \to j}$ in our configuration.

- $\mathcal{X}_{t,i \to j}$: number of packets in $Q_{i \to j}$ at time t.

- $t_k(i \to j)$: the instant preceding the kth visit of the NC server to $Q_{i \to j}$. Assuming that $Q_{1 \to 2}$ is processed at time $t = 0$, and that the server follows the procedure of Alg. 1, $t_k(i \to j)$ is given by

$$t_k(i \to j) = \left((m-1)(n - \frac{m}{2}) + (M - m - 1) \right) T + k\frac{N}{2}T, \qquad (6)$$

where $m = \min\{i, j\}$, $M = \max\{i, j\}$, and $i \neq j$.
For example, for $Q_{1 \to 2}$, the expression reduces to

$$t_k(1 \to 2) = k\frac{N}{2}T, \qquad (7)$$

- $A_{k+1, i \to j}$: number of packets arriving at $Q_{i \to j}$ between the kth and the $(k+1)^{th}$ visit of $Q_{i \to j}$. It follows that

$$A_{k+1, i \to j} = \mathcal{N}_{t_{k+1}(i \to j), i \to j} - \mathcal{N}_{t_k(i \to j), i \to j}. \qquad (8)$$

- $\mathcal{A}$: A random variable representing the number of arrivals in any queue $Q_{i \to j}$ over any period of length $\frac{N}{2}T$. $\mathcal{A}$ has probability mass function $\{p_k\}_{k \in \mathbb{N}}$, hence

$$\mathcal{P}(\mathcal{A} = k) = p_k. \qquad (9)$$

- $A(x)$: the probability-generating function of $\mathcal{A}$, given by

$$A(x) = \sum_{k=0}^{\infty} p_k x^k. \qquad (10)$$

- $(S_{k, i \to j})_{k \in \mathbb{N}}$: infinite series representing the number of packets (i.e., state) of $Q_{i \to j}$ just before the kth visit of the NC server. $(S_{k, i \to j})_{k \in \mathbb{N}}$ is defined by

$$(S_{k, i \to j})_{k \in \mathbb{N}} = \left(\mathcal{X}_{t_k(i \to j), i \to j} \right)_{k \in \mathbb{N}}. \qquad (11)$$

For instance, $Q_{1 \to 2}$ is associated to the series

$$(S_{k, 1 \to 2})_{k \in \mathbb{N}} = \left(\mathcal{X}_{k\frac{N}{2}T, 1 \to 2} \right)_{k \in \mathbb{N}}. \qquad (12)$$

Stability Condition and Throughput. We assume that any $Q_{i \to j}$ receives on average less than one packet in any period of length $\frac{N}{2}T$. Such a condition is reasonable as the NC server processes at most one packet during that period. This stability condition can be expressed as

$$\mathcal{E}(\mathcal{A}) = A'(1) < 1, \qquad (13)$$

where $\mathcal{E}(.)$ denotes the expected value.
With Poisson input traffic, stability requires

$$\lambda \frac{N}{2}T < 1 \qquad (14)$$

Therefore, the maximum system throughput satisfies

$$T^{NC}_{max} < N(\frac{1}{\frac{N}{2}T}) = \frac{2}{T} \qquad (15)$$

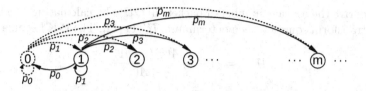

Fig. 3. Markov chain associated to queue $Q_{i \to j}$, with $m > 3$

Markov Chain. Under the procedure of Alg. 1, any queue $Q_{i \to j}$ perceives a single service from the NC server each $\frac{N}{2}T$ period, hence the TDM characterization. If the $(k+1)^{th}$ server visit finds $Q_{i \to j}$ empty (i.e., $S_{k,i \to j} = 0$), its next state $S_{k+1,i \to j}$ will be the number of new packet arrivals ($\mathcal{A}_{k+1,i \to j}$). Otherwise, it will be the sum of previous state and arrivals, minus one served packet.

In other words, for any queue $Q_{i \to j}$, the series $(S_{k,i \to j})$ satisfies

$$S_{k+1,i \to j} = f(S_{k,i \to j}, \mathcal{A}_{k+1,i \to j}) \qquad (16)$$

where

$$f(s, a) = \begin{cases} s + a & \text{if } s = 0, \\ s + a - 1 & \text{otherwise,} \end{cases} \qquad (17)$$

and $\mathcal{A}_{k+1,i \to j}$ is independent from $S_{k,i \to j}$ for any k. It follows that the series $(S_{k,i \to j})$ is a Markov chain with a transition matrix $\mathbf{A}$ given by

$$\mathbf{A} = \begin{pmatrix} p_0 & p_1 & p_2 & p_3 & \cdots \\ p_0 & p_1 & p_2 & p_3 & \cdots \\ 0 & p_0 & p_1 & p_2 & \cdots \\ 0 & 0 & p_0 & p_1 & \cdots \\ \vdots & \vdots & \vdots & \vdots & \ddots \end{pmatrix}. \qquad (18)$$

Fig. 3 illustrates the Markov chain described by $\mathbf{A}$, where each state represents the number of packets waiting in $Q_{i \to j}$. In Fig. 3, the transitions departing from state $S_k = 0$ are dashed whereas those departing from $S_k = 1$ are solid. The transitions departing from all states $S_k \geq 2$ (not shown) are identical to those departing from $S_k = 1$.

Under the stability condition of equ. (13) and Poisson arrivals (equ. (5)), it can be shown that the Markov chain $(S_{k,i \to j})_{k \in \mathbb{N}}$ associated to any queue $Q_{i \to j}$ is irreducible, aperiodic, and positive-recurrent [12]. Furthermore, since queues $Q_{i \to j}$ differ only by their initial conditions (i.e., $S_{0,i \to j}$), we use queue $Q_{1 \to 2}$ as a representative of source-destination queue statistics in the rest of the study.

Total Delay in $Q_{1 \to 2}$. We denote $(\pi_s)_{s \in \mathbb{N}}$ the stationary distribution of the Markov chain $S_{k,1 \to 2}$, and $\Pi(.)$ its probability-generating function, given by

$$\Pi(x) = \sum_{s=0}^{\infty} \pi_s x^s. \qquad (19)$$

We first derive the average number of packets in $Q_{1\to 2}$ by calculating $\Pi(x)$ using the P-K transform equation then determining $\Pi'(1)$ [12]. The P-K formula yields

$$\Pi(x) = (1-\rho)\frac{A(x)(x-1)}{x - A(x)} \tag{20}$$

where ρ is the utilization factor, given by

$$\rho = \mathcal{E}(\mathcal{A}) = A'(1). \tag{21}$$

Under the stability and traffic conditions of Section 3.2, we have

$$A(x) = \sum_{k=0}^{\infty} e^{-\lambda\frac{N}{2}T}\frac{(\lambda\frac{N}{2}T)^k}{k!}x^k = e^{\lambda\frac{N}{2}T(x-1)}. \tag{22}$$

Therefore, equ. (20) yields

$$\Pi(x) = (1 - \lambda\frac{N}{2}T)\frac{(x-1)e^{\lambda\frac{N}{2}T(x-1)}}{x - e^{\lambda\frac{N}{2}T(x-1)}}. \tag{23}$$

From equ. (23), we derive the following expressions for $\Pi(x)$ and $\Pi'(x)$:

$$\Pi(x) = (1 - \lambda\frac{N}{2}T)\frac{1}{1 + x\sum_{i=0}^{\infty}\frac{(-\lambda\frac{N}{2}T)^{i+1}}{(i+1)!}(x-1)^i}; \tag{24}$$

$$\Pi'(x) = -(1 - \lambda\frac{N}{2}T)\frac{\sum_{i=0}^{\infty}\left(1 - \frac{\lambda\frac{N}{2}Tx(i+1)}{i+2}\right)\frac{(-\lambda\frac{N}{2}T)^{i+1}}{(i+1)!}(x-1)^i}{(1 + x\sum_{i=0}^{\infty}\frac{(-\lambda\frac{N}{2}T)^{i+1}}{(i+1)!}(x-1)^i)^2}. \tag{25}$$

Evaluating $\Pi'(x)$ for $x = 1$, we obtain

$$\Pi'(1) = \frac{(1 - \lambda\frac{N}{4}T)\lambda\frac{N}{2}T}{1 - \lambda\frac{N}{2}T}. \tag{26}$$

Hence, for the NC configuration of Fig. 2 (b), the average queuing time is given by

$$W = \Pi'(1) = \frac{(1 - \lambda\frac{N}{4}T)\frac{N}{2}T}{1 - \lambda\frac{N}{2}T}. \tag{27}$$

Total Number of Packets in the System. Let $\mathcal{X}_t$ denote the total number of queued packets in the system at time t, hence

$$\mathcal{X}_t = \sum_{i,j|i\neq j} \mathcal{X}_{t,i\to j}. \tag{28}$$

It can be shown that

$$\lim_{t\to\infty} \max_{[t,t+\frac{N}{2}T]} \mathcal{E}(\mathcal{X}_t) \leq N\Pi'(1). \tag{29}$$

Therefore, we can use $N\Pi'(1)$ as an upperbound for the number of packets in the buffer matrix:

$$N_Q \le \frac{\left(1 - \lambda\frac{N}{4}T\right)\lambda\frac{N^2}{2}T}{1 - \lambda\frac{N}{2}T} \tag{30}$$

4   Numerical Results

4.1   Infinite Queues

In this section, we carry out OPNET [11] simulations in order to validate the results of Section 3 for both configurations of Fig. 2, where all queues are infinite. As for the analysis, we simulate uniform local traffic where input traffic is uniformly distributed over the sources and the destinations. Table 1 shows the main simulation parameters. We call the configurations of Fig. 2 (a) and (b) *native* and *NC-TDM*, respectively. Recall that in NC-TDM, the NC server waits for one packet duration even when both source queues are empty, as per Alg. 1.

Table 1. Simulation Parameters

Number of users	8
Packet size (S_p)	1500 Bytes
Downstream data rate	1 Gb/s
Warmup period	2 s
Data collection period	5 s

Although the simulations illustrated in this section use a warmup period of 2 s, a warmup of 10 s was also implemented for all simulations, with identical results, hence verifying steady-state conditions at all load points. For all simulation plots in this section, we include 95% confidence intervals.

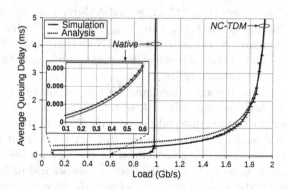

Fig. 4. Average packet delay in native and NC-TDM configurations, for both analysis (dashed) and simulation (solid)

Fig. 4 shows the superposed analysis and simulation plots for average queuing delay (i.e., waiting time) in both configurations. The analytical expressions used for the native and NC-TDM cases are given by equations (3) and (27), respectively. The offered load is increased from 0.1 Gb/s to the maximum stable load, given for the native and NC-TDM cases by equations (1) and (15), respectively. In Fig. 4, the simulation plots match the analysis for both the native and NC-TDM cases, particularly for the more relevant high loads. In the native case, the average difference between analysis and simulation for the highest load quarter (0.75 Gb/s to 1 Gb/s) is 5 μs, a relative difference of 3.6%. In the NC-TDM scheme, the average difference in the highest load quarter (1.5 Gb/s to 2 Gb/s) is 190 μs, a relative difference of 10%.

The NC-TDM plots show that the steady-state queuing delay remains stable up to 2 Gb/s. This indicates that network coding keeps the average queue size within the buffer matrix (i.e., the size of $Q_{i\to j}$) stable for loads above the available downstream data rate. Both analysis and simulation results confirm that network coding is therefore able to support loads up to twice the available downstream data rate under uniform local traffic.

Both analysis and simulation also show that there is a delay penalty incurred by the NC-TDM scheme at all loads below 1 Gb/s. This load penalty remains below 0.5 ms and is due to the TDM process described in Alg. 1: Whereas the native scheme is dynamic in nature, the NC-TDM scheme results in a time-slot without packet transmission for each empty source-destination queue pair. Such inefficiency may be removed using a dynamic NC scheme, as shown in the next section.

4.2   Finite Queues

In this section, we further run OPNET [11] simulations for queues that are limited in size. In addition to applying the parameters of table 1, we limit the total buffer size to N_{max} =1 MByte. Moreover, we implement an additional scheme whereby NC is performed in a dynamic fashion (i.e, no waiting time in Alg. 1). We label this scheme *NC-dynamic*. In the NC configuration of Fig. 2 (b) which applies to both the NC-TDM and NC-dynamic schemes, we limit each source-destination queue ($Q_{i\to j}$) to N_{max}/N in order to have equal total buffer resources compared to the native scheme. Note that the smaller size of the source-destination queues does not affect the maximum attainable throughput in the NC schemes, as is shown below.

Fig. 5 (a) depicts the average throughput for the native, NC-TDM, and NC-dynamic schemes when the total offered load ranges from 0.1 Gb/s to 2.5 Gb/s. As expected from throughput inequalities of equ. (1) and (15), throughput is equal to the offered load until it reaches the stability limit. That limit is equal to the downstream data rate ($\mathcal{T}_{max} = 1$ Gb/s) for the native scheme and reaches twice the downstream rate ($\mathcal{T}_{max}^{NC} = 2$ Gb/s) using network coding (see Fig. 5(a)).

Fig. 5 (b), we plot the average queuing delay in the three simulated schemes. We observe that the average delay curves reach saturation values in all implemented schemes, a consequence of the limits in queue sizes.

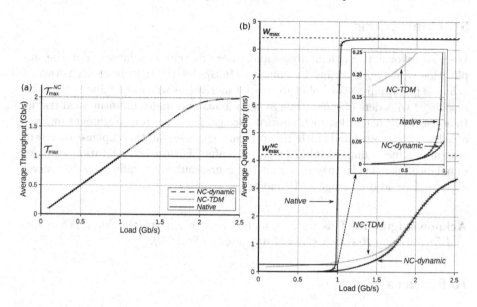

Fig. 5. (a) Average throughput in native (black/solid), NC-TDM (grey), and NC-dynamic (black/dashed) schemes; (b) Average packet delay in native, NC-TDM, and NC-dynamic configurations

At very high loads, incoming packets that are not dropped are likely to see a nearly full queue. In the native scheme, their waiting time is upper-bound by

$$W_{\max} = (N_{\max}/S_p) \times T = 8.3886 \text{ ms}, \qquad (31)$$

where S_p is the packet size and T is the service time (i.e., packet transmission time). In the NC schemes, however, that figure becomes

$$W_{\max}^{NC} = (N_{\max}/NS_p) \times (TN/2) = W_{\max}/2 = 4.1943 \text{ ms}, \qquad (32)$$

accounting for the reduced queue size and the increased service cycle time. Fig. 5 (b) depicts the two computed delay upper-bounds. This theoretical 50% reduction in saturation delay is verified in the simulation results. The *softer saturation* seen in the NC schemes is due to the ability of network coding to drain queues faster, hence preventing the queue size from reaching its maximum level even at very high loads.

More importantly, compared to the NC-TDM scheme, the NC-dynamic scheme effectively eliminates any low-load penalty inherent to the TDM process. This is clear from the low-load inset of Fig. 5 (b). In addition to its improved throughput, the NC-dynamic scheme thus exhibits packet delays that are lower than the native scheme at all loads. At loads slightly above 1 Gb/s, the delay gains of network coding relative to the native scheme attain two orders of magnitude.

5 Conclusions

We have shown through analysis and discrete-event simulation that the application of network coding in Point-to-Multipoint (PMP) broadcast networks achieves potentially a two-fold throughput increase as well as queuing delay gains reaching two orders of magnitude at high loads and under uniform local traffic. In access PMP networks, such performance gains are a strong argument in favor of allocating more bandwidth to upstream channels at the expense of downstream channels, under highly localized traffic. Future invesatigation includes unbalanced pair loads, varying number of users, multicast traffic, new NC server algorithms, and dual-stage PMP models.

Acknowledgment. This work was supported in part by the *Natural Sciences and Engineering Research Council of Canada (NSERC)*.

References

1. Médard, M., Sprintson, A. (eds.): Network Coding: Fundamentals and Applications. Academic Press (November 2011)
2. Ho, T., Lun, D.: Network Coding: An Introduction. Cambridge University Press (April 2008)
3. Fragouli, C., Katabi, D., Markopoulou, A., Médard, M., Rahul, H.: Wireless Network Coding: Opportunities & Challenges. In: Proc. IEEE MILCOM, Orlando, FL, USA, pp. 1–8 (2007)
4. Fragouli, C., Soljanin, E.: Network Coding Applications. Foundations and Trends in Networking 2(2), 135–269 (2007)
5. Katti, S., Rahul, H., Hu, W., Katabi, D., Médard, M., Crowcroft, J.: XORs in the Air: Practical Wireless Network Coding. IEEE/ACM Transactions on Networking 16(3), 497–510 (2008)
6. Effros, M., Ho, T., Kim, S.: A Tiling Approach to Network Code Design for Wireless Networks. In: Proc. Information Theory Workshop, Punta del Este, Uruguay, pp. 62–66 (March 2006)
7. Miller, K., Biermann, T., Woesner, H., Karl, H.: Network Coding in Passive Optical Networks. In: Proc. IEEE International Symposium on Network Coding, Toronto, ON, Canada, pp. 1–6 (June 2010)
8. Belzner, M., Haunstein, H.: Network Coding in Passive Optical Networks. In: Proc. ECOC, Vienna, Austria, pp. 1–2 (September 2009)
9. Fouli, K., Maier, M., Médard, M.: Network Coding in Next-Generation Passive Optical Networks. IEEE Communications Magazine 49(9), 38–46 (2011)
10. Cisco Systems, Cisco Visual Networking Index: Forecast and Methodology, 2009-2014 (June 2010)
11. OPNET Modeler 17.1, http://www.opnet.com
12. Kleinrock, L.: Queueing Systems, Volume I: Theory. John Wiley & Sons (1975)

A Coded DHA FH OFDMA System with a Noncoherent ML Detector under Multitone Jamming

Dmitry Osipov[1,2]

[1] Institute for Information Transmission Problems RAS
(Kharkevich Institute)
[2] National Research Institute Higher School of Economics
Moscow, Russia
d_osipov@iitp.ru

Abstract. In what follows an upper bound for the probability of erroneous decoding in a coded DHA FH OFDMA system with a noncoherent ML detector under multitone jamming is introduced.

Keywords: multiple access, coded DHA FH OFDMA, maximum likelihood, upper bound.

1   Introduction

Dynamic Hopset Allocation Frequency Hopping OFDMA (DHA FH OFDMA) has been initially proposed in [1]. Since then a number of modifications has been considered. Noncoherent DHA FH OFDMA with threshold reception seems the most promising one since it is much less vulnerable to multitone jamming than the conventional FH OFDMA. However, it was shown in [2] that in classical DHA FH OFDMA using q-ary FSK modulation the probability of erasure grows drastically as q grows. Thus in a classical DHA FH OFDMA system the value of q is to be relatively small and therefore the data transmission rate in such a system is bound to be relatively low too. In [3] a modification of a classical DHA FH OFDMA model has been proposed: a coded DHA FH OFDMA model. The basic idea underlying the model under consideration is a combination of q-ary FSK modulation and noncoherent reception utilized in a classical DHA FH OFDMA system with a q-ary error correcting code with good relative distance (e.g. Reed-Solomon code) and correspondingly a replacement of symbol-wise decision by a codeword decoding. Due to additional redundancy in the time domain introduced by an error-correcting code the value of q can be much larger in use in a coded DHA FH OFDMA; and even though additional redundancy is introduced it turns out that the overall transmission rate in a coded DHA FH OFDMA is much higher than that ensured by a classical DHA FH OFDMA system (number of active users, signal-to-noise ratio and signal-to-inference ratio being fixed). Therefore the problem of giving a probabilistic description of a coded DHA FH OFDMA (especially under jamming) is of great importance. In what follows an upper bound for the probability of erroneous decoding

B. Bellalta et al. (Eds.): MACOM 2012, LNCS 7642, pp. 37–48, 2012.
© Springer-Verlag Berlin Heidelberg 2012

in a coded DHA FH OFDMA system with noncoherent ML reception under multitone jamming will be introduced.

This paper is organized as follows. In section 2 a short description of a coded DHA FH OFDMA with a noncoherent ML detector will be given. In section 3 a probabilistic model of the system in question under multitone jamming is introduced. In section 4 the model under consideration will be used to upper bound the probability of erroneous decoding.

2   A Coded DHA FH OFDMA System with a Noncoherent ML Detector

Let us consider a multiple access system in which m active users transmit information via an AWGN channel split into Q identical nonoverlapping subchannels by means of OFDM. Information that is to be transmitted is encoded into a codeword of a (n,k,d) q-ary code ($q \ll Q$).Whenever a user is to transmit a q-ary symbol it places 1 in the position of the vector $\overline{a}_g$ corresponding to the symbol in question within the scope of the mapping in use (in what follows it will be assumed that all positions of the vector are enumerated from 1 to Q, moreover without loss of generality we shall assume that the 1st subchannel corresponds to 0, the 2nd subchannel corresponds to 1 and so on). Than a random permutation of the aforesaid vector is performed and the resulting vector $\pi_g(\overline{a}_g)$ is used to form an OFDM symbol (permutations are selected equiprobably from the set of all possible permutations and the choice is performed whenever a symbol is to be transmitted). Therefore in order to transmit a codeword a user is to transmit n OFDM symbols. A sequence of OFDM symbols, corresponding to a certain codeword that has been sent by a certain user, will be referred to as a frame. Note that frames transmitted by different users need not be block synchronized, i.e. if within the time interval a certain user transmits a frame that corresponds to a codeword, symbols transmitted by another user within the same time period do not necessarily all comprise one codeword. Moreover, it will be assumed that transmissions from different users are uncoordinated, i.e. none of the users has information about the others. In what follows we shall assume that all users transmit information in OFDM frames and the transmission is quasisynchronous. In terms of the model under consideration this assumption means that transmissions from different users are symbol synchronized.

Within the scope of reception of a certain codeword (let us designate it with v_z where z is the number of the codeword) the receiver is to receive n OFDM symbols corresponding to the codeword in question. Note that the receiver is assumed to be synchronized with transmitters of all users. Therefore all the permutations done within the scope of transmission of the codeword in question are known to the user. The receiver applies inverse permutation to each vector b_g corresponding to the respective OFDM symbol thus reconstructing initial order of elements and obtaining vector $\tilde{b}_g = \pi_s^{-1}(b_g)$. Let us designate a matrix that consists of vectors $\overline{a}_g$ corresponding to the codeword v_z with V_z. Furthermore we shall consider a matrix X that consists of vectors $\tilde{b}_g = \pi_s^{-1}(b_g)$ that correspond to the very same codeword v_z. Note that matrix V_z corresponds to the transmitted codeword whereas matrix X corresponds to the received codeword. The detector is to decide on the transmitted codeword matrix. Let us designate each element of matrix X with $X(i, j)$, where i is the column number, whereas j is the row number. Let M be the mapping that associates number t of a certain column of matrix V_z with the number of the nonzero element of the vector in question j_t (i.e. $V_z(t, j_t) = 1$)

$$M(V_z) = [j_1, j_2 \dots j_n] \ \forall t = 1 : \tilde{n} \ \exists! j_t : V_z(t, j_t) = 1,$$
$$V_z(t, j) = 0 \ \forall j \neq j_t. \tag{1}$$

To decide on the codeword transmitted by the active user the detector is to compute the value

$$y_z = \sum_{i=1:n} X^2(i, j_z(i)) \ \overline{j}_z = M(V_z), \tag{2}$$

where $\overline{j}_z$ - is a vector of numbers of rows, corresponding to the nonzero elements of V_z for each codeword v_z. The value y_z is the sum of powers of the elements corresponding to the codeword v_z. Detection boils down to finding $z^* = \arg\max_z(y_z)$.

Since transmissions from different users are uncoordinated it is possible that at some instant more than one user will use a certain subchannel. Thus, the values of the summands in (2) are affected both by the background noise and other users' signals Therefore erroneous decision can occur. It is the probability of erroneous decision that predetermines the capacity of the system under consideration. Therefore the problem of obtaining upper bound on error probability is of great importance. This problem will be considered in what follows.

3 A Coded DHA FH OFDMA System with a Noncoherent ML Detector under Multitone Jamming: A Probabilistic Description

Let us assume that the codeword t is the codeword that was transmitted by the user under consideration. Let us now consider the reception procedure described above. Erroneous decision is possible if

$$\exists z \neq t \ \ y_t - y_z < 0. \tag{3}$$

Probability of (3) can be upper bounded with

$$p_e < \sum_{z \neq t} P \left(\sum_{i=1:n} \left(X^2 \left(i, j_t(i)\right) - X^2 \left(i, j_z(i)\right)\right) < 0 \right). \tag{4}$$

Note that since the minimum distance of the code in use is equal to d any two codewords coincide at most in $n - d$ symbols. Let us designate the set of positions in which codewords v_t and v_z coincide with Θ, while the rest (i.e. those, in which v_t and v_z differ) will be designated by Φ. Let us designate the decision statistic corresponding to the codeword v_z with S_z. This value is given by

$$S_z = \sum_{i=1:n} \left(X^2 \left(i, j_t(i)\right) - X^2 \left(i, j_z(i)\right)\right) = $$

$$= \sum_{i \in \Theta} \left(X^2 \left(i, j_t(i)\right) - X^2 \left(i, j_z(i)\right)\right) + \sum_{i \in \Phi} \left(X^2 \left(i, j_t(i)\right) - X^2 \left(i, j_z(i)\right)\right). \tag{5}$$

Note that $\forall i \in \Theta \ X^2 \left(i, j_t(i)\right) = X^2 \left(i, j_z(i)\right)$. Therefore (5) can be rewritten:

$$S_z = \left(\sum_{i \in \Phi} X^2 \left(i, j_t(i)\right) - \sum_{i \in \Phi} X^2 \left(i, j_z(i)\right)\right). \tag{6}$$

And (4) can be rewritten:

$$p_e < \sum_{z \neq t} P(S_z < 0) = \sum_{z \neq t} P \left(\left(\sum_{i \in \Phi} X^2 \left(i, j_t(i)\right) - \sum_{i \in \Phi} X^2 \left(i, j_z(i)\right)\right) < 0 \right). \tag{7}$$

Note that summands in (7) are statistically independent (though, generally speaking, not identically distributed), and the number of summands in each sum is at least d. Therefore if d is sufficiently great (which is exactly the case that is of interest to us, since to guarantee high data rates and jamming-proofness the minimum distance of the outer code in use is to be great) (7) is well approximated by normal distribution. Note that mean and variance of the distribution of each value S_z depend on the values of means and variances of the summands. In what follows we shall obtain this values   in order to estimate the expression at the right side of (7). Due to random permutations the elements of the matrix X (and thus the summands in (7)) correspond to randomly chosen subchannels. Distributions of the value $X \left(i, j_z(i)\right)$ (and thus the moments of this value) depend on the situation at the subchannel corresponding to the $j_z(i)$ th row of marix at the time interval corresponding to the i th time interval. The element on the matrix can correspond to the subchannel via which an authorized user has transmitted a signal (in what follows we shall assume that the optimal power control is maintained in the system under consideration therefore the amplitude of the signals from all authorized users at the receiver side is A). On the other hand, we assume that there is an intruder in the system that transmits a multitone jamming signal. The jamming signal occupies $\Omega = \lceil \alpha Q \rceil$ subchannels ($\alpha < 1$) and the amplitude of each jamming signal is equal to λ (λ can be any positive number depending on the power available to the intruder). Thus the signal transmitted by a certain user (not necessarily the user under consideration) can be jammed. However since due to the use of random permutations the subchannels that are used by the authorized users are chosen in a random fashion the jamming signal might as well affect the subchannel that has not been used for transmission. Moreover, it is possible that the subchannel corresponding to a certain element of matrix $X\left(i, j_z\left(i\right)\right)$ was not used for information transmission, nor was it jammed. In this case the value $X\left(i, j_z\left(i\right)\right)$ is predetermined by the influence of background noise only.

First of all let us consider the case of jamming. For the case under consideration the received signal is given by

$$\overline{r} = \overline{s} + \overline{s}_j + \overline{\eta} = \overline{s} + \overline{z}, \tag{8}$$

where $\overline{s}$ is a random vector with a constant amplitude $|s| = A$ (i.e. the signal transmitted by the authorized user), $\overline{s}_j$ is the jamming signal, i.e. a random vector with a constant amplitude $|\overline{s}_j| = \lambda A$, $\overline{\eta}$ is the vector corresponding to a two-sided additive white Gaussian noise with a standard deviation σ, $\overline{z} = \overline{s}_j + \overline{\eta}$.

The power of the signal is given by

$$|\overline{r}|^2 = |s|^2 + \left(2 \cdot |s| \cdot |z| \cdot \cos \alpha\right) + |z|^2, \tag{9}$$

where α is the angle between $\overline{s}$ and $\overline{z} = \overline{s}_j + \overline{\eta}$ Note that since phases of the vectors $\overline{s}$, $\overline{s}_j$ and $\overline{\eta}$ are uniformly distributed on $[0, 2\pi]$ α is also uniformly distributed on $[0, 2\pi]$.

Let us find the mean and the variance of the value $|\overline{r}|^2$. The former is given by

$$E\left(|\overline{r}|^2\right) = E\left(|s|^2 + \left(2 \cdot |s| \cdot |z| \cdot \cos \alpha\right) + |z|^2\right) = E\left(|s|^2\right) + E\left(2 \cdot |s| \cdot |z| \cdot \cos \alpha\right) + E\left(|z|^2\right). \tag{10}$$

Note that $|s|, |z|, \alpha$ are uncorrelated random values. Therefore

$$E\left(2 \cdot |s| \cdot |z| \cdot \cos \alpha\right) = 2E\left(|s|\right) E\left(|z|\right) E\left(\cos \alpha\right). \tag{11}$$

Since α is uniformly distributed on $[0, 2\pi]$

$$E(\cos\alpha) = \int_0^{2\pi} \frac{\cos\alpha}{2\pi} d\alpha = 0. \tag{12}$$

Note that $|z|^2$ has a noncentral χ^2 distribution with 2 degrees of freedom and therefore its mean is known [4] and is given by

$$E\left(|z|^2\right) = \lambda^2 A^2 + 2\sigma^2. \tag{13}$$

Thus (10) can be rewritten in the following form:

$$E\left(|\overline{r}|^2\right) = E\left(|s|^2\right) + E\left(|z|^2\right) = A^2 + \lambda^2 A^2 + 2\sigma^2 = \left(1 + \lambda^2\right)A^2 + 2\sigma^2. \tag{14}$$

Let us now find the variance of the value $|\overline{r}|^2$. The latter can be derived as in [5]:

$$D\left(|\overline{r}|^2\right) = E\left(\left(|\overline{r}|^2\right)^2\right) - E\left(|\overline{r}|^2\right)^2. \tag{15}$$

The first summand is given by

$$\begin{aligned}
E\left(\left(|\overline{r}|^2\right)^2\right) &= E\left(\left(\left(|s|^2 + |z|^2\right) + \left(2\cdot|s|\cdot|z|\cdot\cos\alpha\right)\right)^2\right) = \\
&= E\left(|s|^4 + 2|s|^2|z|^2 + |z|^4 + 4\cdot|s|^2\cdot|z|^2\cdot\cos^2\alpha + \left(2\left(|s|^2 + |z|^2\right)\left(2\cdot|s|\cdot|z|\cdot\cos\alpha\right)\right)\right).
\end{aligned} \tag{16}$$

Note that

$$E\left(2\left(|s|^2 + |z|^2\right)\left(2\cdot|s|\cdot|z|\cdot\cos\alpha\right)\right) = 4E\left(\left(|s|^2 + |z|^2\right)\left(|s|\cdot|z|\right)\right)E(\cos\alpha) = 0. \tag{17}$$

Therefore

$$\begin{aligned}
E\left(\left(|\overline{r}|^2\right)^2\right) &= \\
&= E\left(|s|^4\right) + \left(2E\left(|s|^2\right)E\left(|z|^2\right)\right) + E\left(|z|^4\right) + 4E\left(|s|^2\right)E\left(|z|^2\right)E(\cos^2\alpha).
\end{aligned} \tag{18}$$

The last multiplier is given by

$$E\left(\cos^2\alpha\right) = \frac{1}{2\pi}\cdot\int_0^{2\pi}\cos^2\alpha d\alpha = \frac{1}{\pi}\cdot\int_0^{\pi}\cos^2\alpha d\alpha. \tag{19}$$

Note that [6]:

$$\int_0^\pi \cos^2 \alpha d\alpha = \frac{\pi}{2}.$$

$E\left(|z|^4\right)$ is given by [4]:

$$E\left(|z|^4\right) = 4\sigma^4 + 4\sigma^2 \lambda^2 A^2 + \left(2\sigma^2 + \lambda^2 A^2\right)^2 =$$
$$= 4\sigma^4 + 4\sigma^2 \lambda^2 A^2 + 4\sigma^4 + 4\sigma^2 \lambda^2 A^2 + \lambda^4 A^4 = 8\sigma^4 + 8\sigma^2 \lambda^2 A^2 + \lambda^4 A^4 . \tag{20}$$

and $E\left(|s|^4\right) = A^4$. Substituting respective summands in (18) we obtain

$$E\left(\left(|\bar{r}|^2\right)^2\right) = 8\sigma^4 + 8\sigma^2 \lambda^2 A^2 + \lambda^4 A^4 + A^4 + 2\lambda^2 A^4 + 4\sigma^2 A^2 . \tag{21}$$

Now let us consider the second term:

$$E\left(|\bar{r}|^2\right)^2 = \left(\left(1+\lambda^2\right)A^2 + 2\sigma^2\right)^2 = \left(1+2\lambda^2+\lambda^4\right)A^4 + 4\sigma^2\left(1+\lambda^2\right)A^2 + 4\sigma^4 . \tag{22}$$

Therefore $D\left(|\bar{r}|^2\right)$ is given by:

$$D\left(|\bar{r}|^2\right) = 4\sigma^4 + 4\sigma^2 \lambda^2 A^2 . \tag{23}$$

For the sake of convenience let as designate the presence of the signal transmitted by the active user as $S = 1$ and the absence of the signal in question as $S = 0$ whereas the presence and the absence of the jamming signal as $J = 1$ and $J = 0$ respectively; the presence and the absence of the signal transmitted by another authorized user will be designated as $I = 1$ and $I = 0$ respectively . Thus the tuple (S, J, I) describes the respective subchannel completely. Hereinabove it has been shown

$$E(1,1,0) = \left(1+\lambda^2\right)A^2 + 2\sigma^2 \tag{24}$$

and

$$D(1,1,0) = 4\sigma^4 + 4\sigma^2 \lambda^2 A^2 . \tag{25}$$

However since all active users transmit information in uncoordinated fashion the signal is affected by other users' interference, i.e. collision can occur.

For the sake of simplicity we shall further consider only the most probable case, i.e. . collision of multiplicity two (see [1]). However the approach that is to be introduced can be generalized for the case of collision of any multiplicity.

We can use the technique that has been presented hereinabove to obtain the mean and variance of the output of the subchannel described by $(1,1,1)$, i.e. the subchannel where the signal transmitted by the user under consideration has collided with the signal transmitted by another authorized user and was jammed by the signal transmitted by the intruder. The output of the subchannel in the situation under consideration is given by

$$\bar{r} = \bar{s} + \bar{s}_i + \bar{s}_j + \bar{\eta} = \bar{w} + \bar{z}, \tag{26}$$

where $\bar{s}$ is a random vector with a constant amplitude $|s| = A$ (i.e. the signal transmitted by the authorized user), $\bar{s}_j$ is the jamming signal, i.e. a random vector with constant amplitude $|\bar{s}_j| = \lambda A$, $\bar{s}_i$ is the signal transmitted via the same subchannel by another authorized user (i.e. is a random vector with a constant amplitude $|s| = A$), $\bar{\eta}$ is the vector corresponding to the two-sided additive white Gaussian noise, $\bar{z} = \bar{s}_j + \bar{\eta}$, $\bar{w} = \bar{s} + \bar{s}_i$.

Therefore

$$E\left(|\bar{w}|^2\right) = 2A^2 \tag{27}$$

$$E\left(|\bar{w}|^4\right) = 3A^4 \tag{28}$$

$$E(1,1,1) = E\left(|\bar{r}|^2\right) = 2A^2 + \lambda^2 A^2 + 2\sigma^2 \tag{29}$$

$$E\left(\left(|\bar{r}|^2\right)^2\right) = E\left(|w|^4\right) + E\left(|z|^4\right) + 2E\left(|w|^2\right)E\left(|z|^2\right)E\left(\cos^2\alpha\right) =$$
$$3A^4 + 8\sigma^4 + 8\sigma^2\lambda^2 A^2 + \lambda^4 A^4 + 2\lambda^2 A^4 + 4\sigma^2 A^2 = \tag{30}$$
$$= \left(3 + \lambda^4 + 2\lambda^2\right)A^4 + (4 + 8\lambda)\sigma^2 A^2 + 8\sigma^4$$

$$E\left(|\bar{r}|^2\right)^2 = \left(\left(2 + \lambda^2\right)A^2 + 2\sigma^2\right)^2 = 4A^4 + 4\lambda^2 A^2 + \lambda^4 A^4 + 8\sigma^2 A^2 + 4\lambda^2 A^2\sigma^2 + 4\sigma^4 \tag{31}$$

$$D(1,1,1) = E\left(\left(|\bar{r}|^2\right)^2\right) - E\left(|\bar{r}|^2\right)^2. \tag{32}$$

In other cases we are to consider obtaining moments is not that cumbersome. The output of the subchannel described by $(1,0,0)$ is given by

$$\bar{r} = \bar{s} + \bar{\eta}, \tag{33}$$

where $\bar{s}$ is a random vector with a constant amplitude $|s| = A$ (i.e. the signal transmitted by the authorized user), $\bar{\eta}$ is the vector corresponding to the two-sided additive white Gaussian noise. Therefore $|\bar{r}|^2$ has a noncentral χ^2 distribution and its mean and variance are given by [4]:

$$E(1,0,0) = A^2 + 2\sigma^2 \tag{34}$$

$$D(1,0,0) = 4\sigma^2 A^2 + 4\sigma^4 \tag{35}$$

respectively.

The output of the subchannel described by $(0,1,0)$ is given by

$$\bar{r} = \bar{s}_j + \bar{\eta}. \tag{36}$$

Since $\bar{s}_j$ is a random vector this value also has a noncentral χ^2 distribution. Since $|\bar{s}_j| = \lambda A$ the mean and the variance of the value $|\bar{r}|^2$ are given by [4]:

$$E(0,1,0) = \lambda^2 A^2 + 2\sigma^2 \tag{37}$$

$$D(0,1,0) = 4\sigma^2 \lambda^2 A^2 + 4\sigma^4. \tag{38}$$

Finally the output of the subchannel described by $(0,0,0)$ is predetermined by the influence of the additive white Gaussian noise and therefore the value $|\bar{r}|^2$ has a χ^2 distribution. Thus, we can claim that

$$E(0,0,0) = 2\sigma^2 \tag{39}$$

$$D(0,0,0) = 4\sigma^4. \tag{40}$$

4   A Coded DHA FH OFDMA System with a Noncoherent ML Detector under Multitone Jamming: An Upper Bound

Let us once again consider the reception of a codeword by a certain user. Within the scope of the process under consideration the user transmits n signals (n OFDM symbols). As has been stated above it is assumed that the intruder transmits signals in $\Omega = \lceil \alpha Q \rceil$ subchannels within the scope of transmission of every OFDM symbol. Therefore each signal transmitted by the user under consideration is jammed with probability $\dfrac{\Omega}{Q}$. Let us consider two codewords: codeword $\bar{v}_t$ (the one that has been transmitted by the user under consideration) and codeword $\bar{v}_z$. Let us assume that these codewords differ in n positions ($\tilde{n} \geq n \geq d$). The probability of the fact that α of n signals will be jammed is given by

$$p_{SJ}(\alpha) = C_n^{\alpha} \left(\frac{\Omega}{Q}\right)^{\alpha} \left(1 - \frac{\Omega}{Q}\right)^{n-\alpha}. \tag{41}$$

Moreover signals transmitted by the user under consideration can collide with the signals transmitted by other active users (let us further on refer to them as "interfering" users). Since there are $m-1$ interfering users the probability of the fact that a certain signal will collide is given by

$$p_c(m) = 1 - \left(1 - \frac{1}{q}\right)^{m-1}. \tag{42}$$

The probability of the fact that β signals of α signals that were jammed will undergo collision (i.e. the respective signals will interfere both with the intruder and with other authorized users) is given by

$$p_{SJI}(\alpha, \beta) = C_{\alpha}^{\beta} \left(p_c(m)\right)^{\beta} \left(1 - p_c(m)\right)^{\alpha - \beta}. \tag{43}$$

and the probability that γ signals of $n - \alpha$ signals that were not jammed will undergo collision (i.e. the respective signals will be affected by the signals transmitted by other authorized users but not by a jamming signal) is given by

$$p_I(n - \alpha, \gamma) = C_{n-\alpha}^{\gamma} \left(p_c(m)\right)^{\gamma} \left(1 - p_c(m)\right)^{n - \alpha - \gamma}. \tag{44}$$

Note that in this case the mean of the first sum in (7) will be given by

$$E_t(\alpha, \beta, \gamma) = \left(\beta \cdot E(1,1,1)\right) + \left((\alpha - \beta) \cdot E(1,1,0)\right) + \left(\gamma \cdot E(1,0,1)\right) + \left((n - \alpha - \gamma) E(1,0,0)\right) \tag{45}$$

and the variance is given by

$$D_t(\alpha, \beta, \gamma) = \left(\beta \cdot D(1,1,1)\right) + \left((\alpha - \beta) \cdot D(1,1,0)\right) + \left(\gamma \cdot D(1,0,1)\right) + \left((n - \alpha - \gamma) D(1,0,0)\right) \tag{46}$$

Let us now consider the vector of elements corresponding to the second codeword.

Let p_s be the probability of the fact that a elements of the vector correspond to the subchannels, via which only one authorized user has transmitted a signal whereas b elements of the vector correspond to the subchannels were collisions occurred. The probability of this is given by

$$p_s(a,b) = \frac{n!}{a!b!(n-a-b)!} p_1^a (1 - p_1 - p_0)^b p_0^{n-a-b}, \tag{47}$$

where

$$p_1 = C_m^1 \left(\frac{1}{Q-1} \right) \left(1 - \frac{1}{Q-1} \right)^{m-1} \tag{48}$$

$$p_0 = \left(1 - \frac{1}{Q-1} \right)^{m-1}. \tag{49}$$

Now let us assume that f subchannels, via which only one user has transmitted, h subchannels, in which collisions occurred, and u subchannels, via which none of the users transmitted, were jammed. Respective probabilities are given by

$$\tilde{p}_{SJ}(f,a) = C_a^f \left(\frac{\Omega}{Q} \right)^f \left(1 - \frac{\Omega}{Q} \right)^{a-f} \tag{50}$$

$$\tilde{p}_{SJI}(h,b) = C_b^h \left(\frac{\Omega}{Q} \right)^h \left(1 - \frac{\Omega}{Q} \right)^{b-h} \tag{51}$$

$$\tilde{p}_J(u,n-a-b) = C_{n-a-b}^u \left(\frac{\Omega}{Q} \right)^u \left(1 - \frac{\Omega}{Q} \right)^{n-a-b-u}. \tag{52}$$

In this case the mean of the second sum in (7) is given by

$$E_z(a,b,f,g,u) = \big((a-f)E(1,0,0) \big) + \big(f \cdot E(1,1,0) \big) + \big((b-h)E(1,0,1) \big) + \newline + \big(h \cdot E(1,1,1) \big) + \big(u \cdot E(0,1,0) \big) + \big((n-a-b-u) \cdot E(0,0,0) \big) \tag{53}$$

and the variance is given by

$$D_z(a,b,f,g,u) = \big((a-f)D(1,0,0) \big) + \big(f \cdot D(1,1,0) \big) + \big((b-h)D(1,0,1) \big) + \newline + \big(h \cdot D(1,1,1) \big) + \big(u \cdot D(0,1,0) \big) + \big((n-a-b-u) \cdot D(0,0,0) \big) \tag{54}$$

Therefore the decision statistic

$$S_z = \left(\sum_{i \in \Phi} X^2(i, j_t(i)) - \sum_{i \in \Phi} X^2(i, j_z(i)) \right)$$ has a normal distribution with mean

$E = E_t(\alpha,\beta,\gamma) - E_z(a,b,f,g,u)$ and variance $D = D_t(\alpha,\beta,\gamma) + D_z(a,b,f,g,u)$.

Let $\bar{\omega} = [\omega_1,...,\omega_M]$ where $M = q^k$ be the spectrum of the code

Then the probability of error is upper bounded by

$$p \le \sum_{z \ne l} \bar{P}\left(S_z < 0\right) =$$

$$\le \sum_{l \ne t} \sum_{\alpha=0}^{\varpi_i} \sum_{\beta=0}^{\alpha} \sum_{\gamma=0}^{\varpi_i-\alpha} \sum_{a=0}^{\varpi_i-a} \sum_{b=0}^{a} \sum_{f=0}^{b} \sum_{h=0}^{\varpi_i-a-b} \sum_{u=0} \Big[p_{SJ}(\alpha) \cdot p_{SJ}(\alpha,\beta) \cdot p_I(\varpi_i-\alpha,\gamma) \cdot p_s(a,b) \cdot \tilde{p}_{SJ}(f,a) \cdot \tilde{p}_{SJ}(h,b) \times$$

$$\times \tilde{p}_J(u,\varpi_i-a-b) \cdot \left(\int_{-\infty}^{0} f_N\left(x, E_t(\alpha,\beta,\gamma) - E_z(a,b,f,g,u), D_t(\alpha,\beta,\gamma) + D_z(a,b,f,g,u)\right) \right) \Big] dx.$$

where $f_N(x,E,D)$ is probability density function of the normal distribution with mean E and variance D, $\bar{P}$ designates an upper bound on probability P.

5   Conclusion

Hereinabove an upper bound on the probability of erroneous decoding in a DHA FH OFDMA system with a noncoherent ML detector for the case of multitone jamming has been introduced. The approach that has been used to obtain the bound in question can be easily applied to obtain bounds on erroneous decoding probability for other cases (e.g. partial band noise jamming, follower jamming etc.).

References

1. Zyablov, V.V., Osipov, D.S.: On the optimum choice of a threshold in a frequency hopping OFDMA system. Problems of Information Transmission 44(2), 91–98 (2008)
2. Osipov, D.S.: Concatenated codes in multiple access systems. Ph. D. Thesis, IITP RAS, Moscow (2008)
3. Osipov, D.S., Frolov, A.A., Zyablov, V.V.: A jamming-proof q-ary code-based signal-code construction. In: Proc. of ITAS 2011, pp. 167-173, Gelendzhik, Russia (2011) (in Russian)
4. Proakis, J.G.: Digital Communications. McGraw Hill, New York (1983)
5. Feller, W.: An Introduction to Probability Theory and Its Applications. John Wiley & Sons, Inc. (1968)
6. Dwight, H.: Tables of Integrals and other Mathematical Data. The McMillan company, USA (1957)

Analysis of Inter-RSU Beaconing Interference in VANETs*

Carlos Gañán[1], Jonathan Loo[2], Arindam Ghosh[2], Oscar Esparza[1], Sergi Reñé[1], and Jose L. Muñoz[1]

[1] {Universitat Politécnica de Catalunya, Telematics Department, Barcelona Spain
{carlos.ganan,jose.munoz,oscar.esparza,sergi.rene}@entel.upc.edu
[2] Middlesex University, Computer Communication Department, London, UK
{j.loo,a.ghosh}@mdx.ac.uk}

Abstract. Vehicular ad Hoc Networks (VANETs) have emerged as a key technology serving community of peoples in various applications. Providing infotainment and safety services requires the existence of roadside units (RSU) to access to the desired resources. Ideally, the infrastructure should be deployed permeatively to provide continuous connectivity and optimal coverage. This deployment technique increases capacity and coverage at expenses of increasing interference that can severely degrade the performance of the VANET. Moreover, malicious vehicles could mimic the signals of RSUs causing significant performance degradation. In this paper we study the impact of the inter-RSU interference on the beacon broadcasting due to both inefficient deployment and potential RSU emulation attacks (REA). Extensive packet-level simulations have been performed to support the observations made.

Keywords: VANET, RSU interference, RSU emulation attack.

1 Introduction

Vehicular ad hoc networks (VANET) will be deployed around the world within the next years. Covering a very dense environment requires that thousands of road side units have to be placed and set up properly, without interference. Thus, a main requirement of an efficient VANET is adequate coverage where vehicles are able to access (e.g., pervasive computing-enabled) applications and services. The deployment of the infrastructure should reduce the interference as much as possible so as to achieve these functions in a cost-effective and resource-efficient manner.

* This work is funded by the Spanish Ministry of Science and Education under the projects CONSOLIDER-ARES CSD2007-00004, FPU grant AP2010-0244, and TEC2011-26452 "SERVET", and by the Government of Catalonia under grant 2009 SGR 1362.

B. Bellalta et al. (Eds.): MACOM 2012, LNCS 7642, pp. 49–59, 2012.

Regrettably, RSUs will be deployed in an empirical way, manually positioned and located based on the received signal strength. Such an unorganized approach to VANET infrastructure design implies strong channel interference and poor resource utilization. For instance, more RSUs may be used to improve coverage while leaving blind spots or places where there are too many RSUs packed too closely together. This will lead to signal overlap, which in turn will cause interference and waste of resources. In this paper, we address to quantify the impact of this interference on the VANET performance.

The medium access control (MAC) for Wireless Access in Vehicular Environments (WAVE) described in the IEEE 1609.4[1] is unable to cope with the sharp increase in interference caused by these dense deployments. Moreover, most of the applications envisioned for this type of networks require the periodic broadcasting of beacons and WAVE service advertisement (WSA). Beacons are generated with typical frequency of 1-10 Hz; this high generation rate could cause not only the congestion on the control channel (CCH) but also the loss of beacons containing critical information. Moreover, the current standard do not provide any authentication mechanism for the CCH. An adversary equipped with a software defined radio can mimic the transmission characteristics of a RSU in order to emulate its activity. The goal of this attack is to block vehicles from utilizing the idle service channels, thus reducing the available bandwidth and degrading the network performance. The malicious attackers can thus significantly degrade the performances of the well-behaving vehicles by causing additional collisions in the CCH and reserving service channels for their own benefit.

Broadcasting in VANETs has been studied from the vehicle to vehicle (V2V) point of view [2,3], however the role of the RSUs has been neglected. Authors have modeled analytically broadcast transmissions even taking into account he channel switching [4], but only from a V2V perspective. WAVE services will be announced by the infrastructure during the CCH. Though these advertisements will not be as delay-constraint as the safety applications, it is necessary to provide a reliable broadcasting service via RSUs. The lack of an authentication mechanism introduces an entire new suite of threats and tactics that cannot be easily mitigated. RSU emulation attacks (REA) can be easily performed by any malicious vehicle by broadcasting nonexisting or fraudulent WSAs.

In this paper we analyze the unreliable broadcast service from the infrastructure perspective. We show that one of the main issues for broadcast protocols lies in the unreliable packet delivery. While the IEEE 1609.4 uses RTS/CTS handshake mechanism for unicast transmissions to increase reliability, beacons will be broadcasted in the CCH relying only on pure CSMA/CA without RTS/CTS. By means of realistic simulation we show the inability of the broadcasting mechanism to achieve a beacon reception rate close to 100%. Just introducing a single attacker performing a RSU emulation attack could lead to a beacon collision probability above the 35%. We show that this problem is especially critical in VANETs where safety beacons will collide and will not be received in time to prevent accidents.

2   IEEE 1609.4 Broadcasting Limitations

Vehicular denseness will vary from very dense urban areas to sparse highways. Therefore, the MAC layer of the VANET has to be scalable. The IEEE 1609.4 [1] is based on the Distributed Coordination Function (DCF) as MAC technique. DCF employs a CSMA/CA with binary exponential backoff algorithm. This mechanism is enhanced by using the same prioritization techniques than the IEEE 802.11e [5], namely the Hybrid Coordination Function (HCF). Basically, the HCF allows making Arbitration Interframe Space (e.g. AIFS[i]) variable depending on the priority (i) of the packet (see Fig. 1). Also, the length of the contention window varies among different priorities.

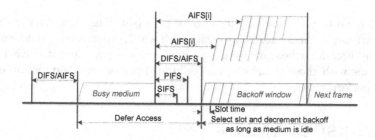

Fig. 1. EDCA channel access prioritization, as specified in [5]

However this MAC mechanism is neither secure nor efficient for dense networks. The CSMA/CA does not totally avoid collisions when broadcasting. Similar to the traditional unicast IEEE 802.11, it presents drastic throughput falls in crowded environments. Moreover, for broadcast communication, there is no error-handling as there are no acknowledgments and hence no exponential backoff growth. In this sense, as the contention window size is not increased, the prioritization is limited and even increases the likeliness of packet collisions. Broadcast beacons suffer from hidden node problems, due to the lack of a RTS/CTS handshake. Moreover, safety beacons are sent with the maximum transmission power, which increased the coverage and, consequently, the inter-RSU interference. According to the different signal strengths, we can distinguish three different ranges (see Figure 2):

- *Communication range*: is the region where both the vehicle's receiver sensitivity threshold and the SINR are met for the payload.
- *Detection range*: is the region where other vehicles can detect an ongoing transmission.
- *Interference range*: is the region starting from the precise location where there is not enough signal power to decode the packet.

Thus, when broadcasting the MAC mechanism described in the IEEE 1609.4 standard will incur in high delays due to channel switching and will suffer from

Fig. 2. Transmitting-RSU ranges

the hidden problem which will lead to beacon collisions. Moreover, as these beacons are not authenticated, any entity with a 802.11p interface could emulate a RSU and broadcast beacons leading to denial of service. Current IEEE 1609.4 cannot cope with these attacks which could lead to a severe degradation of the network performance.

3   Inter-RSU Interference

In this section, the interference between several RSUs is analyzed. Different interference scenarios are distinguished according to the distance, D, between the RSU. These scenarios will appear either to an inefficient RSU deployment or to the existence of attacker performing REA attacks. In this paper, we only take into account the interference from within the communication range of the RSUs. A RSU is said to be interfered by another RSU if the vehicles in its transmission range are able to decode the packets from the interfering RSU.

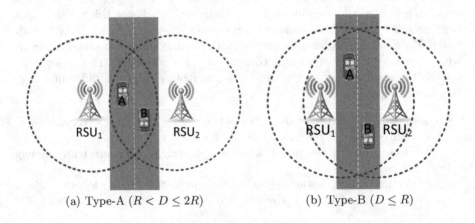

(a) Type-A $(R < D \leq 2R)$ (b) Type-B $(D \leq R)$

Fig. 3. Inter-RSU interference scenarios

Fig. 3 shows two different inter-RSU interference scenarios, i.e., Type-A and Type-B interference scenarios correspond to $R < D \le 2R$ and $D \le R$, respectively, where R is the communication range. Note that for larger distances, there is no interference between both RSUs. Before delving further into the characteristics of each interference scenario, we define the overlapping region O as the intersection region of the transmission range of the RSUs.

In Type-A scenarios, RSUs are not within communication range of each other and this cannot decode each other's transmitted beacons. Although the RSUs can hear from the vehicles of the interfering RSU, the interfering RSU and the vehicles in its range can become hidden nodes. For instance, as in Fig. 3(a), when RSU_1 and RSU_2 are broadcasting beacons, these beacons could potentially collide as both RSUs are hidden nodes one to the other. Thus, both vehicles in region O will suffer from beacon losses. Therefore, the beacon transmission from RSU_1 is not successful at vehicle A due to a colliding transmission from RSU_2. Traditionally this problem is addressed by the RTS/CTS/DATA/ACK handshake. However, when broadcasting the IEEE 1609.4 standard does not use this handshake. Therefore, the hidden RSU effect will be one of the main reasons for packet loss in vehicular communication.

For Type-B (see Fig. 3(b)), a RSU can receive direct transmissions from the interfering RSU and some or all of the vehicles in its range. The problem faced by Type-B interference scenario is that all the entities in the transmission range of either one of the RSUs (i.e. vehicles or the interfering RSU) can become potential hidden nodes to the ongoing transmission. As RTS/CTS is not used when broadcasting, vehicles may be exposed to a beacon drop in the message queue in high load scenarios where the carrier is nearly all the time found busy. The connection to packet loss here is that for the exposed RSUs the local message queue becomes full. In the worst case, not even one beacon can be sent. Such a situation can be described as local beacon congestion. Beacon loss then occurs depending on the packet dropping strategy. If we now consider highly varying RSU densities this consideration also reveals that even in locally low densities RSUs may be exposed if there are high densities within carrier sensing range. In this case, some RSUs would be blocked from transmission unnecessarily. Therefore, in both type of interference scenarios, it is clear that a significant number of beacon collisions will occur when broadcasting.

4   Evaluation

In this section, extensive packet-level simulations are performed to validate the observations made in the previous section. We use the VeinS simulator to evaluate the impact of the inter-RSU interference. VeinS [6] is an inter-vehicular communication simulation framework that integrates the OMNeT++/ INET [7] network simulator and the SUMO [8] road traffic microsimulation tool. VeinS implements a multi-channel simulation model for IEEE 1609.4/802.11p allowing to fully capture the distinctive properties of this radio technology.

We use two real scenarios (each one representing a different interference Type) to evaluate the inter-RSU interference (see Fig. 4). First, we evaluate a urban

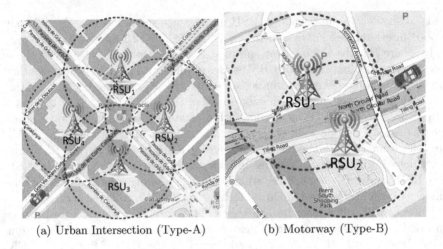

(a) Urban Intersection (Type-A)   (b) Motorway (Type-B)

Fig. 4. Simulation scenarios

intersection of the Spanish city of Barcelona. According to the Spanish transport authority, annually, in Barcelona from 70 to 100 intersections are detected with more than ten accidents, with a total of 1,500 accidents, near 60% of those produced in the entire city. Typically, these accidents are concentrated at intersections of roads with two lanes. The second scenario is a urban motorway located in the city of London. Due to the high density of cars and roads in this area, it is foreseeable that the RSU will overlap as in a Type-B interference scenario. The configuration parameters of the RSUs/vehicles are shown in Table 2. Note that cars are placed in each scenario moving across the intersection in the Type-A scenario and moving through the motorway in the Type-B scenario. Each RSU broadcast beacons in the CCH with the highest priority. SUMO [8] is used to recreate a realistic traffic environment.

Table 1. RSU configuration parameters

Parameter	Value
Transmission Power	20 mW
Bit rate	18 Mbps
Sensitivity	-94.0 dBm
Thermal Noise	-110.0 dBm

Table 2. Vehicle profile

Parameter	Value
Speed	20 m/s
Max. Acceleration	5 m/s
Max. Deceleration	3 m/s
Channel bandwidth	10 MHz
OBU receiver sensitivity	-94.0dBm

4.1 Performance Metrics

We define four different metrics to evaluate the inter-RSU interference:

- *Beacon Collision Probability* (P_{col}): probability that a beacon broadcasted by RSU_j collides with another beacon broadcasted by RSU_i.
- *Delay*: elapsed time since the creation of the beacon from RSU_j and the reception at $vehicle_i$. This is only calculated for received beacons.
- *Per-vehicle Throughput* (T): size of the beacons delivered to a particular vehicle over a period of time.
- *Inter-arrival Time* (τ): amount of time between two successive beacon receptions at $vehicle_i$. This is important from the point of view of a real-time applications. Ideally, the inter-arrival time would equal the beacon generation interval.

4.2   Simulation Results

Beacon Collision Probability. Fig. 5 shows P_{col} for different beacon sizes (b_s) ranging from 100 to 800 bytes, and different beacon generation frequencies (BGF) raging from 1 to 10 Hz. As expected, the collision probability increases with both b_s and BGF. It is worth noting that P_{col} is higher in the Type-A scenario as all the RSUs are hidden one to each other. Thus, the collision avoidance mechanism is totally inefficient, and P_{col} achieves values higher than the 70%. In the Type-B scenario, the hidden terminal problem is not that frequent. Therefore, the collision probability is lower.

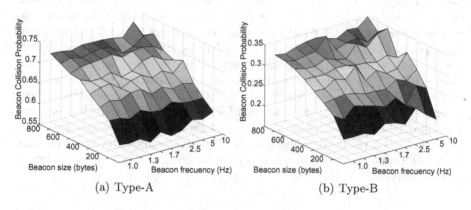

(a) Type-A   (b) Type-B

Fig. 5. Beacon Collision Probability P_{col}

The scenario with $b_s = 800$ bytes and BGF $= 10Hz$ is shown in Fig. 6. In this case, it is clear than when a vehicle is in range of 4 RSUs, the number of collision highly increases. In the London motorway, the CSMA/CA avoids most of the collisions but it is not able to avoid that some of the beacons collide.

The required reception probability depends on the type of application supported by the vehicular network. However, for safety application P_{col} should not exceed the 1%. As shown this requirement not met when the vehicle is in range

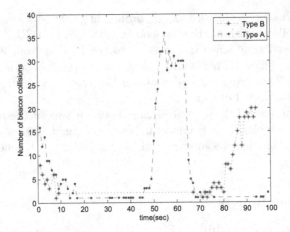

Fig. 6. Number of beacon collisions for $b_s=$ 800 bytes and BGF=10 Hz

of two or more hidden RSUs. The simulation results show that a P_{col} below 1% is only achieved in Type-B scenarios when the BGF is under 10Hz and the beacon are smaller than 200 bytes.

Delay Analysis. We furthermore analyzed the beacon delay, i.e., the time from the generation of a beacon message at the RSU to its actual reception at the vehicle under different BGF. We visualized our findings in Fig. 7. As shown in Fig. 7, while for low frequencies (BGI< 10 Hz) the differences between Type-A and Type-B scenarios are very small. Significant differences appear when the BGF> 10Hz. This is due to the impossibility to distribute the beacons over only Control Channel intervals. With this BGF, all beacons generated during a Service Channel interval have to wait for the next CCH interval to be sent. Therefore, a beacon has to wait at most of 54 ms until it is sent. Note also, that for BGF> 10 Hz the delay is higher in the Type-B scenario. The reason for that is that in Type-B when a RSU detects that the channel is busy it enters into a back-off interval.

Per-vehicle Throughput. Fig. 8 shows the impact of the BGF on per-vehicle throughput. As expected, when beacons are generated more frequently, the throughput increases. However, this increment is not directly proportional to the BGF as there are more collisions when BGF increases. Note that, while in the Type-B scenario the throughput remains roughly constant during the simulation time, in the Type-A scenario the throughput varies over time.

Fig. 9 shows the throughput for $b_s=$ 800 bytes and BGF=10Hz. Note that in the case of the Type-A scenario, when the vehicle is in range of the four RSUs, the throughput decreases drastically. This is due to the high number of collisions. After 40s, the vehicle is at the intersection and the 4 RSUs are broadcasting

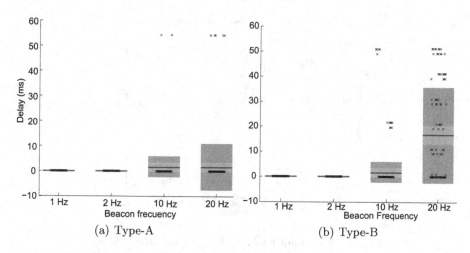

Fig. 7. Delay Box-Plot for $b_s = 800$ bytes

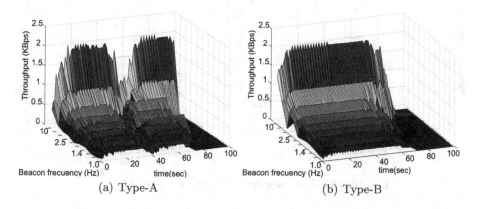

Fig. 8. Throughput evolution vs BGF

beacons as if the medium was idle. Thus, almost all the beacons collide (see Fig. 6) and the throughput drops to almost 0 KBps.

Inter-arrival Time. Fig. 9 shows the empirical cumulative distribution function (ECDF) of τ for different BGF. As the BGF increases P_{col} increases, with a detrimental effect on the inter-arrival time of beacons. Thus, τ increases for larger BGF values. This is a direct consequence of the beacon collisions. When a RSU transmits a beacon and this beacon is lost, it is not retransmitted. At the next beacon issuing instant, the RSU will transmit a new beacon with updated information. This effect is more evident in Type-A as there are more collisions. Due to this periodicity, the ECDF of τ adopts a staircase shape. In the Type-B scenario, τ is lower (as there are fewer collisions).

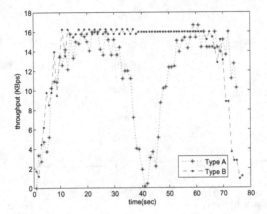

Fig. 9. Throughput for $b_s =$ 800 bytes and BGF 10 Hz

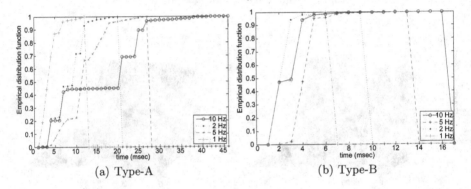

(a) Type-A   (b) Type-B

Fig. 10. ECDF of Inter-arrival times for $b_s =$ 800 bytes

5   Conclusions

In this paper, we have shown that inter-RSU interference will appear due to either inefficient RSU deployment or the existence of RSU emulation attacks. We have shown that current IEEE 1609.4 medium access technique is not able to cope with the interference caused by overlapping RSUs. The analysis of the beacon collision probability shows that the broadcast performance drops below 30% when a vehicle is in range of four RSUs that are hidden one to the other. Moreover, due to the channel switching scheme defined in the IEEE 1609.4, the delay can exceed the 54 ms, making unfeasible the deployment of a safety applications.

The insights gained from this analysis not only lead to a better understanding of the impact of inter-RSU interference on VANETS but also can be used to design improved beaconing techniques to mitigate the RSU emulation attacks.. Future work includes identifying REA attackers and exclude them from the network.

References

1. IEEE draft standard for wireless access in vehicular environments (WAVE) - multi-channel operation. IEEE 1609.4/D8.0, pp. 1–92 (June 2010)
2. Vinel, A., Koucheryavy, Y., Andreev, S., Staehle, D.: Estimation of a successful beacon reception probability in vehicular ad-hoc networks. In: Proceedings of the 2009 International Conference on Wireless Communications and Mobile Computing: Connecting the World Wirelessly, IWCMC 2009, pp. 416–420 (2009)
3. Campolo, C., Molinaro, A.: On vehicle-to-roadside communications in 802.11p/wave vanets. In: 2011 IEEE Wireless Communications and Networking Conference (WCNC), pp. 1010–1015 (March 2011)
4. Campolo, C., Koucheryavy, Y., Molinaro, A., Vinel, A.: Characterizing broadcast packet losses in ieee 802.11p/wave vehicular networks. In: 2011 IEEE 22nd International Symposium on Personal Indoor and Mobile Radio Communications (PIMRC), pp. 735–739 (September 2011)
5. IEEE Standard for Information Technology - Telecommunications and Information Exchange between systems - local and metropolitan area networks - specific requirements. IEEE Std 802.11e-2005 (Amendment to IEEE Std 802.11), pp. 1–189 (November 2005)
6. Sommer, C., German, R., Dressler, F.: Bidirectionally coupled network and road traffic simulation for improved ivc analysis. IEEE Transactions on Mobile Computing 10(1), 3–15 (2011)
7. Vargas, A.: Objective modular network testbed in c++ (omnet++). version 4.2, http://www.omnetpp.org
8. Krajewicz, D., Hertkorn, G., Rössel, C., Wagner, P.: SUMO (simulation of urban mobility); an open-source traffic simulation. In: 4th Middle East Symposium on Simulation and Modelling (MESM 2002), pp. 183–187 (2002)

Survey of Energy Efficient Tracking and Localization Techniques in Buildings Using Optical and Wireless Communication Media

Tom M. Bruintjes, André B.J. Kokkeler, Georgios Karagiannis,
and Gerard J.M. Smit

University of Twente, Hallenweg 19, 7522 NH Enschede, The Netherlands
t.m.bruintjes@utwente.nl
http://caes.ewi.utwente.nl/

Abstract. This paper presents a survey of beamforming, beamsteering and mobile tracking techniques. The survey was made in the context of the SOWICI project. The aim of this project is to reduce power consumption of data exchanging devices within houses. An optical fiber network is used for data transport to and from rooms whereas wireless transceivers communicate with appliances within the rooms. Using this approach, the aim is to reduce power consumption and exposure to electromagnetic radiation. To realize this, beamforming will be used to only radiate energy in, and receive signals from, the direction of interest. Because appliances within households can move, some of them even relatively fast, the pointing direction of the beam should be steerable. The pointing direction can be deduced from the communication link (beamsteering) or via separate mobile tracking techniques.

Keywords: beamforming, beamsteering, mobile tracking.

1 Introduction

Today's society is confronted with immense challenges such as climate change, depletion of resources and aging society. This has triggered a change in mindset from continuous growth to sustainability (e.g., smart buildings and smart mobility). Today's homes and buildings are responsible for 41% of the energy consumption in the European Union. They contain many functionalities like domestic appliances, heating, air-conditioning, lighting, electronics and wireless systems that are not responding adequately to actual situations; they do not adapt to actual energy needs and mostly they are not aware of each other due to a lack of overall coordination and control. This leads to unnecessary energy consumption.

Especially in homes and buildings, energy can be saved by using modern technology with situational-aware devices that are able to communicate. Home automation encompasses the increased automation of appliances in residential dwellings through electronic means, to meet the specific needs of the inhabitants. The term "home automation" is used in contrast to the more mainstream

B. Bellalta et al. (Eds.): MACOM 2012, LNCS 7642, pp. 60–74, 2012.

"building automation", which refers to similar technology for general needs, particularly the automatic or semi-automatic control of lighting, doors and windows, heating, ventilation, air conditioning, etc.. Both home and building automation heavily rely on sensors and actuators that interchange information with control units via reliable communication links. For efficiency reasons, the communication for home/building automation should preferably be integrated with the communication system used for data exchange and multi-media entertainment, which is not the case today. Needless to say that the integrated system should be reliable, flexible, scalable and of course it should consume minimal power. It should support fixed and mobile devices as well as low and high bit-rate devices efficiently. Finally, the wireless communication should work reliably with a minimum of electro-magnetic (EM) emission for energy-efficiency and to eliminate potential health hazards due to exposure to EM radiation in a world full of wireless devices.

By using 60GHz radio transmission in room-sized pico-cells in combination with adaptive radio pencil beams which are steered to pin-point the (mobile) wireless devices, considerable savings in the energy consumption of the network itself can be achieved. The main goal of this paper is to provide an overview of energy efficient localization and tracking techniques that can be applied in buildings when using optical and wireless communication media. In particular, in this paper, we first introduce the SOWICI project [1] which aims at using energy efficient tracking techniques based on these communication media. Second, as part of this project, existing solutions are surveyed in the areas of Beamforming (section 3), Beamsteering (section 4) and Mobile Tracking (section 5) with an emphasis on the latter. At the end of this paper, we will draw conclusions, relevant to the SOWICI project, based on this survey.

2   The SOWICI Project

Within the SOWICI project, which started in 2011, a novel hybrid optical/wireless network architecture is proposed that integrates the home automation network with the high bit-rate in-home network for data transfer and entertainment in a very energy-efficient way. In particular, this integrated network features an optical fiber network backbone between a central control unit and all rooms with wireless transmission inside the rooms. SOWICI supports 60GHz radio transmission in combination with beamforming to save energy consumption. In addition, the exposure of humans to EM radiation is reduced to a bare minimum. We expect to reduce the radio emission by at least three orders of magnitude.

The general infrastructure, researched within the SOWICI project is depicted in Fig. 1. Wireless transmitters (Radio Access Points, RAPs) are placed in a (4×4) rectangular planar array configuration such that beamforming becomes possible by means of constructive interference. Pointing the beams to the Mobile Devices (MDs) present in a room will yield considerable savings in the energy consumption of the network. However, MDs can move around in the building. Beamforming therefore needs to be adaptive.

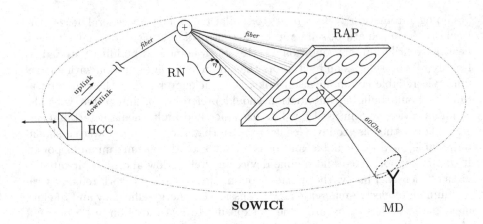

Fig. 1. SOWICI Infrastructure

To steer and/or shape a beam, a variable delay τ and gain η need to be applied to each of the antenna elements of the RAP. To drive the antenna elements with the appropriate delay and gain, an integrated optical circuit is used. Although this Reconfigurable Node (RN) is responsible for physically inducing the delays needed for constructive interference, the control intelligence for localization and tracking is located in the centralized Home Communication Center (HCC). The fiber that connects the HCC to the different RAPs therefore conveys both the actual data for the MDs and the RN configuration information to control the angle and shape of the beam remotely from the HCC. To check the appropriateness of the proposed infrastructure, a survey of existing alternatives in beamforming and tracking mobiles in general was made.

3   Beamforming

Radio beams can be steered by using beamforming techniques, often also referred to as phased array techniques. Basic theory on this subject can be found in [56]. Until recently, mainly narrowband beamforming has been considered because of ease of implementation. The term 'narrowband' is used for signals whose bandwidth is much smaller than their center frequency (generally 1% or less). In other cases, a signal is 'wideband'. Wideband beamforming techniques are studied in detail more and more [32]. In phased array antennas, differences in the phases (narrowband beamforming) or time (wideband beamforming), determine the shape and direction of the beam. For this, accurate and tuneable shifting of phases or time delays need to be accomplished, which is particularly challenging when microwave radio signals with complex modulation formats are involved and fast beamsteering is required.

Traditionally, beamforming is realized in electronic circuits in contrast with optical beamforming discussed later on. A time delay or phase shift can be realized at different stages [57].

- RF beamforming realizes beamforming at RF frequencies and is done fully analogue [44].
- LO Beamforming performs the beamforming operation at intermediate frequencies (IF) where phase shifts are introduced in the local oscillator (LO) signals. This type of beamforming is inherently narrowband.
- IF beamforming performs beamforming at intermediate frequencies (IF) and generally in the digital domain. This has the advantage that the flexibility and computational capacity of digital processors can be exploited to the full.
- Beamforming by optical techniques was achieved by deploying bulky dispersive fiber delay lines, and dispersive micro-ring structures [36][33]. Only 1-dimensional beamsteering was addressed.

There are several application areas for beamforming.

- One of the first areas to adopt these techniques was radar. Phased arrays for radar have been used since the 1950s to detect, locate and follow reflecting objects or targets [58] .
- Phased arrays are also used to construct images of celestial object within radio astronomy. A Radio Telescope for astronomy, exploiting phased array technology that is currently operational is LOFAR [58].
- Within telecommunications, beamforming is used within GSM and UMTS networks mainly in the downlink (from base station to mobile) [21][20][41], within WLAN [62] and LTE [8]. During the last few years, multi-antenna techniques at both the transmitter and receiver have also been introduced in the latest wireless standards (e.g., IEEE803.11n [7]). However, these techniques are applied in a highly scattering environment where signals arrive from different directions. In this case, the techniques used are generally referred to as MIMO [19].

A significant challenge associated with beamforming is how to form the beam in such a way that the phased array antenna can transmit (almost) simultaneously different content towards multiple mobile devices located in a room. Two alternatives can be distinguished:

- For each mobile device located in a room a time slot is allocated. During a time slot a beam is formed in such a way that the phased array antenna can transmit only to one mobile device. The disadvantages of this solution are (1) the switching in time; (2) the reconfiguration of the phased array antenna elements; (3) transmission of the information needs to be accomplished within the given time slot.
- More than one beams are formed simultaneously and sent to the different mobile devices in the room. The main disadvantage of this option is that each beam is formed using a smaller in size phased array (i.e., only a subset of the phased array antenna elements are used).

Furthermore, we intend to stay IEEE 802.15.3C [18] compliant within SOWICI. The IEEE 802.15.3C standard defines a central controlled network topology and a TDMA based MAC protocol for Wireless Personal Area Networks (WPANs) operating in the unlicensed 60GHz band. It also specifies an optional *codebook beamforming* protocol, which is based on scanning discrete sectors (section 5.2).

4   Beamsteering

For stationary devices their location can be detected at the start of a communication session during a training sequence [47]. However, for moving mobile devices the position needs to be tracked continuously. Algorithms that adapt steering vector weights (τ and η) to steer the beam are called adaptive beamforming algorithms. These type of algorithms can be classified into three subclasses [2]: Temporal reference beamforming algorithms, Spatial reference beamforming algorithms and Blind beamforming algorithms.

- In Temporal reference beamforming, known temporal signal properties are used to adjust the beamsteering [61].
- Spatial reference beamforming uses Direction-of-Arrival (DoA) algorithms to estimate the direction of the impinging signal. Well-known examples of DoA algorithms are MUSIC [47] and ESPRIT [46]. Most spatial reference algorithms are inappropriate for real-time beamsteering because of their high computational costs.
- Blind beamforming algorithms use statistical properties of the desired signal to determine the angle of arrival of the signal. An example of a blind beamforming algorithm is the Constant Modulus Algorithm (CMA) [49][50]. Blind beamforming algorithms are efficient since they do not need a-priori information about channel characteristics. Thus, the initial training phase of an adaptive equalizer is avoided, eliminating potential losses in channel capacity. An extended version of CMA can be used to adapt the steering vector weights to compensate for movement of mobiles [49][50], but such an algorithm is quite computationally intensive.

5   Mobile Localization and Tracking

Instead of using one of the beamsteering algorithms mentioned above, a separate mobile tracking technique can be used to obtain the information about the desired pointing direction of the beamformer. In this section, a broad survey of mobile tracking techniques is presented. The purpose is to become familiar with mobile tracking in a broad sense and to assess the applicability of (parts of) the techniques to be used within the SOWICI project.

Currently mobile users can roam ubiquitously and have access from many locations. Therefore, the knowledge of the physical locations of mobile user devices, such as phones, laptops, is important in network operation & planning and in several applications such as location based services and low enforcement services. The procedure required for the estimation of such physical locations (e.g., longitude, latitude, altitude) is usually denoted as localization, which is estimated relative to a reference position. The wireless device whose location is to be estimated is usually called Localization Node (LN) and the network entity with known location is usually called Localization Base Station (LBS). One important performance measure of localization schemes is the achieved accuracy on estimating the exact physical position of devices. Several surveys and classification on localization solutions have been published, such as [38][35][10].

5.1 Classification of Localization Schemes

Localization is classified based on (a) area of deployment, (b) used wireless technology physical layer, (c) measured localization physical parameter, (d) location lookup table, (e) the estimation technique, (f) the localizing entity and (g) the supported security.

Area of Deployment. Localization schemes depend on the area of deployment, due to the differences in network topology, number of users and available resources for such networks. This category can be subdivided into Wide Area Localization (WAL), Local Area Localization (LAL) and Ad-Hoc Localization (AHL). The WAL category is characterized by predominantly outdoor deployments, such as:

- Global Navigation Satellite System (GNSS) Galileo [14] and Global Positioning System (GPS) [22], Differential GPS [25], Assisted GPS [17].
- Cellular network based localization solutions [55].

The LAL category is characterized by predominantly indoor deployments, such as:

- Active Batch [13].
- Wireless LAN localization solutions [39].

The AHL category is characterized by the use of ad-hoc networks and wireless sensor networks which typically are power constrained and may be heterogeneous in nature. Examples of localization solutions that are based on wireless sensor networks are described in [35], which can be:

- Centralized based, where centralized information already exists such as road traffic monitoring, health monitoring and where the measurement data of all nodes are collected in a central processing unit [29].
- Distributed based, where each node relies on self-localization using the measured distances and the local information from its neighbouring nodes [28].

Example solutions that are based on mobile ad-hoc networks are e.g., [11].

Used Wireless Technology. The used wireless technology and in particular its physical layer, influences significantly the localization solution. This category can be subdivided into:

- Infrared (IR) solutions [59].
- Ultrasound (US), where the signals can propagate through walls [43].
- Radio Frequency (RF), which is the most commonly used type, e.g., GPS based systems [22][17].

Measured Localization Physical Parameter. The measured localization physical parameter of the used radio link between the LN and multiple LBSs is used to estimate the location of LN. Several physical parameter values can be used to estimate the location of the LN. The most common are:

- Signal Strength (SS) or Received Signal Strength Indicator (RSSI) [5].
- Link Quality Indicator (LQI), which is a metric of the current quality of the received signal. Not purely based on RSSI but often a combination of RSSI and Signal to Noise Ratio (SNR) [53].
- Time of Arrival (ToA), which is the time taken by wireless packets (or signals) to travel from a transmitter to a receiver at a certain distance [37]. Differential Time of Arrival (DTOA) is used to avoid complex time synchronization [60]. Two signals traveling at different propagation speeds are sent out and then quantify the difference in time of arrival. If both signal propagation speeds are known, a distance can be derived from the difference measurement.
- Connectivity (Cnn), which indicates that the LN is in the transmission range of an LBS [59].
- Fingerprinting uses a signature (or a fingerprint), such as radio link, optical, acoustic, or motion attributes, to identify a certain logical location [4].
- The techniques discussed in section 4 can be considered as techniques that measure physical parameters as well.

Location Lookup Table (LLT). The location lookup table (LLT) is used to map the physical parameter values onto the various locations within the deployment site and prior to the actual localization process. Different types of LLTs are known. The most common ones are:

- Measurement based, where the physical parameter at various locations on the deployment site is measured in order to construct the LLT [3].
- Agent based, where the LLTs is built using readings from agents that are placed at various locations to perform certain automatic measurements without requiring extensive manual costs [31].
- Model based, where analytical/empirical models are used to estimate the values of the physical parameter at any location within the deployment site [5].

Estimation Technique. An estimation technique can be used to calculate the position of the LN based on the available LLT and the current measurements of the physical parameter within the deployment site. The current location of the LN is estimated to be the physical location that has physical parameter values closest to the current measured values. Two types of estimation techniques are used:

- Deterministic estimation, where statistical parameters such as measured physical parameter mean or median between LN and multiple LBSs are used for a robust multilateral estimation [12].
- Probabilistic estimation, where the position of LNs can be estimated based on the statistical distribution of the physical parameter at different locations within the deployment site [13].

Localizing Entity. The described estimation techniques can be carried out by either the LN or the LBS. Further subdivision is possible by distinguishing between:

- Client based localization, where the LN determines its position by monitoring the signals and/or messages received from the LBSs [13].
- Network based localization, where the network determines the position of a LN by measuring the physical parameter values of the signals and/or messages sent by the LN towards several LSBs [5].

Supported Security. The security category is characterized by whether a localization technique is resistant to location spoofing and to security attacks. This category is subdivided in:

- Open, where security is not supported meaning that devices could easily spoof their position to various locations [59].
- Secure, where location spoofing and security attacks on a localization scheme are protected [3].

5.2   Indoor Localization Techniques

Most applicable to SOWICI are indoor localization techniques. Such mechanisms have been studied extensively in [23] and [35]. Focusing on wireless technology, the following can be distinguished:

- GPS-based using an indoor GPS technique [6].
- RFID-based using RSS information to calculate the location of RFID tags [9].
- Cellular-based using the mobile cellular network to estimate indoor positioning, when considering that the building is covered by several LBSs [54].
- Ultra Wide Band(UWB)-based using ultra-short pulses with a low duty cycle permitting an accurate determination of the Time of Arrival [34].

- WLAN-based using IEEE 802.11 for positioning by e.g., adding a location server [5].
- Bluetooth-based using e.g., RSSI values for locating specific Bluetooth tags [52].
- IEEE 802.15.4-based [26]. Several tracking techniques are developed to measure the distance between two or more IEEE 802.15.4 compliant sensor devices. Such techniques are based on (1) combination of signal time-of-flight and phase measurements [48], (2) RSSI measurements [45][45][15] (3) Time (Difference) of Arrival [42] [51], (4) using Ultra Wide Band [40], (5) using Angle of Arrival [40], (6) using Radio Interferometric Positioning (RIP) [24][16].

Localization using phased arrays is possible by:

- Direction or Angle of Arrival (AoA) algorithms such as MUSIC [47] and ESPRIT [46]. In order to derive the direction of arrival these algorithms consider that the received signals are narrowband and that phase differences between the individual elements or the array are measurable.
- The extended Constant Modulus Algorithm (CMA), see section 4, can be used for beamsteering and mobile tracking, which is able to adapt the steering vector weights to compensate for movement of the LNs [49][50][30]. This algorithm also considers that the received signals are narrowband and that phase information is available.
- Systematically scanning an area by changing the beam direction, using an antenna array, and by measuring the signal strength [33]. The LN is located in the direction where the signal strength is the highest. Such scanning techniques require a search algorithm to be able to localize LNs that are fast moving but do not require that the received signals are narrowband. An example of such an algorithm can be found in the the IEEE 802.15.3C standard [27]. A beamforming protocol (codebook beamforming) is proposed, which is based on scanning sectors with increasing granularity. The protocol consists of three stages: sector-level (coarse) training, beam-level (fine) training, and an optional tracking phase. The division of the stages facilitates a significant reduction in setup time compared with beamforming mechanisms using exhaustive searching. Moreover, the protocol employs only discrete phase shifts, which simplifies the problem compared to continuously tuneable beamforming. Scanning algorithms often assume a discrete beamformer (i.e., the best beam is selected from a limited set of beam patterns).
- Applying small perturbations to the current steering weights and evaluating if and in which direction the RSS/RSSI is better [18]. Perturbation techniques are closely related to scanning but are usually applicable to continuous beamformers.

5.3   Localization Selection Criteria

In order to select a localization scheme several criteria can be applied:

- Cost of deployment, which constitutes the initial deployment costs along with maintenance costs.
- Required accuracy, which is influenced mainly by the choice of the applied wireless technology physical layer, measured localization physical parameter and the estimation technique.
- Resource requirements and computational complexity, which measures the computation complexity and the resources, such as radio resources, required by a certain localization scheme.
- Effects on underlying network, which measures the impact of a localization scheme on the used underlying communication network.
- Security and privacy, which measures whether a localization scheme is resistant to e.g., intruders that try to gain access and disrupt the operation of a system and whether a localization scheme protects the identity of users while they are being localized.
- Type of environment, which affects the choice of the wireless technology physical layer, localization lookup table and the estimation technique. Some significant characteristics that need to be taken into account when considering the use of a multi-array receiver antenna for localization are related to whether the localization algorithm can receive/measure the phase information of the received signals and whether the received signals are narrowband or wideband.
- Effects on energy consumption, which measures the impact of a localization scheme on the consumed energy

5.4   Identifying the Appropriate Techniques for SOWICI

From the selection of criteria mentioned in the previous section, energy consumption is the most important for SOWICI. The resource requirements and computational complexity of the technique used are closely related to energy consumption. Hence, these are our primary concerns at this early stage in the research. Ideally we would like SOWICI to localize MDs using only the phased array. The other techniques that have been discussed need additional equipment which is likely to increase the costs of deployment. In addition we think that a mixture of techniques will result in a less elegant solution. However, if

Table 1. Selection Criteria applied to Indoor Localization Techniques

	Cost	Accuracy	Resources	Environment	Energy
GPS	✓✗	✓✗	✓✗	✗✗	✗✗
RFID	✓	✓	✓✗	✓✓	✓✓
GSM	✓✗	✓✗	✓✗	✗✗	✗✗
WiFi	✓	✓✗	✓	✓✓	✓✗
Bluetooth	✓✓	✓	✓	✓✓	✓
IEEE 802.15.4	✓✓	✓✓	✓✓	✓✓	✓✓
IEEE 802.15.3C (beamforming)	✓	✓✓	✓✗	✓✓	✓✓

complementary techniques add up to the energy consumption or help reduce it remains to be answered. Because we intend to bring energy consumption to a bare minimum, other solution have to be considered.

Table 1 shows the selection criteria from section 5.3 that we think are most important for SOWICI applied to the techniques enumerated in section 5.2. From the techniques that are complementary to the phased array, IEEE 802.15.4 based technology appears to match best with the goals of the SOWICI project.

6   Conclusion and Future Work within SOWICI

This paper presents a survey of beamforming, beamsteering and mobile tracking techniques. The information presented in this paper has been used within the SOWICI project to identify two main beamsteering and mobile tracking research directions. The first direction is to use the communication signals themselves for directing the beam. In SOWICI, beamforming is realized optically (RF beamforming) and is aimed to comply with the IEEE 802.15.3C standard [18]. This means signals are wideband and phase information is lost due to signal summation before analogue to digital conversion. Under these conditions none of the matured Direction-of-Arrival techniques like MUSIC, ESPRIT or CMA can be employed. Within this direction further research will therefore focus on other techniques that are based on RSSI measurements. Such techniques are for example scanning or the approaches based on perturbation, which were discussed in section 5.2. The second direction is to use a separate indoor localization technique to determine the position of the MD and then use this information to point the beam. One of the options that will be considered for further research is localization by means of IEEE 802.15.4 based technology. The final SOWICI architecture will be assessed based on the selection criteria mentioned in the previous section with an emphasis on energy consumption.

References

1. SOWICI (2011), http://www.sowici.nl
2. Allen, B., Ghavami, M.: Adaptive Array Systems: Fundamentals and Applications. John Wiley & Sons Inc. (2005)
3. Anjum, F., Pandey, S., Agrawal, P.: Secure localization in sensor networks using transmission range variation. In: IEEE International Conference on Mobile Adhoc and Sensor Systems Conference, p. 9. IEEE (2005)
4. Azizyan, M., Constandache, I., Roy Choudhury, R.: Surroundsense: mobile phone localization via ambience fingerprinting. In: Proceedings of the 15th Annual International Conference on Mobile Computing and Networking, MobiCom 2009, pp. 261–272. ACM, New York (2009), http://doi.acm.org/10.1145/1614320.1614350
5. Bahl, P., Padmanabhan, V.: Radar: An in-building rf-based user location and tracking system. In: Nineteenth Annual Joint Conference of the IEEE Computer and Communications Societies (INFOCOM 2000), vol. 2, pp. 775–784. IEEE (2000)

6. Barnes, J., Rizos, C., Wang, J., Small, D., Voigt, G., Gambale, N.: High precision indoor and outdoor positioning using locatanet. Journal of Global Positioning System 2(2), 73–82 (2003)
7. Behzad, A.: Radio design for mimo systems with an emphasis on ieee 802.11n. In: Course Presented at IEEE International Solid-State Circuits Conference, San Francisco (2007)
8. Boudreau, G., Panicker, J., Guo, N., Chang, R., Wang, N., Vrzic, S.: Interference coordination and cancellation for 4g networks. IEEE Communications Magazine 47(4), 74–81 (2009)
9. Bouet, M., Dos Santos, A.: Rfid tags: Positioning principles and localization techniques. In: Wireless Days (WD 2008), pp. 1–5. IEEE (2008)
10. Boukerche, A., Oliveira, H., Nakamura, E., Loureiro, A.: Localization systems for wireless sensor networks. IEEE Wireless Communications 14(6), 6–12 (2007)
11. Boukerche, A., Oliveira, H., Nakamura, E., Loureiro, A.: Vehicular ad hoc networks: A new challenge for localization-based systems. Computer Communications 31(12), 2838–2849 (2008)
12. Čapkun, S., Hamdi, M., Hubaux, J.: Gps-free positioning in mobile ad hoc networks. Cluster Computing 5(2), 157–167 (2002)
13. Castro, P., Chiu, P., Kremenek, T., Muntz, R.: A Probabilistic Room Location Service for Wireless Networked Environments. In: Abowd, G.D., Brumitt, B., Shafer, S. (eds.) UbiComp 2001. LNCS, vol. 2201, pp. 18–34. Springer, Heidelberg (2001)
14. Commission, E., et al.: Galileo-mission high level definition. EMRF Doc. 5(5), 2 (2002)
15. Dil, B., Havinga, P.: On the calibration and performance of rss-based localization methods. In: Internet of Things (IOT 2010), pp. 1–8. IEEE Computer Society (November 2010)
16. Dil, B., Havinga, P.: Stochastic radio interferometric positioning in the 2.4ghz range. In: Proceedings of the 9th ACM Conference on Embedded Networked Sensor Systems, SenSys 2011, pp. 108–120. ACM, New York (2011)
17. Djuknic, G., Richton, R.: Geolocation and assisted gps. Computer 34(2), 123–125 (2001)
18. Fakharzadeh Jahromi, M.: Optical and Microwave Beamforming for Phased Array Antennas. Ph.D. thesis, University of Waterloo (2010)
19. Gesbert, D., Shafi, M., Shiu, D., Smith, P., Naguib, A.: From theory to practice: an overview of mimo space-time coded wireless systems. IEEE Journal on Selected Areas in Communications 21(3), 281–302 (2003)
20. Godara, L.: Applications of antenna arrays to mobile communications ii. beamforming and direction-of-arrival considerations. Proceedings of the IEEE 85(8), 1195–1245 (1997)
21. Godara, L.: Applications of antenna arrays to mobile communications i. performance improvement, feasibility, and system considerations. Proceedings of the IEEE 85(7), 1031–1060 (1997)
22. NAVSTAR GPS: User equipment introduction. Department of Defense Document MZ10298 1 (1996)
23. Gu, Y., Lo, A., Niemegeers, I.: A survey of indoor positioning systems for wireless personal networks. IEEE Communications Surveys & Tutorials 11(1), 13–32 (2009)
24. Havinga, P., et al.: A feasibility study of rip using 2.4ghz 802.15.4 radios. In: IEEE 7th International Conference on Mobile Ad Hoc and Sensor Systems (MASS), pp. 690–696. IEEE (2010)

25. Hofmann-Wellenhof, B., Lichtenegger, H., Collins, J.: Global positioning system. theory and practice. Global Positioning System. Theory and Practice 1 (1993)
26. IEEE: Ieee standard for information technology - telecommunications and information exchange between systems - local and metropolitan area networks specific requirements part 15.4: Wireless medium access control (mac) and physical layer (phy) specifications for low-rate wireless personal area networks (lr-wpans). IEEE Std 802.15.4-2003, pp. 1–670 (2003)
27. IEEE: Wireless medium access control (mac) and physical layer (phy) specifications for high rate wireless personal area networks (wpans) amendment 2: Millimeter-wave-based alternative physical layer extension. IEEE Std 802.15.3c-2009 (Amendment to IEEE Std 802.15.3-2003), pp. 1–187 (December 2009)
28. Ihler, A., Fisher III, J., Moses, R., Willsky, A.: Nonparametric belief propagation for self-localization of sensor networks. IEEE Journal on Selected Areas in Communications 23(4), 809–819 (2005)
29. Kannan, A., Mao, G., Vucetic, B.: Simulated annealing based localization in wireless sensor network. In: The IEEE Conference on Local Computer Networks, pp. 15–22. IEEE (2005)
30. Blom, K.C.H., van de Burgwal, M.D., Rovers, K.C., Kokkeler, A.B.J., Smit, G.J.M.: Angular cma: A modified constant modulus algorithm providing steering angle updates. In: The Seventh International Conference on Wireless and Mobile Communications (ICWMC 2011), pp. 42–47. ThinkMind (June 2011)
31. Krishnan, P., Krishnakumar, A., Ju, W., Mallows, C., Gamt, S.: A system for lease: Location estimation assisted by stationary emitters for indoor rf wireless networks. In: Twenty-Third Annual Joint Conference of the IEEE Computer and Communications Societies (INFOCOM 2004), vol. 2, pp. 1001–1011. IEEE (2004)
32. Liu, W., Weiss, S.: Wideband Beamforming: Concepts and Techniques. Wiley (2010)
33. Madsen, C., Lenz, G.: Optical all-pass filters for phase response design with applications for dispersion compensation. IEEE Photonics Technology Letters 10(7), 994–996 (1998)
34. Mahfouz, M., Fathy, A., Kuhn, M., Wang, Y.: Recent trends and advances in uwb positioning. In: IEEE MTT-S International Microwave Workshop on Wireless Sensing, Local Positioning, and RFID (IMWS 2009), pp. 1–4. IEEE (2009)
35. Mao, G., Fidan, B., Anderson, B.: Wireless sensor network localization techniques. Computer Networks 51(10), 2529–2553 (2007)
36. Meijerink, A., Roeloffzen, C., Zhuang, L., Marpaung, D., Heideman, R., Borreman, A., van Etten, W.: Phased array antenna steering using a ring resonator-based optical beam forming network. In: Symposium on Communications and Vehicular Technology, pp. 7–12. IEEE (2006)
37. Nájar, M., Huerta, J., Vidal, J., Castro, J.: Mobile location with bias tracking in non-line-of-sight. In: IEEE International Conference on Acoustics, Speech, and Signal Processing (ICASSP 2004), vol. 3, pp. iii–956. IEEE (2004)
38. Pandey, S., Agrawal, P.: A survey on localization techniques for wireless networks. Journal of the Chinese Institute of Engineers 29(7), 1125–1148 (2006)
39. Pandey, S., Kim, B., Anjum, F., Agrawal, F.: Client assisted location data acquisition scheme for secure enterprise wireless networks. In: IEEE Wireless Communications and Networking Conference, vol. 2, pp. 1174–1179. IEEE (2005)

40. Patwari, N.: Location Estimation in Sensor Networks. Ph.D. thesis, University of Michigan (2005)
41. Pedersen, K., Mogensen, P., Ramiro-Moreno, J.: Application and performance of downlink beamforming techniques in umts. IEEE Communications Magazine 41(10), 134–143 (2003)
42. Pichler, M., Schwarzer, S., Stelzer, A., Vossiek, M.: Positioning with moving ieee 802.15.4 (zigbee) transponders. In: IEEE MTT-S International Microwave Workshop on Wireless Sensing, Local Positioning and RFID (IMWS 2009), pp. 1–4. IEEE (2009)
43. Priyantha, N., Chakraborty, A., Balakrishnan, H.: The cricket location-support system. In: Proceedings of the 6th Annual International Conference on Mobile Computing and Networking, pp. 32–43. ACM (2000)
44. Razavi, B.: RF Microelectronics. Prentice Hall (2011)
45. Robles, J., Tromer, S., Hidalgo, J., Lehnert, R.: A high configurable protocol for indoor localization systems. In: International Conference on Indoor Positioning and Indoor Navigation (IPIN), pp. 1–7. IEEE (2011)
46. Roy, R., Kailath, T.: Esprit-estimation of signal parameters via rotational invariance techniques. In: IEEE International Conference on Acoustics, Speech, and Signal Processing (ICASSP 1989), vol. 37(7), pp. 984–995 (1989)
47. Schmidt, R.: Multiple emitter location and signal parameter estimation. IEEE Transactions on Antennas and Propagation 34(3), 276–280 (1986)
48. Schwarzer, S., Vossiek, M., Pichler, M., Stelzer, A.: Precise distance measurement with ieee 802.15.4 (zigbee) devices. In: IEEE Radio and Wireless Symposium, pp. 779–782. IEEE (2008)
49. Silva, M., Miranda, M.: Tracking issues of some blind equalization algorithms. IEEE Signal Processing Letters 11(9), 760–763 (2004)
50. Silva, M., Nascimento, V.: Tracking analysis of the constant modulus algorithm. In: IEEE International Conference on Acoustics, Speech and Signal Processing (ICASSP 2008), pp. 3561–3564. IEEE (2008)
51. Stelzer, A., Pourvoyeur, K., Fischer, A.: Concept and application of lpm—a novel 3-d local position measurement system. IEEE Transactions on Microwave Theory Techniques 52, 2664–2669 (2004)
52. Subramanian, S., Sommer, J., Zeh, F., Schmitt, S., Rosenstiel, W.: Pbil pdr for scalable bluetooth indoor localization. In: Third International Conference on Next Generation Mobile Applications, Services and Technologies (NGMAST 2009), pp. 170–175. IEEE (2009)
53. Tang, L., Wang, K.C., Huang, Y., Gu, F.: Channel characterization and link quality assessment of ieee 802.15.4-compliant radio for factory environments. IEEE Transactions on Industrial Informatics 3(2), 99–110 (2007)
54. Varshavsky, A., de Lara, E., Hightower, J., LaMarca, A., Otsason, V.: Gsm indoor localization. Pervasive and Mobile Computing 3(6), 698–720 (2007)
55. Venkatraman, S., Caffery Jr., J.: Hybrid toa/aoa techniques for mobile location in non-line-of-sight environments. In: IEEE Wireless Communications and Networking Conference (WCNC 2004), vol. 1, pp. 274–278. IEEE (2004)
56. Visser, H.: Array and Phased Array Antenna Basics. John Wiley & Sons Inc. (2005)
57. van Vliet, F.: Trends in wideband phased-array front-ends. In: European Radar Conference (EuRAD 2007), pp. 154–157. IEEE (2007)
58. de Vos, M.: Lofar: the first of a new generation of radio telescopes. In: IEEE International Conference on Acoustics, Speech, and Signal Processing (ICASSP 2005), vol. 5, pp. 865–868. IEEE (2005)

59. Want, R., Hopper, A., Falcao, V., Gibbons, J.: The active badge location system. ACM Transactions on Information Systems (TOIS) 10(1), 91–102 (1992)
60. Whitehouse, K., Culler, D.: Calibration as parameter estimation in sensor networks. In: Proceedings of the 1st ACM International Workshop on Wireless Sensor Networks and Applications, WSNA 2002, pp. 59–67. ACM, New York (2002), http://doi.acm.org/10.1145/570738.570747
61. Winters, J.: Signal acquisition and tracking with adaptive arrays in the digital mobile radio system is-54 with flat fading. IEEE Transactions on Vehicular Technology 42(4), 377–384 (1993)
62. Zetterberg, P., Bengtsson, M., McNamara, D., Karlsson, P., Beach, M.: Performance of multiple-receive multiple-transmit beamforming in wlan-type systems under power or eirp constraints with delayed channel estimates. In: IEEE 55th Vehicular Technology Conference (VTC Spring 2002), vol. 4, pp. 1906–1910. IEEE (2002)

Network Coding as a WiMAX Link Reliability Mechanism: An Experimental Demonstration

Surat Teerapittayanon[1], Kerim Fouli[1], Muriel Médard[1],
Marie-José Montpetit[1], Xiaomeng Shi[1], Ivan Seskar[2], and Abhimanyu Gosain[3]

[1] Research Laboratory of Electronics (RLE), Massachusetts Institute of Technology
(MIT), Cambridge, MA 02139, USA
{steerapi,fouli,medard,mariejo,xshi}@mit.com
[2] WINLAB, Rutgers University, Piscataway, NJ 08854, USA
seskar@winlab.rutgers.edu
[3] Raytheon BBN Technologies, Cambridge, MA 02138, USA
agosain@bbn.com

Abstract. Our demonstration showcases a network-coding (NC)–
enabled reliability architecture for next generation wireless networks. Our
NC architecture uses a flexible thread-based design, applying systematic
intra-session random linear network coding as a packet erasure code at
the IP layer. Using GENI WiMAX platforms, a series of point-to-point
transmission experiments are conducted to compare NC with Automatic
Repeated reQuest (ARQ) and Hybrid ARQ (HARQ). At the application
layer, *Iperf* and *UFTP* are used to measure throughput, packet loss and
file transfer delay. In our selected scenarios, NC offers up to 5.9 times gain
in throughput and 5.5 times reduction in file transfer delay, compared
to HARQ and joint HARQ/ARQ. Our demonstration hence illustrates
that lower-layer redundancy mechanisms such as HARQ and ARQ incur
high cost since they operate at the packet-level. Conversely, running NC
at higher layers (e.g., IP) amortizes the cost of redundancy over several
packets, thus leading to higher efficiency.

Keywords: ARQ, GENI, HARQ, Network Coding, WiMAX.

1 Introduction

NC enables nodes to combine or separate transient bits, packets, or flows through
coding and decoding operations, in addition to storing and forwarding [1]. Despite the demonstrated effectiveness of NC in WLANs [1], NC for Wireless
Metropolitan Area Networks (WMANs) has gained attention only recently, as
the telecommunication industry moves toward next generation wireless networks
such as 4G Worldwide Interoperability for Microwave Access (WiMAX) [2].

To ensure the fast and reliable transfer of information between wireless nodes,
we propose an NC architecture using a flexible thread-based design, with each
encoder-decoder instance applying systematic intra-session random linear network coding as a packet erasure code at the IP layer. In our selected scenarios,

B. Bellalta et al. (Eds.): MACOM 2012, LNCS 7642, pp. 75–78, 2012.

the proposed architecture substantially decreases packet loss from around 11-32% to nearly 0%. Compared to the HARQ and joint HARQ/ARQ mechanisms, the NC architecture offers up to 5.9 times gain in throughput and 5.5 times reduction in end-to-end file transfer delay [3,4].

In this demonstration, we implement our NC-enabled reliability architecture in a WiMAX platform provided by the Global Environment for Network Innovations (GENI) collaborative research framework [5] and located at Rutgers University's WINLAB, New Jersey, USA. Our friendly web-interface enables the demonstrator to select a reliability configuration, run the corresponding experiment remotely, and compare the results of different reliability configurations.

The targeted audience for the demonstration includes the GENI and MACOM communities and other academic researchers involved in NC. We also believe the demonstration to be useful for network operators and equipment providers who want to experiment with NC before development or deployment decisions.

2   NC-Enhanced Architecture

Our proposed NC-enabled reliability architecture is implemented in the form of an NC module at the IP layer of the network protocol stack, as shown in Fig. 1. In the NC-enhanced architecture, ARQ and HARQ, run from the upper and lower MAC sublayer respectively, are switched off.

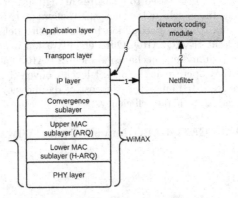

Fig. 1. IP-based NC architecture: 1) A Linux packet filtering framework (*netfilter*) [6] intercepts and forwards IP packets to the NC module. 2) Implemented in user-space, the latter acts as an encoder at the base station (BS) or as a decoder at the subscriber station (SS). 3) The NC module then injects processed packets back into the IP layer.

The NC module uses a flexible thread-based design, where N_p parallel encoding-decoding instances are generated to process packets concurrently and systematic intra-session random linear network coding is applied [3,4]. The encoding process comprises the following steps: **(1)** Incoming IP packets are buffered at the master thread, forming a coding buffer list. **(2)** At each worker thread, the list is concatenated into a coding block. **(3)** The number of segments and segment length are determined, then byte padding is added. **(4)** The block is segmented. For each systematic block to be transmitted, N_m coded redundancy segments are generated. **(5)** Coded segments are encapsulated into coded IP packets and queued for transmission. More detail on the designed encoding, decoding, and feedback mechanisms can be found in [3,4].

3 Demonstration Setup

We implement our architecture over a GENI WiMAX IEEE-802.16 downlink. More details on the testbed hardware can be found at [7].For our demonstration, one fixed downlink Modulation and Coding Scheme (MCS) and transmission power level (64 QAM CTC 5/6 at 20 dBm) is available at the BS. When using HARQ or ARQ, the default settings of the GENI BS are employed [3,4].

The available reliability configurations include a number of ARQ, HARQ and NC arrangements, where the different NC configurations use a varying number of redundancy segments transmitted with each fixed block of 120 systematic segments (N_m). Furthermore, a fixed packet size of 1400 bytes and a single thread $(N_p = 1)$ are used. More detail on the implemented PHY, MAC and reliability configurations is given in [3,4].

For each of the reliability configurations, two transmission trials may be conducted through Iperf [8] and UDP-based File Transfer Protocol (UFTP [9]) so as to measure throughput/loss and file transfer delay, respectively. An application-layer load of 6 Mbps is offered for both. Each individual Iperf trial is terminated after a fixed duration of 30 seconds, whereas the UFTP transmissions are run until a 10 MByte file is successfully transferred.

4 Demonstration Interface and Requirements

The demonstration interface is a web application that allows the demonstrator to schedule experiments on the WiMAX GENI platform at WINLAB (Rutgers University, NJ, USA) and view live results. This demo hence requires a reliable high-speed Internet connection to WINLAB.

Fig 2 represents the configuration screen and a sample result from our demonstration interface. The demonstrator chooses between two types of experiments: *Throughput and Loss* (Iperf trial) and *File Transfer* (UFTP trial). Furthermore, three different base station configurations are available: *HARQ/ARQ, HARQ only* and *NC* where the BS is configured to use both HARQ and ARQ, only HARQ and only NC with neither HARQ or ARQ, respectively. If *NC* is selected, the demonstrator is able to specify the redundancy percentage (i.e., $N_m/120$): The web interface suggests a redundancy percentage from the available 10%–100% range, based on the most recent loss measurement.

The result of each experiment is be fed back live to the web application for audience to view. Once the demonstrator schedules an experiment, the status

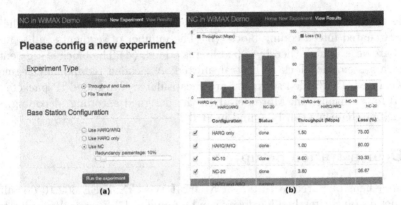

Fig. 2. Demonstration Interface: (a) configuration and (b) result screen, showing throughput (left) and application-layer packet loss (right) in four scenarios

and result of the experiment can be found under the *Scheduled Experiments* tab, where viewers can also compare results of the different reliability configurations.

5   Conclusion and Future Work

With the NC demonstration, we provide easy access to our results and illustrate the advantages of NC in future 4G networks. In particular, we show that the use of NC makes lower-layer error management mechanisms unnecessary and leads to major bandwidth performance improvements. Our demonstration provides a tool for researchers and developers alike to evaluate the impact of NC. In the future, we intend to expand the use cases supported by the demo to include, for example, live and on-demand video streaming, peer-to-peer (P2P) and machine-to-machine (M2M) communications, as these represent future traffic patterns.

References

1. Médard, M., Sprintson, A. (eds.): Network Coding: Fundamentals and Applications. Academic Press (2011)
2. Andrews, J., Ghosh, A., Muhamed, R.: Fundamentals of WiMAX: understanding broadband wireless networking. Prentice Hall (2007)
3. Teerapittayanon, S., Fouli, K., Médard, M., Montpetit, M.J., Shi, X., Seskar, I., Gosain, A.: Network coding as a WiMAX link reliability mechanism. Arxiv (2012)
4. Teerapittayanon, S.: Performance enhancements in next generation wireless networks using network coding: A case study in WiMAX. Master's thesis, MIT (2012)
5. Global Environment for Network Innovations (GENI), http://www.geni.net
6. The netfilter.org project, http://www.netfilter.org
7. ORBIT testbed, http://www.orbit-lab.org/wiki/Hardware/gDomains/dSB4
8. Iperf, http://sourceforge.net/projects/iperf/
9. Bush, D.: UFTP, http://www.tcnj.edu/~bush/uftp.html

Spectrum Sensing with USRP-E110

Luis Sanabria-Russo, Jaume Barcelo, Albert Domingo, and Boris Bellalta

Universitat Pompeu Fabra
Carrer de Tànger 122 – 150, 08018 Barcelona, Spain
{luis.sanabria,jaume.barcelo,albert.domingo,boris.bellalta}@upf.edu

Abstract. Spectrum sensing is one of the key topics towards the implementation of future wireless services like SuperWiFi. This new wireless proposal aims at using the freed spectrum resulting from the analog-to-digital transition of TV channels for wireless data transmission (UHF TV White Spaces). The benefits range from better building penetration to longer distances when compared to the set of IEEE 802.11 standards. Nevertheless, the effective use of the available spectrum is subject to strict regulation that prohibits unlicensed users to interfere with incumbents (like wireless microphones). Cognitive Radios (CR) and dynamic spectrum allocation are suggested to cope with this problem. These techniques consist on frequency sweeps of the TV-UHF band to detect White Spaces that could be used for SuperWiFi transmissions. In this paper we develop and implement algorithms from GNURadio in the Ettus USRP-E110 to build a standalone White Spaces detector that can be consulted from a centralized location via IP networks.

Keywords: USRP, GNURadio, Spectrum Sensing, TV White Spaces, Energy detection.

1 Introduction

TV White Spaces refer to free spectrum available in the TV band. These range from VHF to UHF bands, although in this paper only those in UHF will be considered (from 471.25 to 863.25 MHz). The switchover from analog to digital television increased the number of TV White Spaces, which are going to be used for upcoming wireless standards, like IEEE 802.22 and SuperWiFi.

The benefits of attempting data transmission over these frequencies include longer ranges and better building penetration compared with the unlicensed 2.4 GHz and 5 GHz bands used in the set of IEEE 802.11 protocols. Along with these benefits, a variety of technical and regulatory challenges surface, involving spectrum sensing, channel availability and incumbent avoidance.

The technical difficulties involving spectrum sensing vary with each technique [1]. Some of the more popular are energy detection [2][3], cyclostationary detection [4] and locking detection [5].

In this work, an energy detection-based approach is implemented due to its low complexity. It is built using a standalone Universal Software Radio Peripheral (USRP) Ettus USRP-E110 [6] and the open source Software Defined Radio

B. Bellalta et al. (Eds.): MACOM 2012, LNCS 7642, pp. 79–84, 2012.
© Springer-Verlag Berlin Heidelberg 2012

(SDR) project GNURadio [7]. USRP-E110 is a popular SDR platform that acts as a radio front-end for embedded applications. Furthermore, it is equipped with the USRP Hardware Driver (UHD) [8] that allows the writing of GNURadio programming code at a separate host computer and then to transfer it to the USRP-E110 via a standard Secure Shell (SSH) tunnel (see the connections layout in Fig. 1).

Results show a clear image of the studied spectrum that provides the opportunity to recognize unused TV channels.

Apart from signal processing, the combination USRP-GNURadio has a steep learning curve that requires familiarity with Python and C/C++ programming languages.

In Sect. 2 the connection layout between a PC and the USRP-E110 is described. A proposal for identification and selection of White Spaces in a standalone Ettus USRP-E110 is presented in Sect. 3. Section 4 summarizes the results of this paper and highlights the future work pending in this area.

2   Spectrum Sensing

TV channels are 6 and 8 MHz wide in USA and Europe respectively. TV White Spaces, which are of the same bandwidth, are shared with other transmitters like microphones and radio astronomy. The main objective of an effective spectrum sensing is to avoid the channels where these incumbents are transmitting.

In spite of the technical challenges, there are several techniques available to aid the task of finding an empty channel. The proposed approach gathers the Power Spectral Density (PSD) of a set of samples taken every SampleStep (SS) Hertz in a determined frequency band. After the gathering, post-processing carries the task of identifying which power levels could be considered as noise based on the statistics of the sampled spectrum.

The identification of White Spaces is performed in a standalone USRP-E110 using GNURadio [7] and a modified example code for spectrum sensing [9][10] to account for different RF daughterboards and antennas. Figure 1 presents the connection layout between the USRP-E110 and a PC. This connection was used to transmit the executable code to the USRP and then to retrieve the White Spaces estimation file.

Both the PC and USRP-E110 belong to the same subnet and the communication was established inside a standard SSH tunnel.

3   Using the USRP-E110 as a Standalone White Spaces Detector

The USRP is equipped with an Ettus WBX daughterboard [11] that allows the reception of all TV channels in the UHF band. The setup is also composed by a log-periodic directional antenna [12] which is connected to the USRP via a SMA-M to SMA-M cable.

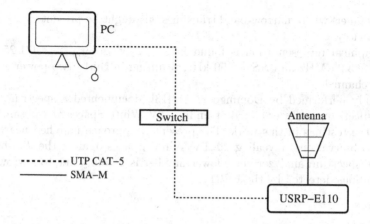

Fig. 1. PC-USRP connections layout

3.1   Spectrum Sense in USRP via UHD

UHD [8] allows the configuration of the USRP via SSH or USB through its console port. It is installed by default in current versions of the different US-RPs models available and provides support for operations like spectrum sensing controlled from a remote location.

In order to gather the signal power in the UHF TV band, the example spectrum sensing code [9] is modified to comply with the proposed task [10]. Developing on what was mentioned in Sect. 2, the algorithm measures the signal power at a center frequency f_o for a fixed *dwelling time* $d_w = 0.001$ s, moving from f_{min} towards f_{max} at SS frequency intervals. We denote the signal power at interval i as P_i and $T = (f_{max} - f_{min})/SS$ samples are taken in total. Since SS is typically smaller than the width of a TV channel, several samples are taken for each TV channel.

The procedure described above is conventionally performed using a spectrum analyzer. The resolution bandwidth in the spectrum analyzer is equivalent to our SS. In our prototype, there is not a concept equivalent to the spectrum analyzer's video bandwidth, as we do not apply any further filtering on the P_i values.

3.2   Identifying TV White Spaces

After all the signal power readings (or collection) are contained in a file, a threshold (γ in (1)) is defined.

$$\gamma = avg(\min P_i, \max P_i) \tag{1}$$

If a received power in the collection (P_i, $i = 1, 2, ..., T$) is greater than γ, then the whole channel at which the sample belongs to is considered *occupied*. On the contrary case, it is considered *free* if $P_i \leq \gamma$. This measure is used in order to avoid channels where narrow-band transmissions might be present (like wireless microphones).

A graphical representation is found in Fig. 2, where $f_{min} = 471.25$ MHz, $f_{max} = 863.25$ MHz and $SS = 250$ kHz, resulting in thirty two power samples per TV channel.

A study performed by Domingo *et al.* [13], documented a spectrum sweep with a spectrum analyzer aimed at finding TV White Spaces at the same location as the testings in this work. The presented approach matched nearly 70% of their observations, revealing 29 TV White Spaces against the 35 observed with the spectrum analyzer. This lower number is possibly due to narrow-band transmissions detected by the USRP.

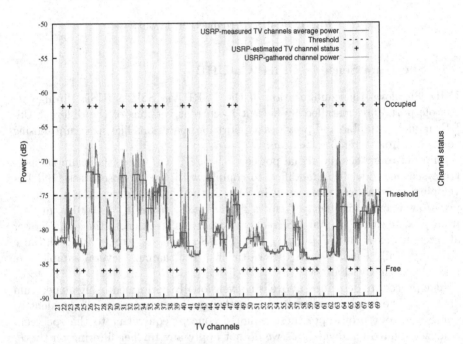

Fig. 2. USRP-estimated TV White Spaces

4   Conclusions and Future Work

The proposed identification of TV White Spaces with USRP-E110 enables the execution of a spectrum sensing algorithm via SSH, allowing the USRP to be located at convenient locations.

It is possible to build a Radio Environment Maps (REM) [14] from samples gathered by geographically distributed USRPs controlled from a centralized location, increasing the efficiency and boosting the implementation of cognitive networks.

In order optimize the spectrum sensing algorithm, better signal processing techniques are expected to be implemented in the near future [1]. Also it is planned to add a second step in the analysis that involves time domain samples gathering in order to perform stochastic analysis of the signal. All of this in the attempt to differentiate noise from TV broadcast signals.

Acknowledgements. This work has been partially funded by the European Commission (grant CIP-ICT PSP-2011-5) and the Spanish Government (TEC2008-0655, Plan Nacional I+D). The views expressed in this work are solely those of the authors and do not represent the views of the European Commission nor of the Spanish Government.

References

1. Shellhammer, S.J., Sadek, A.K., Zhang, W.: Technical Challenges for Cognitive Radio in the TV White Space Spectrum. In: Information Theory and Applications Workshop, pp. 323–333. IEEE (2009)
2. Cabric, D., Tkachenko, A., Brodersen, R.W.: Experimental Study of Spectrum Sensing based on Energy Detection and Network Cooperation. In: Proceedings of the First International Workshop on Technology and Policy for Accessing Spectrum, p. 12. ACM (2006)
3. Sarijari, M.A., Marwanto, A., Fisal, N., Yusof, S.K.S., Rashid, R.A., Satria, M.H.: Energy detection sensing based on GNU radio and USRP: An analysis study. In: Proceedings of the 2009 IEEE 9th Malaysia International Conference on Communications, pp. 338–342. IEEE (2009)
4. Kyouwoong, K., Akbar, I.A., Bae, K.K., Jung-sun, U., Spooner, C.M., Reed, J.H.: Cyclostationary Approaches to Signal Detection and Classification in Cognitive Radio. In: 2nd IEEE International Symposium on New Frontiers in Dynamic Spectrum Access Networks, DySPAN, pp. 212–215 (2007)
5. Cabric, D., Tkachenko, A., Brodersen, R.W.: Spectrum Sensing Measurements of Pilot, Energy, and Collaborative Detection. In: Military Communications Conference, MILCOM 2006, pp. 1–7. IEEE (2006)
6. Ettus Research: USRP-E110. Ettus Research LLC,
   https://www.ettus.com/product/details/UE110-KIT
7. Blossom, E.: GNU Radio: Tools for Exploring the Radio Frequency Spectrum. Linux Journal 2004, 4 (2004)
8. Ettus Research: USRP Hardware Driver. Ettus Research LLC,
   http://ettus-apps.sourcerepo.com/redmine/ettus/projects/uhd/wiki
9. GNURadio: USRP Spectrum Analyzer Example,
   http://gnuradio.org/cgit/gnuradio.git/tree/gr-uhd/examples/python/usrp_spectrum_sense.py
10. Sanabria, L.: Detecting TV White Spaces by Energy Detection with USRP-E110 [C/C++ code], http://github.com/SanabriaRusso/USRP-GNURadio.git
11. Ettus Research: WBX USRP RF Daughterboard. Ettus Research LLC,
    https://www.ettus.com/product/details/WBX

12. Ettus Research: Log Periodic PCB Antenna. Ettus Research LLC,
    https://www.ettus.com/product/details/LP0410
13. Domingo, A., Bellalta, B., Oliver, M.: White Spaces in UHF band: Catalonia case
    study and impact of the Digital Dividend. In: 18th EUNICE 2012 Conference on
    Information and Communications Technologies, Budapest (2012)
14. Youping, Z., Morales, L., Gaeddert, J., Bae, K.K., Jung-Sun, U., Reed, J.H.: Ap-
    plying Radio Environment Maps to Cognitive Wireless Regional Area Networks,
    pp. 115–118. IEEE (2007)

Power Control for Wireless Networks with a Limited Number of Channels

Atuletye Burton Mwamila, Jaeseon Hwang, Taejin Ha, and Hyuk Lim*

School of Information and Communications
Gwangju Institute of Science and Technology (GIST)
Gwangju 500-712, Republic of Korea
{atubm,jshwang,tjha,hlim}@gist.ac.kr

Abstract. In wireless networks, interferences from adjacent nodes that are concurrently transmitting can cause packet reception failures and thus result in significant throughput degradation. The interference can be simply avoided by assigning different orthogonal channel to each interfering node. However, if the number of orthogonal channels is smaller than that of adjacent nodes, this simple channel assignment method does not work. In this paper, we propose a vertex coloring based power control algorithm for wireless networks with a limited number of channels. In order to maintain high data transmission rate between two nodes, the transmission power is increased as long as different orthogonal channel is assigned to each adjacent node. We show that the proposed algorithm significantly improves the network throughput performance for various wireless network topologies with different number of orthogonal channels.

Keywords: channel assignment, power control, interference avoidance, topology control, wireless networks.

1 Introduction

In wireless networks, interferences can be excessively increased as adjacent nodes perform concurrent transmissions. Because the interferences disturb successful packet receptions, they significantly reduce the network throughput performance. One of interference reduction techniques is to exploit multiple orthogonal channel. Note that transmissions on an orthogonal channel do not interfere with the other orthogonal channels. In graph theory [1], a network can be represented in a graph where *vertices* denote the nodes, and *edges* denote the links that connect the nodes. Once a wireless network is represented as a graph, vertex coloring can be used for channel assignment. It determines colors to be assigned to vertices, and the colors are assigned to corresponding nodes [1]. In [2], Kim *et al.* assumed that each node has a fixed transmission power, which is gradually obtaining by allowing a certain amount of the increase of interferences. In this paper, we use a protocol interference model to investigate the effect of interferences among the pairs of nodes, and propose a vertex coloring based power control algorithm.

---

* Corresponding author.

B. Bellalta et al. (Eds.): MACOM 2012, LNCS 7642, pp. 85–88, 2012.
© Springer-Verlag Berlin Heidelberg 2012

Algorithm 1. Centralized power control algorithm

1: **input:** C, N, P_{min}, and P_{max}
2: **output:** P_t
3: $P_t = P_{min}$
4: **while** $P_t \leq P_{max}$ **do**
5:    Create an interference graph $G(V, E)$
6:    Compute a maximum degree Δ from $G(V, E)$
7:    **if** $(\Delta + 1) \leq C$ **then**
8:      $P_t = P_t + \epsilon$
9:    **else**
10:     break
11:   **end if**
12: **end while**

2   Power Control with a Limited Number of Channels

2.1   Interference Graph

Consider a set of N nodes, randomly distributed in a wireless network. The SNR at a receiver j [4] is expressed as a function of the transmission power P_t, which is given by

$$SNR(j) = \frac{P_t}{N_0(d_c)^\eta},\tag{1}$$

where N_0 is the thermal noise power spectral density, d_c is the connectivity range, and η is the path loss exponent. When SNR is equal to the communication threshold γ_c, the connectivity range d_c can be computed using Eq. (1), as follows:

$$d_c = (P_t/(N_0 * \gamma_c))^{1/\eta}.\tag{2}$$

Based on the protocol interference model [3] that considers the interference between a transmitter and its interferer, the interference range d_I [4] can be computed by

$$d_I = d_c(\gamma_c/\gamma_i)^{1/\eta},\tag{3}$$

where γ_i is the interference threshold. To identify the interference between nodes i and j, we use the following relationship between the connectivity and interference range:

$$d_c < D(i, j) \leq d_I,\tag{4}$$

where $D(i, j)$ is the distance between nodes i and j. Then the network coordinator can create the interference graph $G(V, E)$ [3], representing the edge of interference. If $D(i, j) < d_c$, nodes i and j are linked to represent the edge of connectivity.

2.2   Power Control Algorithm

Based on the interference graph, we propose a centralized power control algorithm for wireless networks with a limited number of channels, which improves the network throughput performance while ensuring high network connectivity with high transmission power. Algorithm 1 describes the proposed power control algorithm for all nodes. We assume that all nodes have an equal transmission power P_t, and the available number of channels is C. Initially, the minimum transmission power P_{min} is provided, then the interference graph is generated. From this, the maximum node degree of interference Δ can be computed. The transmission power P_t is then increased by the incremental value ϵ until the maximum transmission power P_{max} is reached. However, if condition $\Delta + 1 \leq C$ is not satisfied, the transmission power is not increased any further, and the current P_t is regarded as the final transmission power. Therefore, when any two nodes are out of the connectivity range and interfere with each other, different channels can be assigned to each node depending on the maximum number of channels in the network.

3 Numerical Results

We have conducted performance evaluation with MATLAB, with the random topologies of 25, 50 and 100 nodes distributed uniformly. The data rate is fixed at 1 Mb/s, P_{min} is 2 dBm, P_{max} is 100 dBm, ϵ is 0.5, γ_c is 2 dB, γ_i is 0.5 dB, N_0 is 3 dBm, and η is 2. Based on the interference graph, the edge of connectivity assigns the same channel, while the edge of interference assigns different channels for nodes that share the edge. According to Bianchi's model [5], the aggregate throughput performance is numerically calculated by considering the number of nodes within connectivity range that share the same channel.

Figure 1 shows the transmission power resulting from the proposed algorithm with respect to the number of channels. If nodes are allowed to use more channels, nodes can further increase transmission power because multiple channels eliminate the effect of higher interference by different channel assignment of nearby nodes. As the number of nodes increases in the network, each node requires higher transmission power in order to increase connectivity. In Figure 2, as more nodes perform data transmissions in the proposed algorithm, we observe that the throughput performance also increases because nodes can transmit packets in a

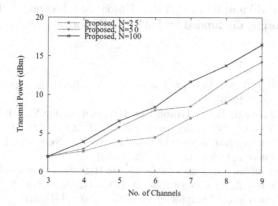

Fig. 1. Transmit power with respect to the number of channels

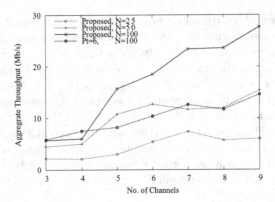

Fig. 2. Aggregate throughput performance with respect to the number of channels

wider connectivity range with the high transmission power as shown in Figure 1. However, because the connectivity range remains the same in the fixed power approach, the node degree of connectivity also remains the same and thus the throughput is not increased significantly.

4   Conclusion

In this paper, we proposed a power control algorithm for wireless networks with a limited number of channels in order to improve network throughput performance by mitigating the interferences. With the proposed power control, we were able to significantly reduce the interference as we assigned multiple orthogonal channels to interfering nodes. Through numerical validations, we showed that the network throughput performance increases as more channels are available.

Acknowledgments. This research was supported by Leading Foreign Research Institute Recruitment Program through the NRF funded by MEST (K2090300 1804-11E0100-00910) and by the UTRC (Unmanned Technology Research Center) at KAIST, originally funded by DAPA, ADD of the Korean government.

References

1. Bondy, J.A., Murty, U.S.R.: Graph Theory with Applications. The Macmillan Press Ltd., Great Britain (1976)
2. Kim, G., Li, Q., Negi, R.: A Graph-based Algorithm for Scheduling with Sum-Interference in Wireless Networks. In: IEEE GLOBECOM (2007)
3. Cardieri, P.: Modeling Interference in Wireless Ad Hoc Networks. IEEE Communications Surveys and Tutorials 12, 551–572 (2010)
4. Gore, A.D., Karandikar, A., Jagabathula, S.: On High Spatial Reuse Link Scheduling in STDMA Wireless Ad Hoc Networks. In: IEEE GLOBECOM (2007)
5. Bianchi, G.: Perfomance Analysis of the IEEE 802.11 Distributed Coordination Function. IEEE Journal on Selected Areas in Communications 18, 535–547 (2000)

A Measurement Study for Predicting Throughput from LQI and RSSI

Krzysztof Wolosz*, Ulf Bodin, and Laurynas Riliskis

Department of Computer Science, Electrical and Space Engineering
Luleå University of Technology, 971 87 Luleå, Sweden
{krzysztof.wolosz,ulf.bodin}@ltu.se
www.ltu.se

Abstract. Wireless sensor networks (WSN) commonly use ZigBee to communicate, especially when low power consumption is demanded. ZigBee may however provide unpredictable throughput although transmission distances are short. This is especially evident in difficult environments with complicated reflections and various materials through which radio signals need to pass through. Distributed scheduling based on cognitive networking principles may improve both network predictability and overall throughput. This paper presents measurements of key parameters for such cognitive scheduling, and discusses their potential for predicting suitable per-node transmission rates. Results include variability of throughput, RSSI and LQI observed for different transmission powers, transmission ranges, and number of transmitting nodes.

Keywords: WSN, RSSI, LQI, Throughput.

1   Introduction

Miniaturized and portable wireless sensor nodes are suitable for many different tasks. Such sensors often communicate their sensed data wirelessly and participate for that purpose together with other nodes in wireless sensor networks. Wireless communication brings many advantages, among them easiness in quickly mounting nodes for various measurement tasks.

This paper focus on communication properties over short distances and evaluates key parameters for predicting transmission capacity between one or more data sources sending data to a common sink. The experiments included up to six Mulle sensor nodes serving as transmitters equipped in Low Power radio Zigbee AT86RF230.

Our results indicate that RSSI can be more reliable than LQI for predicting throughput. RSSI may hence be useful for distributed scheduling based on cognitive networking principles to improve both network predictability and overall throughput.

---

* Corresponding author.

B. Bellalta et al. (Eds.): MACOM 2012, LNCS 7642, pp. 89–92, 2012.

In [1], the relationships between RSSI, LQI and Packet Reception Rate were verified. Lin et. al. [2] show how to adjust the transmit power during measurements based on RSSI and LQI. Papers [3] and [4] concentrated on the distance, outdoor and indoor localization impact on the LQI and RSSI indicators. The results showed that it is efficient to utilize two proposed factors in the object tracking methods. None of the above-mentioned papers consider the predictability of throughput based on WSN parameters (i.e. RSSI and LQI), which is the focus of this paper.

2   Test Results and Applicability Discussion

We are targeting a scheduler that distributes forwarding capacity at a time scale for which throughput can be statistically predicted from LQI, RSSI or both. We expect that we will need to account for throughput variability at shorter times scales when designing the cognitive and distributed scheduler, while throughput at longer time scales may be used as reference, or target values. The variability can for example be handled by aiming at target values lower than reference target values to trade capacity for predictability. Further work will focus on finding an attractive solution to this problem.

Figure 1(a) shows the throughput as the load increases with number of nodes transmitting at their individual full speed. Nodes transmitting are sending at their full capacity. It can be seen that throughput increases to reach its maximum at the load produced by two nodes, to thereafter decrease as load increase further. The reason for this is that with greater number of nodes transmitting the single sink node is not able to correctly receive that amount of data. Another reason is that some packets are corrupted because of frequent collisions. RSSI as presented in Figure 1(c) shows similar behavior with high values at lower loads, i.e. one to three nodes transmitting, and lower values as load increases.

LQI on the other hand shows a different behavior in Figure 1(e) than throughput does in Figure 1(a), with values on LQI dropping drastically at three nodes transmitting although throughput is still high at that level of load. Also LQI values increase slightly at high loads although throughput continues to decrease with increasing load. This indicates that RSSI is a more promising parameter than LQI to predict throughput. Reasons for that LQI shows less correlation with throughput likely include that background noises impacting channel quality causing higher variability in LQI. The used hardware does not guaranty the stable functionality, which may also result in more varying LQI.

Assuming that RSSI is a good parameter for predicting throughout we need to make sure that assumption holds as other parameters are varied. As a first step we study how payload size impacts the reliability of RSSI as a parameter for throughput prediction. Figure 1(b) shows the throughput at different payload sizes, ranging from 10 to 80 Bytes. It can be seen that throughput decreases as payload size increase. The reason is that the transmitter and receiver need more time to process larger packets, which results in decreased throughput. Hence the load decreases as payload size is increased.

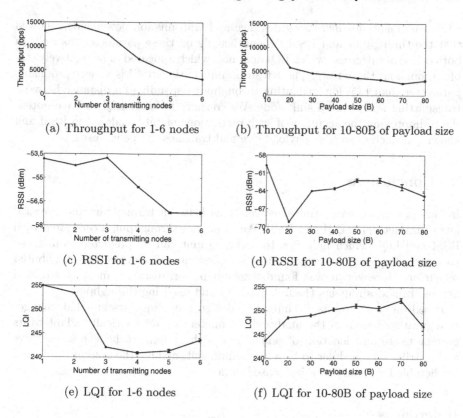

(a) Throughput for 1-6 nodes

(b) Throughput for 10-80B of payload size

(c) RSSI for 1-6 nodes

(d) RSSI for 10-80B of payload size

(e) LQI for 1-6 nodes

(f) LQI for 10-80B of payload size

Fig. 1. Correlation between RSSI, LQI and Throughput

Figure 1(d) reveals that RSSI not only reflect throughput but also other parameters like payload size. It can be seen that RSSI first drop when payload size is increased from 10 to 20 bytes, to thereafter increase again with slightly increasing variability. From this we conclude that we need to account for other parameters like payload size in combination with RSSI to accurately predict throughput. Looking at Figure 1(f) we can see that LQI in this case of varying payload size show a closer relation to throughput than RSSI appear to have. This may indicate that LQI in combination with knowledge of parameters such as payload size can be of use to make predictions based on RSSI more reliable.

From Figure 1(b), 1(d) and 1(f) we conclude that the increasing sizes of packets cause less corruptions simply because less packets are sent. This leads to lower probability of interference and better quality of the link. We observed that for packet sizes equal or smaller than 30 bytes the RSSI, LQI and throughput change values rapidly. For the middle sizes of the payload, the characteristics of the graphs are getting much more smother and aligned. This indicates that it may be possible to estimate the fluctuations of the throughput based on RSSI and LQI.

Measurements for increasing distance and transmission power index showed that the throughput and RSSI depend heavily on these parameters as well. In both cases they decrease which LQI does not, which appeared to be relatively stable throughout those tests. These results confirm that RSSI is a more promising parameter than LQI for estimating throughput depending on distance between transmitting nodes and a sink node. We consider however LQI to have potential to improving the accuracy of such predictions mainly made using RSSI and known parameters such as payload size and transmission power used.

3   Conclusions

In this paper, we have studied correlations between throughput and physical layer parameter, i.e. LQI and RSSI. We show that throughput is correlated with RSSI and LQI, which indicates that throughput can be predicted from those parameters and may hence prove useful in designing a cognitive and distributed scheduler. Moreover, it was found transmit power, distance, message size and number of nodes impacts the link capacity and resulting throughput.

Based on these results we intend to design a dynamic system that changes configuration based on the analyzed parameters to automatically adapt to its current usage and location of nodes. For such system we believe a cognitive and distributed scheduler to be a key component, making the system stable and predictable for communicating sensed data.

References

1. Srinivasan, K., Levis, P.: RSSI is Under Appreciated. In: Proceedings of the Third Workshop on Embedded Networked Sensors, EmNets (2006)
2. Lin, S., Zhang, J., Zhou, G., Gu, L., He, T., Stankovic, J.A.: ATPC: adaptive transmission power control for wireless sensor networks. In: Proceedings of the 4th International Conference on Embedded Networked Sensor Systems, SenSys 2006, p. 223 (2007)
3. Halder, S.J., Park, J.G., Kim, W.: Adaptive Filtering for Indoor Localization using ZIGBEE RSSI and LQI Measurement. In: Garcia, L. (ed.) Adaptive Filtering Applications. InTech (2011) ISBN: 978-953-307-306-4
4. Miluzzo, E., Zheng, X., Fodor, K., Campbell, A.T.: Radio characterization of 802.15.4 and its impact on the design of mobile sensor networks. In: Proc. of 5th European Workshop on Wireless Sensor Networks (EWSN), Bologna, Italy, pp. 171–188 (2008)

Reality Considerations When Designing
a TDMA-FDMA Based Link-Layer for Real-Time WSN

Laurynas Riliskis[1,*], Jan Berdajs[2], Evgeny Osipov[1], and Andrej Brodnik[2]

[1] Department of Computer Science and Electrical Engineering
Luleå University of Technology, 971 87 Luleå, Sweden
laurynas.riliskis@ltu.se
[2] University of Ljubljana, Faculty of Computer and Information Science
Tržaška 25, 1000 Ljubljana, Slovenia

Abstract. In this article we elaborate on reality considerations when designing and implementing application tailored TDMA-FDMA medium access protocol with guaranteed end-to-end delay. We highlight importance of considering underlaying hardware and software components when designing communication protocols for resource constrained platforms. We also show that by combining medium access protocol, bootstrapping, and time synchronization mechanisms within the link-layer, we can limit on average clock drift in the network to 0.5 μs, as well as achieve 81% energy efficiency while keeping collision probability at its minimum of 1%. Finally, we conclude with challenges and lessons learned in real-world deployment of TDMA/FDMA based link-layer with guaranteed end-to-end delay in WSN.

Keywords: Dependable protocol, medium access control, bootstrapping, time synchronization, wireless sensor network, wsn.

1 Introduction

Time synchronization is a crucial requirement when using TDMA/FDMA protocols [1, 2]. Ofter research publications consider operations of MAC protocols separately from the issues related to the time synchronization. In this paper we show that when integrated the MAC functionality and the time synchronization mutually affect each other performance. This conclusion come as a result of our work on practical deployment of a TDMA – FDMA test network with strict end-to-end delay requirements.

Our main conclusion is that it is feasible to deploy WSN with strict end-to-end delay requirement. The main prerequisite for achieving this is performance of hardware components and execution time of concurrent software modules already at the design stage of the link layer.

---

* Corresponding author.

B. Bellalta et al. (Eds.): MACOM 2012, LNCS 7642, pp. 93–96, 2012.

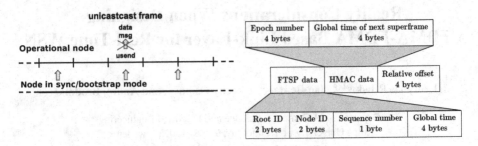

Fig. 1a. Possible collision when FTSP operates as a service   **Fig. 1b.** FTSP message piggybacking in HMAC

2   Link Layer: TDMA/FDMA MAC, Bootstrapping, and Time Synchronization

For medium access a TDMA/FDMA scheme called HMAC proposed in [3,4] is used. We outline main functionality below. In Section 3 we report on the performance of the integrated link layer.

The time in HMAC protocol is divided in enumerated epochs which contain n superframes. The superframe is divided into slots, the length of the slot depends on the size of the message and number of the slots is selected depending on the number of neighboring nodes to minimize the collision probability in time and frequency domains. The main feature of HMAC protocol is the distributed consensus scheduling i.e. based on the epoch number, the sender's, and receiver's ID nodes calculated the time and frequency slot for the transmission. Each b superframes all nodes enter the bootstrapping phase in which new nodes can join network and synchronize to the current epoch number.

The target application uses a line topology of seven nodes and has requirement on one second end-to-end delay. In order to satisfy the delay requirement the per-node delay should be less then 166 ms to transmit five bytes of measured data. This results in having 20 unicast slots per superframe. With four contenders for 20 unicast slots the collision probability in time and frequency is 1%, which makes an error free relay probability sufficiently high.

To achieve target requirements strict time synchronization is needed. The instance of HMAC protocol was designed to guarantee end-to-end delay with known traffic pattern. Introducing haphazard communications from time synchronization protocol would disturb normal operation of the protocol as shown in Fig.1a. Therefore, we modify time synchronization protocol FTSP [5] to operate only during the bootstrap phases and piggyback FTSP data in bootstrap messages as shown in Fig. 1b.

3   Protocol Performance

Clock Accuracy. In order to determine the time error and needed frequency for synchronization we measured the difference between time approximations and actual time of the root node. This difference is the global time error. The measurements are repeated over 30 min window which is shown in Figure 1c.

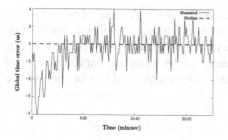 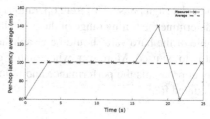

Fig. 1c. FTSP average global time error measured over 30 minutes

Fig. 1d. Average per-hop latency in detail over 30 seconds

We found that when performing synchronization every 10 seconds we could achieve maximum measured error of 8 microseconds. The median of the error rarely exceeded 4 microseconds. Thus, the average error during the whole evaluation was 0.5 microseconds. Our conclusion is that when piggybacking and controlling time synchronization protocol from the link layer, the clock drift does not have seriously affects performance of the protocol.

Per-hop Latency in a Multi-hop Network. During implementation phase we encountered additional internal node time delays which affected HMAC planning. Especially, radio state switching was effecting negatively on the overall performance. Therefore, we introduced a 20 ms start frame to allow for initialization of the protocol and hardware components. The unicast slots needed to be extended, beside accounting for time error, to account for time consumed during channel switching. Thus, the resulting unicast frames of 20 ms was used for packet exchange, resulting in a 420 ms superframe. As a result we were forced to reconsider the core protocol functionality as described in poster.

The measured per-hop latency average is shown in Figure 1d for a 30 second subportion of evaluation. During the whole 30 minute period, we observed a per-hop latency of 100 ms on average. This latency is caused mainly by application processing time and also by HMAC unicast slot rules.

The worst-case measured latency was 141 ms. Additional delays can be caused by several factors such as processing time, superframe transition (20 ms delay for start frame) and bootstrap phase (420 ms). Most of these occur with a pre-defined frequency and can only occur once during the forwarding of one packet, as per protocol design.

The results of evaluation – end-to-end delay can be achieved in this application on average below 1 second. However, if a bootstrap phase occurs during packet forwarding, a packet from node 1 will arrive at node 7 after 1020 ms. In worst case scenario the packet will arrive after 1272 ms or 852 ms. On average, the packet will arrive at node 7 after 600 ms.

4 Conclusions

In order to satisfy dependability requirements, the performance of the hardware platform and core software components should be assessed experimentally as part of the protocol design phase. Different operations should be profiled on a set of nodes in order to determine the timing range of the target hardware. It is important to note that the time profile of the hardware should be established while it is running the operating system that is to be used. Moreover, when matter comes to designing and implementing time critical protocols the performance and influence of the additional services needs to be accounted for.

References

1. Mottola, L., Picco, G.P.: Programming wireless sensor networks: Fundamental concepts and state of the art. ACM Comput. Surv. 43(3), 19:1– 19:51 (2011),
   http://doi.acm.org/10.1145/1922649.1922656
2. Elson, J., Römer, K.: Wireless sensor networks: a new regime for time synchronization. SIG-COMM Comput. Commun. Rev. 33(1), 149–154 (2003),
   http://doi.acm.org/10.1145/774763.774787
3. Osipov, E., Riliskis, L.: On synthesis of dependable MAC protocol for two real-world WSN applications. In: 2011 Baltic Congress on Future Internet Communications (BCFIC Riga), pp. 41–49 (February 2011)
4. Riliskis, L.: On design of dependable communication protocols for wireless sensor networks. Lule tekniska universitet (2011)
5. Maróti, M., Kusy, B., Simon, G., Lédeczi, A.: The flooding time synchronization protocol. In: Proceedings of the 2nd International Conference on Embedded Networked Sensor Systems, Ser. SenSys 2004, pp. 39–49. ACM, New York (2004),
   http://doi.acm.org/10.1145/1031495.1031501

Wireless Groupcast Routing with Palette of Transmission Methods*

Alexander Safonov[1], Andrey Lyakhov[1],
Anastasia Urgenson[2], and Olga Sokolova[2]

[1] IITP RAS (Kharkevich Institute), Moscow, Russia
{safa,lyakhov}@iitp.ru
http://www.iitp.ru,
[2] ICM & MG SB RAS, Novosibirsk, Russia
{nastya,olga}@rav.sscc.ru
http://www.sscc.ru,

Abstract. We study the problem of wireless groupcast routing when multiple transmission methods are available. The paper is inspired by GroupCast with Retries (GCR) methods appeared in IEEE 802.11aa in 2012. The paper contributes with comparative analysis of GCR methods in a wireless multihop network from the groupcast routing perspective. It also addresses the issue of possible benefit for a routing protocol to account for this palette of transmission methods.

Keywords: Groupcast Routing, Groupcast with Retries (GCR).

1 Introduction

The problem of groupcast routing, i.e. routing same packets to multiple destinations, has been studied for decades and even a short overview of various problem statements and their solutions would require writing a book. A generalized problem statement is to find a route on the graph representing the network, minimizing a cost function which value is the criterion of the overall routing efficiency. The graph edges are usually weighted in a metric which contributes to the cost function, and a common approach to solve such a problem is to find the route of minimal cost, e.g. in the class of treelike routes, to find the Steiner tree [1] with an approximate algorithm which is a simplicity-accuracy trade-off.

This approach was developed at the days when broadband wireless networks did not exist. For example, the first polynomial algorithm to find the Steiner tree was proposed by Takahashi and Matsuyama in [2] in 1980.

In wired networks, groupcast packets are naturally transmitted in an individual way on each edge covered by the tree. With such transmission method, the metric values on the graph edges are independent in the sense that it does not matter which other edges are covered by the tree. The contribution of two edges

---

* This work has been carried out partially as part of European Project FP7-ICT FLAVIA, contract no. 257263 (http://www.ict-flavia.eu).

B. Bellalta et al. (Eds.): MACOM 2012, LNCS 7642, pp. 97–108, 2012.

to the cost function equals the sum of individual contributions of these edges, including the case when the edges are adjacent.

Such view on calculating the route cost is also justified in wireless networks when the packets are transmitted to each recipient individually. At the same time, such a view does not account for and does not take advantage of the broadcast nature of wireless transmission.

Broadcast nature of wireless transmission is obviously taken into account with the broadcast transmission method. Ruiz et al. show in [3] that the Steiner tree is not so minimal with this method in the sense that a single transmission made by a node covers all edges incident to the node and its contribution to the cost function is less than a sum of contributions which would be made by individual transmission over each edge. Ruiz et al. propose their algorithm aimed at minimizing the number of forwarders.

Though broadcast method is known to be unreliable and the proposed algorithm is probably inapplicable in many scenarios, the results obtained by Ruiz et al. are very important. By proving that the benefit from accounting for broadcast nature of wireless transmission is considerable, they inspired this paper.

Also inspiring is the appearance of an alternative transmission method for group-addressed frames in IEEE 802.11aa amendment [4] to widely known IEEE 802.11 specification [5]. The method is called Groupcast with Retries (GCR) and supports two policies, namely unsolicited retries and block acknowledgement. Addressing the reliability-overhead trade-off, the method itself is pretty much general, i.e. applicable to other network protocols. That is why in this paper we study the method in an abstract wireless multihop network, leaving aside peculiarities of IEEE 802.11 such as interframe spaces and length of specific frames. With that, we refer to this method as GCR.

To estimate the immediate benefit of using GCR method, we carried out the following study. With a classical algorithm to find a Steiner tree on a weighted graph (we choose Takahashi and Matsuyama algorithm as probably the simplest one), we find the tree on the graph which edges are weighted in well-known Air Time Link (ATL) metric [6]. Let us refer to this route as to *reference route* and its weight in ATL metric as to *reference weight*. We compare the weights of the reference route when different transmission methods are used, normalized to the reference weight. With that, we assume that it is necessary and sufficient to deliver groupcast packets to each destination with the loss ratio less than a given threshold dictated by the traffic quality-of-service requirements.

This preliminary study shows that GCR method is efficient, and efficient by itself, i.e. even on the reference route which was found without any knowledge of the used transmission method. The key question this paper aims to answer is shall the routing protocol account for the palette of transmission methods, or how much the cost saving would be when it does account for the methods?

To answer the question, we propose a simple extension to Takahashi and Matsuyama algorithm, to get rid of the assumption on the independence of the metric values on the graph edges in the sense discussed above. We designed the extension with GCR in mind, but it appears to be general and potentially may be used for other methods. Eventually, the extension reduces the route cost as it enables the algorithm to find routes optimized for the transmission method in use. Also, we propose more complex algorithms, to give the ultimate answer for the posed question by estimating the upper bound of cost saving.

Comparative analysis of the trees found by the proposed algorithms for different transmission methods reveals that the tree weight is sensitive to the success probabilities on its edges and the degree of each node. Values of these parameters may vary considerably among nodes and edges of the tree, so it is natural to allow nodes to choose the transmission method at each hop independently from previous and further hops. In this paper, we also address this issue.

The rest of the paper is organized as follows. In Section 2, we introduce notation and terminology as well as state formally the groupcast routing problem. Section 3 describes various transmission methods, derives equations to calculate the cost of adding a node to the tree, and provides an analysis of transmission methods by comparing the cost of the same reference tree, depending on the used transmission method. In Section 4, we present and analyze a simple extension to Takahashi and Matsuyama algorithm as well as more complex algorithms aimed at further reducing the tree weight. Section 5 concludes the paper with a short discussion on directions of further study.

2   Notation and Terminology

Let the network be represented as a directed graph $G(V, E)$ with the set of vertices V, representing nodes, and the set of edges $E \subseteq \{(i, j) : i, j \in V\}$, representing links. Every edge (i, j) is assigned the failure probability p_{ij} of a transmission attempt from node i to node j.

The groupcast packets source node is denoted as $s \in V$, and the set of sink (destination) nodes is denoted as $D \subset V, s \notin D$. In this paper, we consider groupcast routes in the class of treelike subgraphs, so a route is a tree $T \subseteq G$ with root s, covering all nodes in D.

It is common to think of a unicast route as the sequence of hops which are joint edges. In the case of groupcast route, each hop of the route turns into a *cluster*, i.e. the collection of vertices consisting of vertex $i \in T$ and i's child vertices $J = \{j_1, j_2, \ldots, j_k\}$.

Let us weight vertices on the tree, so that for vertex i the weight is $C(i) = c(i, J)n(i, J)$, where $n(i, J)$ is the number of transmission attempts on the vertex, and $c(i, J)$ is the cost of an attempt. For leaves, obviously $n = 0$, so $C(i) = 0$. For any other vertex $i \in T$, the values of $c(i, J)$ and $n(i, J)$ are connected with $\{p_{ij_1}, \ldots, p_{ij_k}\}$ by equations which define one of the transmission methods described in detail in Section 3. Then, the tree weight representing the groupcast route cost is the sum of the weights of vertices covered by the tree.

In this paper, we state the following problem. Among treelike routes, such that the packet loss ratio on each link of the route is less than a threshold value q, find a route, such that the cost function reaches the minimum. To define the cost function, let us look closer at IEEE 802.11s mesh networking amendment which is now included in IEEE 802.11-2012 [5].

Leaving aside the conversion of groupcast packets into unicast at the source node, the only transmission method defined for groupcast packets is pure broadcast with a single transmission attempt per packet. No cost function is considered at all due to best-effort nature of broadcast transmission. For unicast packets, IEEE 802.11s defines the cost function, though implicitly in the form of an additive ATL metric, as the average channel occupancy time for successful packet delivery, taking into account the transmission rate and the average number of transmission attempts under the assumption that the possible number of attempts is not limited.

In this paper, we extend the definition of the metric to account for the fact that the metric value shall be assigned to a node, not a link, as it depends on the cluster of the node on the route. As already mentioned above, the form of this dependence is defined by equations reflecting the structure of groupcast transmission methods defined in IEEE 802.11aa [4]. In Section 3, we model these methods to estimate the weights of vertices on the route, i.e. the average channel occupancy time to deliver a packet in each cluster on the route.

3   Models of Groupcast Transmission Methods

In this section, we present the models of three methods to deliver groupcast packets at a hop of a network. In the framework of IEEE 802.11 specification, one of the methods, namely Directed Multicast Service (DMS), was initially defined in IEEE 802.11v which is now a part of IEEE 802.11-2012 [5]. DMS is also supported in IEEE 802.11aa [4] where two other methods, GCR with Unsolicited Retries and GCR with Block Ack, are defined.

3.1   Directed Multicast Service

DMS converts groupcast packets into unicast. Then each node $i \in T$ delivers the unicast packets individually to neighbors $J = \{j_1, j_2, \ldots, j_k\}$ in its cluster, and each $j \in J$ replies with an acknowledgement. Node i makes additional transmission attempts of unacknowledged packets, so the actual number of transmission attempts to each neighbor is random.

To minimize the average channel occupancy time and at the same time to ensure the packet loss ratio less than q to each $j \in J$, let us limit the number of possible transmission attempts to $\lceil \log_{p_{ij}} q \rceil$, where $\lceil x \rceil$ is the minimal integer not less than x. Then, the total average number of transmission attempts of node i to recipients in its cluster is

$$n_D(i, J) = \sum_{j \in J} \frac{1 - p_{ij}^{\lceil \log_{p_{ij}} q \rceil}}{1 - p_{ij}} . \tag{1}$$

The structure of DMS implies that the cost of a transmission attempt is proportional to the sum $l + \xi$, where l is the packet length and $\xi = \xi_D > 0$ is the constant reflecting the overhead caused by transmission of acknowledgements and interframe spaces. In turn, the coefficient of proportionality reflects the transmission rate, so assuming that all nodes transmit at the same rate, without loss of generality, we consider the coefficient of proportionality equal to one.

The value of $\eta = l/\xi$ determines the traffic type in our model. For voice packets, which are relatively short, we consider $\eta_{voice} \simeq 1$. For video packets, η_{video} may be greater by an order of magnitude compared with η_{voice}. We will use $\eta_{video} = 10\eta_{voice}$ in numerical analysis below.

So, the weight of node $i \in T$ when it uses DMS in its cluster is

$$C_D(i, J) = n_D(i, J)(l + \xi) .\tag{2}$$

Note that with $q \to 0$ the numerator in each fraction in (1) turns to one, and the route weight $\sum_{i \in T} C_D(i, J)$ takes the form of the cost function used in IEEE 802.11 [5].

3.2   GCR with Unsolicited Retries

Groupcast with Unsolicited Retries (GCR-U) delivers a groupcast packet with some pre-established fixed number of transmission attempts. Receivers of the packet do not acknowledge any transmission.

Consider a cluster with node $i \in T$ making $H(i)$ transmission attempts to nodes $J = \{j_1, j_2, \ldots, j_k\}$. Obviously, the probability that a packet is not delivered to the recipient in the worst channel conditions is $p^{H(i)}$, where $p = \max_{j \in J} \{p_{ij}\}$. Then, the minimal number of transmission attempts which ensures the packet loss probability less than q equals

$$n_U(i, J) = \lceil \log_p q \rceil .\tag{3}$$

GCR-U uses no Ack frames, so the transmission attempt cost is only proportional to l, while $\xi = 0$ (compare with DMS). Then, the weight of node $i \in T$ when it uses GCR-U in its cluster is

$$C_U(i, J) = n_U(i, J)l .\tag{4}$$

3.3   GCR with Block Ack

GCR with Block Ack (GCR-B) delivers a block of groupcast packets before asking for acknowledgements from recipients. Node $i \in T$ transmits b packets in a raw and then requests each of its recipients which or those b packets are delivered, by transmitting a Block AckReq frame. Recipients reply with Block Ack frames and node i retransmits packets which are unacknowledged by at least one of the recipients. As in the case of DMS, the number of transmission attempts appears to be random.

GCR-B method is very flexible. The implementor may choose between the delivery probability and overhead in wide range, varying the block length, the number of recipients which are requested to acknowledge packets, the policy to choose those recipients, etc. [7].

In this paper, we consider the case when node i requests *all* child nodes in its cluster. As in the case of DMS, the number of possible transmission attempts per packet shall be limited to some value, $H(i)$, to minimize the average channel occupancy time and ensure the probability to deliver the packet to each child node $j \in J$ is not less than $1 - q$. In much the same way as in the previous section, we obtain $H(i) = \lceil \log_p q \rceil$. The probability that at least one node $j \in J$ does not receive a packet after h transmission attempts is

$$\pi_h(i) = 1 - \prod_{j \in J} \left(1 - p_{ij}^h\right),$$

where $\pi_h(i)$ may be also thought as the probability that h attempts were not enough to deliver the packet and next attempt (with number $h + 1$) is needed. Then, the average number of transmission attempts is

$$n_B(i, J) = 1 + \sum_{h=1}^{H(i)-1} \pi_h(i) = H(i) - \sum_{h=1}^{H(i)-1} \prod_{j \in J} \left(1 - p_{ij}^h\right). \tag{5}$$

The cost to transmit a packet in a block (per packet cost) is proportional to $l + k\xi_B/b$ (remember that we assume the coefficient of proportionality equals one). In the structure of GCR-B method two frames are needed (Block AckReq and Block Ack) to acknowledge a packet reception by each of k recipients in contrast to DMS where one frame is only needed. So, we assume $\xi_B = 2\xi_D$, ignoring the difference in the frames length.

So, the weight of node $i \in T$ when it uses GCR-B in its cluster is

$$C_B(i, J) = n_B(i, J)(l + k\xi_B/b). \tag{6}$$

3.4   Benchmark Analysis

Simulation Setup. In numerical analysis in this section and further in the paper, we consider the network of $N \times N$ grid topology. We vary the network density by varying the grid spacing, r, in the range $\{r_0, r_1 = r_0/\sqrt{2}, r_2 = r_0/2, r_3 = r_0/\sqrt{5}, r_4 = r_0/2\sqrt{2}\}$, where r_0 is the maximal possible spacing when neighboring nodes in the grid are still in the radio range of each other. To violate the grid symmetry, we assign random (with uniform distribution) failure probabilities $p_{ij} \in \mathbb{P}$ of transmission attempt from node i to its neighbor j. In this paper, we show the results for $N = 9$, $r \in \{r_0, r_4\}$, and $\mathbb{P} \in \{(0; 0.3), (0.3; 0.6)\}$.

The source is one of the nodes in the grid corner. The sinks are chosen randomly with uniform distribution among other nodes in each run. We consider the cases when the number of sinks $|D| = \{3, 10, 20, 40, 70\}$. For each $(r, \mathbb{P}, |D|)$, we generate a set of topologies, different in the values of $p_{ij} \in \mathbb{P}$ and in the distribution of sinks over the grid; for each of these topologies, with the algorithms described in Section 4 (the reference route is found with Takahashi and Matsuyama algorithm, see Section 4.1) we find a Steiner tree; finally, we find the average route cost, by averaging out over the considered topologies. In each of

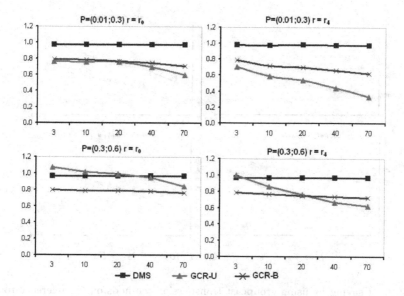

Fig. 1. The average reference route weight, normalized to the reference weight

such scenarios, we vary the packet length $l \in \{1, 10\}$ to cover the cases of voice and video packets, with $\xi_B = 2\xi_D = 2$. In all scenarios, $q = 0.05$ and $b = 3$.

Numerical Results. Fig. 1 shows the results of using groupcast transmission methods, defined in IEEE 802.11aa and described above, over the reference route used as the benchmark (the same transmission method is used on every link of the route) when $l = 1$. The results show how much lower the average weight is of the reference route compared with the average reference weight, i.e. the route weight when DMS with unlimited number of transmission attempts is used (100% reliability). DMS makes little change to the route weight, compared to the reference weight, because the constraint $\lceil \log_{p_{ij}} q \rceil$ to the number of transmission attempts is loose due to small q. At the same time, considerable effect is achieved when the broadcast nature of wireless transmission is taken into account, regardless of the method (GCR-U or GCR-B).

The key difference in the structure of GCR-U and GCR-B transmission methods is the feedback between the transmitter and the receiver. The feedback, on the one hand, contributes to the method overhead, but, on the other hand, allows making retransmissions when and only when they are needed. Due to no overhead connected with the feedback, GCR-U appears to be more efficient than GCR-B when failure probability p is low and the average number of transmission attempts is small. GCR-B efficiency increases with the density of the network and the number of sinks. When p is high, the feedback between the transmitter and the receiver is needed and GCR-B appears to be more efficient (unless the number of sinks is greater than the half number of nodes in the network).

If one designs an ideal algorithm to choose an optimal transmission method among described above, how much cost effective would it be? Solid lines in Fig. 2

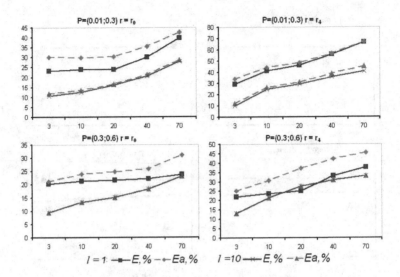

Fig. 2. Cost saving by using groupcast transmission methods on the reference route, depending on the number of sink nodes

show the cost saving calculated as $E = 100\%(W_{ref} - \min\{W_u, W_b\})/W_{ref}$, where W_{ref} is the average reference weight and W_u or W_b are the weights when GCR-U or GCR-B are used, taken for the set of same routes. The effect of using GCR-U or GCR-B increases with the network density and the number of sinks as the out-degree of vertices in the network graph also increases and accounting for broadcast nature of wireless transmission becomes more and more justified. In particular, in the shown numerical analysis, the cost saving is 20 - 30% for low network density ($r = r_0$) and reaches 70% for high density ($r = r_4$).

The relative efficiency of GCR-U and GCR-B transmission methods appears to be quite sensitive to the success probability on the network links, see Fig. 1. So, would it be possible to choose the transmission method *in each cluster* of the route independently from previous and further clusters, it is natural to expect additional cost saving on the route. Dashed lines in Fig. 2 show the results of such *adaptive* transmission method choice. The cost saving is calculated as $E_a = 100\%(W_{ref} - W_a)/W_{ref}$, where W_a is the average route weight with adaptive choice. Numerical results in this paper show that in most cases the effect caused by transmission method adaptive choice is quite modest: in the best case the contribution to cost savins is some 12% percentage points. This may be explained by the fact that in the presented numerical analysis the network grid is quite homogeneous in terms of success probabilities on its links.

Though, the results obtained with transmission method adaptive choice are convenient to use as a benchmark in further analysis. The obtained value of E_a is the maximum cost saving which may be reached on a route found with a classical route search algorithm unaware of the broadcast nature of wireless transmission.

4   Groupcast Routing Algorithms

4.1   Takahashi and Matsuyama Algorithm

The first approximate algorithm for finding Steiner tree which complexity is polynomial was proposed by Takahashi and Matsuyama in [2] in 1980. The algorithm operates on graphs with weighted edges. In this paper, we use Takahashi and Matsuyama algorithm to find the reference route, weighting edges in the ATL metric. For edge e_{ij}, ATL metric can be written in the form:

$$a_{ij} = \frac{l + \xi_D}{1 - p_{ij}}. \tag{7}$$

Let us denote by D_0 the set of sink nodes not covered yet, i.e. not included in the tree T, and by (td) the path starting in vertex t and ending in vertex $d \in D_0$. The algorithm consists of the following steps.

1. *Initialization:* $T = \{s\}$, $D_0 = D$; each edge $e_{ij} \in E$ is assigned weight a_{ij} calculated according to (7).
2. *Next sink node addition:* Find the shortest path (t^*d^*) and include it into the tree; $D_0 = D_0 \backslash \{d^*\}$.
3. *End of the work:* If $D_0 = \varnothing$, then end the work, else go to step 2.

4.2   Modified Takahashi and Matsuyama Algorithm

In this section, we propose a modified Takahashi and Matsuyama algorithm which allows to derive the minimum weight tree, taking into account the usage of one of groupcast transmission methods described in Section 3. Specifically, with this modification we consider the groupcast route cost as the sum of vertices weights based on the weights of edges outgoing from the vertices.

1. *Initialization:* $T = \{s\}$, $D_0 = D$; each edge $e_{ij} \in E$ is assigned the weight equal to the weight $C(i, J = \{j\})$ of vertex i when vertex j is the only child of i. Here and further in the section, $C(i, J)$ is calculated by (2), (4) or (6), depending on the applied groupcast transmission method.
2. *Next sink node addition and graph edges re-weighting:* Find the shortest path (t^*d^*) and include it into the tree; $D_0 = D_0 \backslash \{d^*\}$. Every edge e_{ij} such that $i \in (t^*d^*), j \notin T$, is assigned the weight equal to $C(i, J \cup \{j\}) - C(i, J)$ where $J = J(i)$ is the current set of i's children in the tree partially built at the given algorithm iteration.
3. *End of the work:* If $D_0 = \varnothing$, then end the work, else go to step 2.

4.3   Re-clusterization

The algorithm described in the previous section is quite approximate, and, as we will show in Section 4.4, the found set of clusters representing hops of the route may be far from optimal. So, taking the tree T built by the modified Takahashi algorithm as a start point, it is reasonable to try moving some vertices to another clusters to decrease the groupcast transmission cost. In this section, we propose 2 algorithms of such re-clusterization, Path Change Algorithm and Node Deletion Algorithm, and carry out them sequentially while the route cost improves.

Path Change Algorithm.

1. *Initialization:* For temporary Re-Weighting (RW) of graph edges we carry out the following procedure.

   RW procedure. Each edge $e_{ij} \in E$ is assigned the weight equal to: (a) the weight $C(i, J = \{j\})$ of vertex i when vertex j is the only child of i, if i does not have children in the current tree T; (b) $C(i, J \cup \{j\}) - C(i, J)$ if $i \in T$ and the set $J = J(i)$ of i's children is not empty.

   Then we assign the infinite weight to all $e_{ij} \in T$.
2. *Path change in the tree:* For any $d \in D$, we find the closest d's parent $t'(d)$ which is either a branch point or a destination node. Using the Floyd algorithm [8], we find the shortest paths (td) for all $t \in T$ and $d \in D$, choose such path (t^*d^*) which addition to the tree instead of $(t'(d^*)d^*)$ gives the maximal tree cost saving, and change the tree correspondingly.
3. *End of the work:* If no path changes have been made, end the work, else return to step 1.

Node Deletion Algorithm.

1. *Initialization:* Consider all vertices $v' \in T$ (except for s and leaves) in the ascending order of their out-degrees.
2. *Node deletion:* We delete v' from the tree. As a result, the tree is divided into 2 subsets: $T = T_1 \cup T_2$, where T_1 is a connected tree with root s and T_2 is the remaining part of T. Let $V'' \subseteq T_2$ be the set of vertices which were children of v' (if $v'' \in V''$, $v'' \notin D$, and v'' has only one child $\hat{v}$, we replace v'' by $\hat{v}$ in V'' and remove v'' from T_2, etc.). Similarly, if $v' \notin D$ we remove parents of v' from T_1 until either a branch point or a destination node is reached.
3. *Tree re-assembling:* We carry out RW procedure, assign the infinite weight to all $e_{ij} \in T_1 \cup T_2$ and all $e_{v'j}$; using the Floyd algorithm, we find the shortest paths (t_1v'') for all $t_1 \in T_1$ and $v'' \in V''$, choose the minimal cost path, and include it to the tree. We repeat these actions until all $v'' \in V''$ become connected to T_1.
4. *End of the work:* If the re-assembled tree cost is less than the current tree cost, we consider the former one as the current tree. If all vertices $v' \in T$ have been considered, end the work; otherwise, we return to step 2.

4.4   Numerical Results

To compare results obtained with the proposed algorithms and the original Takahashi and Matsuyama algorithm, we considered the same scenarios as in Section 3.4. Due to limited paper size, we present only results obtained with adaptive transmission method choice.

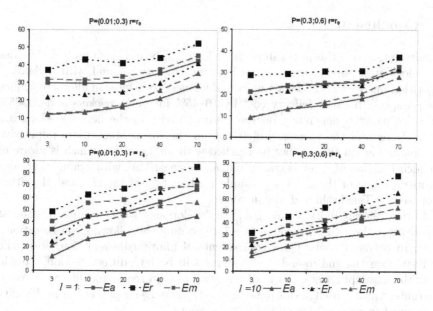

Fig. 3. Cost saving by using proposed algorithms

Fig. 3 shows the results of using the original and modified Takahashi algorithms and re-clusterization algorithms. Dashed curves show the cost saving achieved by using the modified Takahashi algorithm: $E_m = 100\%(W_{ref} - \min\{W_{ua}^m, W_{ba}^m\})/W_{ref}$, where W_{ua}^m and W_{ba}^m are the average weights of routes built by using first the modified Takahashi algorithm (with GCR-U and GCR-B methods taken correspondingly) and then the adaptive transmission method choice. Dotted curves show the cost saving E_r achieved by re-clusterization and calculated in similar way. Cost saving E_a obtained with the original Takahashi algorithm (as in Fig. 2) is shown by solid curves.

We can see that the modified Takahashi algorithm improves the cost saving (comparing with the original Takahashi algorithm) quite modestly in case of low network density: the improvement achieves 10 percentage points only with a large number of sink nodes. With high network density, such improvement is observed in a wide range of the number of sink nodes and failure probability values; in some network topologies, the modified Takahashi algorithm improves the cost saving by 20 percentage points.

Re-clusterization algorithms improve the cost saving greatly (in 1.5–2 times) almost with any network density, failure probability and packet length. However, these algorithms are quite resource-extensive and can hardly be used for dynamic routing. Nevertheless, they are useful in estimating a potential effect that can be achieved by a groupcast routing algorithm which accounts for groupcast transmission method and outperforms the algorithm in Section 4.2.

5   Conclusion

Results obtained in this paper show the following. The usage of unsolicited retries and block transmission methods on a route which was found with a classical algorithm unaware of broadcast nature of wireless transmission allows to reduce the groupcast packets delivery cost by 10–45% for video packets and 20–65% for voice packets, depending on the ratio of nodes in the network which are destinations and the success probability on the links. Much more impressive cost reduction (in times) may be reached with an algorithm which is aware of broadcast nature of wireless transmission. We contribute with examples of such algorithms, one of them being a simple modification of the classical algorithm proposed by Takahashi and Matsuyama.

As the future activity, we are going to develop algorithms aware of broadcast nature of wireless transmission to take into account the following considerations. First, to better describe QoS requirements of multimedia real time flows, the limitation on the end-to-end packet delay will be introduced. Second, we will relax the assumption of uniform distribution of QoS requirements over links on the route, which is used in this paper as the threshold q for packet loss probability is assumed to be equal for all links on the route.

References

1. Winter, P.: Steiner problem in networks: a survey. Networks 17, 129–167 (1987)
2. Takahashi, H., Mastsuyama, A.: An approximate solution for the Steiner problem in graphs. Math. Japonica 24, 573–577 (1980)
3. Ruiz, P.M., Gomezskarmeta, A.F.: Approximating optimal multicast trees in wireless multihop networks. In: 10th IEEE Symposium on Computers and Communications (ISCC), pp. 686–691 (2005)
4. IEEE Std 802.11aa-2012. IEEE Standard for Information technology – Telecommunications and information exchange between systems – Local and metropolitan area networks – Specific requirements Part 11: Wireless LAN Medium Access Control (MAC) and Physical Layer (PHY) specifications. Amendment 2: MAC Enhancements for Robust Audio Video Streaming. IEEE Computer Society (2012)
5. IEEE Std 802.11-2012. IEEE Standard for Information technology – Telecommunications and information exchange between systems – Local and metropolitan area networks – Specific requirements Part 11: Wireless LAN Medium Access Control (MAC) and Physical Layer (PHY) Specifications. – Revision of IEEE Std 802.11-1999. IEEE, N.Y. (2012)
6. Akyildiz, I.F., Wang, X.: Wireless Mesh Networks. Wiley (2009)
7. Lyakhov, A., Yakimov, M.: Analytical Study of QoS Oriented Multicast in Wireless Networks. EURASIP Journal on Wireless Communications and Networking 11, 1–13 (2011)
8. Floyd, R.W.: Algorithm 97: Shortest Path. Communications of the ACM 5(6), 345 (1962)

Concurrent Access Control Using Subcarrier Signature in Heterogeneous MIMO-Based WLAN[*]

Hu Shen[1,**], Shaohe Lv[2], Yanqiang Sun[1], Xuan Dong[1],
Xiaodong Wang[1], and Xingming Zhou[1]

National Key Laboratory of Parallel and Distributed Processing
Institute of Network Information and Security
National University of Defense Technology, Changsha, P.R. China, 410073
{shenhu,shaohelv,dongxuan,xdwang,xmzhou}@nudt.edu.cn,
syqester@gmail.com

Abstract. In recent WLAN standards (such as IEEE 802.11n), MIMO (Multiple Input Multiple Output) is deployed to provide high data transmission rate. It is however challenging to efficiently share the channel resources among different stations/users. In this paper, we study the MAC protocol in heterogeneous MIMO-based WLAN to effectively exploit the capability of concurrent transmission. We propose a novel subcarrier encoding method, which uses frequency signatures to perform the control message exchange between the AP and multiple stations simultaneously. Afterwards, a MAC protocol, HT-MIMO MAC, is presented to support concurrent transmission in both the uplink and downlink directions. HT-MIMO MAC supports link adaptation and is completely compatible with legacy stations. We evaluate the performance of the HT-MIMO MAC protocol and find that it outperforms the existing 802.11 MAC protocol with SU-MIMO and the downlink MU-MIMO MAC protocol in [9] with a remarkable throughput gains up to 86%.

Keywords: MAC protocol, heterogeneous MIMO, subcarrier signature.

1 Introduction

WLAN (IEEE 802.11 standard serials) has been widely deployed in the past 15 years, however it hardly suffice the vast data transmission demands, raised by increasingly fashionable applications such as multimedia streaming, picture sharing, online gaming, real-time map data, etc. To fulfill these data transmission requirements, many advanced physical techniques, MIMO, OFDM (Orthogonal Frequency Division Multiplexing) and channel binding, for instance, have been introduced in the latest IEEE 802.11n standard [1] and its future version 802.11ac [2]. But as we know, with

---

[*] This work was supported by the National Natural Science Foundation of China under Grant No. 61070203, No. 61202484, and Excellent Graduate Innovation Foundation of NUDT (National University of Defense Technology, China) under Grant No. B120608.
[**] Corresponding author.

B. Bellalta et al. (Eds.): MACOM 2012, LNCS 7642, pp. 109–121, 2012.
© Springer-Verlag Berlin Heidelberg 2012

physical rate of WLAN rapidly increasing from tens of Mbps to hundreds of Mbps, or even higher (>1Gbps) in coming years, the increase of data throughput or network throughput will not correspond with the same speed due to various MAC protocol overheads, including the cost of time induced by preamble, inter-frame space, contention period, handshake messages and acknowledgement confirmation, etc.

The intrinsic reason for the abovementioned inefficiency is the inconsistency between current MAC protocols and physical foundation. The upper state-of-the-art MAC protocols ignore potential concurrent transmission opportunities provided by underlying physical layer. For example, in heterogeneous MIMO-based WLAN, where the AP (access point) employs richer antenna resources than those of stations, the state-of-the-art 802.11 MAC protocol in WLAN permit only one single station to communicate with the AP in one period, thus it's a huge waste to the AP's abundant antenna resources.

However, it is challenging to synchronize and coordinate distributed stations for the concurrent transmission in the heterogeneous MIMO-based WLAN, and it's also difficult for negotiation about the channel matrix and which antenna elements to be activated between the AP and stations.

In this paper, the focus of our work is to design a MAC protocol to improve the data-to-overhead ratio and fully exploit as much concurrent transmission as permitted by MIMO-based WLAN nodes, which are with different number of antennas. The main contributions of this paper are as follows: First, we employ a novel subcarrier encoding method, which uses frequency signatures to encode protocol control messages, for handshake and acknowledgement between the AP and multiple stations simultaneously. Second, we propose an efficient MAC protocol in heterogeneous MIMO-based WLAN. So far as we know, in such network environment, our proposed protocol is the first one to achieve multiple stations concurrent transmission in both uplink and downlink directions. Our design supports link adaptation, and is compatible with 802.11 legacy stations.

The remainder of the paper is organized as follows. Section 2 provides a general overview for heterogeneous MIMO-based WLAN and formalizes the problem we dedicate to solve; Section 3 presents our design in detail; Section 4 develops a performance analysis model; Section 5 demonstrates our performance evaluation for our proposed protocol using simulation; Section 6 discusses the related work and finally we conclude our paper in Section 7.

2   System Model

Due to economic feasibility and existing legacy, the nodes in WLAN can be very heterogeneous and are equipped with different number of antennas. Consider a WLAN system with one AP and N stations as illustrated in Figure 1. The AP is equipped with M antennas, and station j employs k_j antennas, where $0 < j \leq N, 0 < k_j \leq K$ (in 802.11n standard, the maximum value of both M and K is 4; in 802.11ac draft, 8 and 4, respectively).

We assume the channel state between two antennas in a pair is symmetrical and the link data rate function takes the channel state as its variable. We denote the link between the ith antenna on the AP and the kth antenna on the jth station by l_{ijk}, where $0 < i \leq M$, $0 < j \leq N$, $0 < k \leq k_j$, and the corresponding channel state and link data rate at the tth transmission interval of scheduling duration T are denoted by $h_{ijk}(t)$ and $dr(h_{ijk}(t))$, respectively. At last, we define $\sigma_{ijk}(t)$ as the state of l_{ijk} at the tth transmission interval: when l_{ijk} is in activation, $\sigma_{ijk}(t)$ equals to 1; otherwise, $\sigma_{ijk}(t)$ equals to 0.

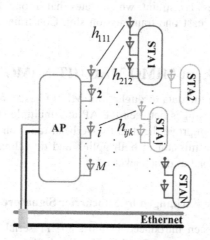

Fig. 1. Heterogeneous MIMO-based WLAN System

Then the throughput optimization problem with link adaptation in heterogeneous MIMO-based WLAN can be formalized as an integer programming problem with the objective function in (1) subject to constraints (2)-(4).

$$\max \quad \sum_{t=1}^{T}\sum_{i=1}^{M}\sum_{j=1}^{N}\sum_{k=1}^{k_j} dr(h_{ijk}(t))\sigma_{ijk}(t) \tag{1}$$

$$subject \quad to: \ \forall t \begin{cases} \sum_{i=1}^{M}\sum_{j=1}^{N}\sum_{k=1}^{k_j}\sigma_{ijk}(t) \leq M & uplink \\[4mm] \sum_{i=1}^{M}\sum_{j=1}^{N}\sum_{k=1}^{k_j}\sigma_{ijk}(t) \leq \min_{j^*,s.t.\sum_{k=1}^{k_{j^*}}\sigma_{ij^*k}(t)\geq 1}(k_{j^*}) & downlink \end{cases} \tag{2}$$

$$\forall j \quad \sum_{t=1}^{T}\sum_{i=1}^{M}\sum_{k=1}^{k_j}\sigma_{ijk}(t) \geq 1 \tag{3}$$

$$\forall i,j,k,t \quad \sigma_{ijk}(t) \in \{0,1\} \tag{4}$$

The objective function in (1) demonstrates that to achieve optimal throughput in heterogeneous MIMO-based WLAN, link activation parameter $\sigma_{ijk}(t)$ requires appropriate scheduling based on current channel matrix $h_{ijk}(t)$. Constraint (2) is called the DOF constraint, and states that the sum of the number of antennas used for reception of all active links in the collision region of one WLAN must not exceed the number of available antenna elements on every receive node of active links. Constraint (3) is called the relative fairness constraint, which states that in one scheduling duration T, every station obtains at least one transmission slot. Constraint (4) states $\sigma_{ijk}(t)$ is a binary variable.

3   High Throughput MIMO MAC (HT-MIMO MAC)

We dedicate to improve the data throughput of MIMO-based WLAN in two aspects: on one hand, control messages between the AP and multiple stations are exchanged simultaneously so as to improve the data-to-overhead ratio; on the other hand, every potential concurrent transmission in both uplink and downlink is fully exploited to increase equivalent payload of data packet.

3.1   Control Message Exchanged by Subcarrier Signature

OFDM technique has been introduced in most 802.11 serial WLAN PHY (except early 802.11 basic and 802.11b). OFDM PHY splits the frequency band into multiple subcarriers, which are orthogonal and hence non-interfering, and each subcarrier can be manipulated independently. For example, in 802.11n, the 20MHz channel is divided into 57 subcarriers whose serial number is ranged from -28 to 28, and the 40 MHz channel is divided into 117 subcarriers from -58 to 58 [1].

According to the above nature of OFDM subcarrier, we can use subcarriers' 0/1 status depicted by their different energy levels to encode control messages. We take the case of the 20MHz channel of 802.11n into consideration. And we must note that our method can also be extended into the wider channel case of 802.11n and cases of 802.11ac easily.

With 4 subcarriers (No. -28, -14, 14, 28) acting as pilot carriers, we are able to assign a set of 13 subcarriers to the link corresponding to each antenna on the AP: subcarriers from No. -27 to No.-15 are assigned to the first antenna on the AP, and subcarriers from No. -13 to No.-1, subcarriers from No. 1 to No.13, subcarriers from No. 15 to No.27 are assigned to the second, third, fourth antenna on the AP one by one. And each set of 13 subcarriers can encode three segment messages: the first 8 subcarriers to code the sequence number of stations; the middle 2 subcarriers to code the sequence number of antennas on the station; the last 3 subcarriers to code the type of control messages. Hence, a mapping constituted by 4 antennas on the AP, at most 4 antennas on 256 stations and at most 8 types of control messages is encoded. Thus control messages such as RTS/CTS and ACK between the AP and at most 4 stations can be exchanged simultaneously. In this way, all the abundant antenna resources on the AP are used.

As illustrated in Figure 2 for example, the code of the set of subcarriers from No.1 to No.13 is 0000011010001, and it demonstrates a RTS message is sent from the 3th antenna on the AP to the 2th antenna on the 7th station.

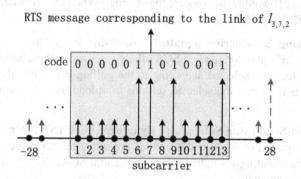

Fig. 2. Example of control message exchange using subcarrier signature

To satisfy the need of pre-coding at transmitter, current channel states $h_{ijk}(t)$ must be measured before data transmission. Here, we adopt the method of effective wireless channel measurement as depicted in [3]. In following formulation (5) and (6), $BER(\ )$ and $BER^{-1}(\ )$ is the bit error rate function with the channel state as its variable and the corresponding reverse function, $\psi(i)$ denotes the set of subcarriers assigned to the ith antenna on the AP, and $h_{ijk}^{s}(t)$ denotes the channel state of l_{ijk} at the tth time interval measured on the sth subcarrier.

$$BER_{eff,i} = \frac{1}{|\psi(i)|} \sum_{s \in \psi(i)} BER(h_{ijk}^{s}(t)) \tag{5}$$

$$h_{ijk}^{eff}(t) = BER^{-1}(BER_{eff,i}) \tag{6}$$

According to the effective channel state $h_{ijk}^{eff}(t)$, the link data rate $dr(h_{ijk}^{eff}(t))$ for data transmission can be adjusted dynamically. Considering frequency diversity[3], we interleave isolated subcarriers to each $\psi(i)$, for example, the actual set of subcarriers of $\psi(1)$ will be the set of {-28, -24, -19, -15, -11, -6, -2, 3, 8, 12, 16, 20, 25}.

3.2   Uplink Concurrent Transmission

To synchronize distributed stations for concurrent transmission, we design HT-MIMO MAC protocol in a similar way to 802.11 Point Coordination Function (PCF) [4]: In our HT-MIMO transmission model, WLAN adopts a contention-free media access mechanism, and stations can only access the channel by the AP's permit.

In uplink transmission, concurrent transmission of multiple antennas on multiple stations is allowed to efficiently exploit all potential transmission opportunities. The uplink concurrent transmission diagram is shown in Figure 3, and we will introduce detailed procedure step by step as follows.

Step 1 Channel Contention: After the channel has been idle for a DIFS period, the AP starts its backoff window to compete the channel. When the AP's backoff window decreases to 0, the step of channel contention is over.

Step 2 Poll using SubCarrier signature (SC-Poll): When the AP competes the channel successfully, the AP sends a SC-Poll message to multiple antennas on multiple stations, which are selected according to the polling list of uplink. The purpose of the SC-Poll is to permit the selected stations to upload their data with the corresponding antennas.

Step 3 Clear-To-Send using SubCarrier signature (SC-CTS): After the step of SC-Poll and an idle period of SIFS, if the stations permitted to access the channel are in possession of data waiting for upload, they will send a SC-CTS reply to the AP with the corresponding antennas.

Step 4 uplink DATA Concurrent Transmission (CT-DATA): After the step of SC-CTS and an idle period of PIFS, the stations upload their data simultaneously through the links established by step 2 and step 3.

Step 5 ACKnowledgement using SubCarrier signature (SC-ACK): After step of CT-DATA and an idle period of SIFS, the AP will send a SC-ACK message to confirm the data received successfully. Then a whole uplink concurrent transmission period is finished.

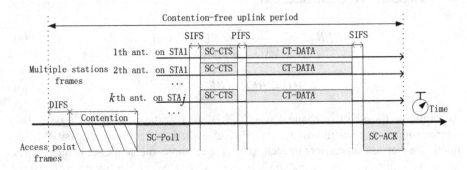

Fig. 3. Uplink concurrent transmission

3.3   Downlink Concurrent Transmission

In downlink transmission, as stations are much weaker than the AP in terms of the capacity of signal processing, concurrent transmission from the AP to multiple stations may interfere with each other. For example, supposed that the AP delivers data to two stations simultaneously, one of which employs one antenna, and the other employs two antennas. Generally speaking, the station with only one antenna would not be able to decode its received data due to the interference caused by concurrent transmission of the other station. To break through this limit, we can adopt the method of transmitter-side interference suppression in [5] to minimize the interference brought to the weaker station by using the AP's abundant antenna resources. The downlink concurrent transmission diagram is shown in Figure 4 and its procedure as follows.

Step 1 Channel Contention: This step is the same with that of uplink's.

Step 2 Request-To-Send using SubCarrier signature (SC-RTS): Firstly, the AP sends a SC-RTS message to multiple antennas on multiple stations, which are selected according to the transmission list of downlink. The purpose of the SC-RTS is to inform the selected stations to prepare to receive data with the corresponding antennas.

Step 3 Clear-To-Send using SubCarrier signature (SC-CTS): After the step of SC-RTS and an idle period of SIFS, the stations which are informed to receive data will send SC-CTS messages to the AP with the corresponding antennas.

Step 4 downlink DATA Concurrent Transmission (CT-DATA): After the step of SC-CTS and an idle period of SIFS, the AP begins to transmit data to multiple stations concurrently.

Step 5 ACKnowledgment using SubCarrier signature (SC-ACK): After the step of CT-DATA and an idle period of SIFS, the stations will send SC-ACK to confirm the data received successfully with the corresponding antennas. Then a whole downlink concurrent transmission period is finished.

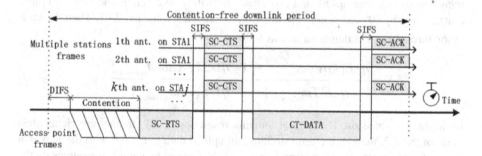

Fig. 4. Downlink concurrent transmission

3.4   Other Design Details

We have finished the main body of HT-MIMO MAC protocol, and there are still some trivial but important details left to discuss about.

Switch Transmission between Uplink and Downlink: From section 3.(2) and 3.(3), we know that both uplink and downlink transmission are initiated by the AP, so it's determined by the AP when to switch transmission between uplink and down-link. The fundamental consideration is to keep balance between uplink and downlink according to their relative traffic load, quality of service, etc.

Optimal Link Activation: As shown in formulation (1)-(4), it is clear that the scheduling problem has to determine that the value of the parameter set { $\sigma_{ijk}(t)$ } to assign a transmission opportunity to an appropriate wireless link in order to maximize the total throughput of the network. In our scenario, we just use a simple centralized greedy selection algorithm which considers node relative fairness and traffic queuing, while much more complex distributed scheduling algorithms can be found in [6].

Interoperation with Legacy: If the AP detects the existence of legacy stations, the AP will alternately perform HT-MIMO model and 802.11 basic Distributed Coordination Function (DCF) model. In both models, the AP's channel contention performs the same way with legacy stations, thus legacy stations can access the channel for uploading their data to the AP; and if the AP operates in 802.11 DCF model, data can be delivered to legacy stations. So HT-MIMO MAC protocol can interoperate with legacy stations.

4   Performance Analysis

We develop the performance analysis model to derive the saturation throughput [7] of heterogeneous MIMO-based WLAN using the proposed protocol. For simplicity, we consider that HT-MIMO MAC protocol operates in HT-MIMO model only, and all data packets have the same fixed size. We leave the more complex cases to our future work.

As HT-MIMO MAC protocol operates in HT-MIMO model, the AP switches transmission between uplink and downlink alternately. We denote the ratio of uplink transmission by η and denote the function of expected value by $E[\cdot]$. Then the saturation throughput S is demonstrated as follows.

$$S = \frac{\eta \cdot E[Payload_{uplink}] + (1-\eta) \cdot E[Payload_{downlink}]}{\eta \cdot E[Time_{uplink}] + (1-\eta) \cdot E[Time_{downlink}]} \tag{7}$$

In uplink transmission, if the total antenna resources of all stations are richer than those of the AP, then all the time stations can upload data to the AP with the maximal value of concurrent spatial streams, denotes by M, limited by antenna resources on the AP. In addition, δ denotes the propagation delay and $S_{payload}$ denotes the payload size of data packet.

$$E[Payload_{uplink}] = \begin{cases} S_{payload} \cdot \sum k_j & others \\ M \cdot S_{payload} & if \sum k_j > M \end{cases} \tag{8}$$

$$E[Time_{uplink}] = DIFS + E[T_{contention}] + T_{SC-Poll} + \delta + SIFS + T_{SC-CTS} + \delta \\ + PIFS + E[T_{DATA-packet}] + \delta + SIFS + T_{SC-ACK} + \delta \tag{9}$$

In downlink phase, limited by the weakest stations (in terms of antenna resources), the number of concurrent spatial streams, denoted by k, will be smaller than the maximal value M, and the probability of k, denoted by P_k, is determined by the distribution of stations' type.

$$E[Payload_{downlink}] = \sum_{k=2}^{M} k \cdot P_k \cdot S_{payload} \tag{10}$$

$$E[Time_{downlink}] = DIFS + E[T_{contention}] + T_{SC-RTS} + \delta + SIFS + T_{SC-CTS} + \delta$$
$$+ SIFS + E[T_{DATA-packet}] + \delta + SIFS + T_{SC-ACK} + \delta \tag{11}$$

As only the AP will attempt to compete for the channel and all Poll or RTS messages are also initialed by the AP (in other words, stations are entirely coordinated by the AP), thus there will be no collision and contention windows of the AP will be kept at the minimum value, denoted by CW_{min}.

$$E[T_{contention}] = CW_{min} \cdot T_{slot} / 2 \tag{12}$$

Finally we take the overhead of PHY header and MAC header of data packet into consideration, and we also consider the impact of link adaptation.

$$E[T_{DATA-packet}] = T_{PHY-hdr} + T_{MAC-hdr} + \max_{\forall \sigma_{ijk}(t)=1} \{T_{S_{payload}}^{l_{ijk}(t)}\} \tag{13}$$

$$T_{S_{payload}}^{l_{ijk}(t)} = \frac{S_{payload}}{dr(h_{ijk}^{eff}(t))} \tag{14}$$

5   Evaluation

We evaluate the performance numerically based on the above model with Matlab 7.10. We consider a heterogeneous MIMO-based 802.11n WLAN system, where half of stations are equipped with only one antenna, a quarter of stations with two antennas and others with four antennas, the same as the AP. Related PHY and MAC parameters of 802.11n WLAN are presented in Table 1.

Table 1. 802.11n WLAN Parameters for Simulation

Parameter	Value	Parameter	Value
Slot Time	20 μs	PIFS	8 μs
MAC hdr	36 bytes	SIFS	10 μs
PHY hdr	40 μs	DIFS	50 μs
CW_{min}	16	RTS	20bytes+PHY hdr
δ	1 μs	CTS	20bytes+PHY hdr
η	0.5	ACK	14bytes+PHY hdr
station number	40	max payload size	7935 bytes
available PDR[a]		6.5, 13, 19.5, 26, 39, 52, 58.5, 65Mbps	

a. PDR is the abbreviation for "physical data rate"

To be noted here is that depicted by SORA platform [8], scanning a subcarrier in the 20 MHz channel requires 0.03 μs, and the switch time between two subcarriers is about $0.6\,\mu s$, so we can calculate $T_{SC\text{-}Poll}$, $T_{SC\text{-}RTS}$, $T_{SC\text{-}CTS}$, and $T_{SC\text{-}ACK}$ as the following formulation (15).

We compare the performance of HT-MIMO MAC protocol with the state-of-the-art 802.11 MAC protocol and downlink MU-MIMO (muti-user MIMO) MAC protocol proposed in [9]. To be fair, we implement the later two MAC protocols based on PCF model as to eliminate the impact of contention among nodes, and 802.11 MAC protocol can operate in SU-MIMO (single user MIMO) model.

$$T_{SC-Poll} = T_{SC-RTS} = T_{SC-CTS} = T_{SC-ACK}$$

$$= 0.03 \cdot \left(\sum_i | \psi(i) | + n_{pilot-carrier}\right) + 0.6 \cdot \left(\sum_i | \psi(i) | + n_{pilot-carrier} - 1\right) \qquad (15)$$

$$= (13x4+4)x0.03 + (13x4+4-1)x0.6 = 34.68 \mu s$$

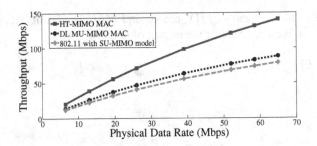

Fig. 5. Average throughput vs. PDR with max payload size

The relationship between the network saturation throughput and the physical data rate of transmission links is illustrated in Figure. 5. We can observe that in all PDR cases, HT-MIMO MAC outperforms the two comparisons, and the improvements are 74% and 53% on average, respectively.

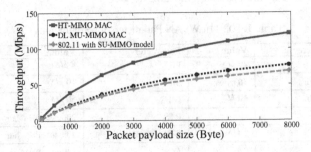

Fig. 6. Average throughput vs. payload size with PDR =52Mbps

The relationship between the network saturation throughput and the payload size of data packet is shown in Figure. 6. We can observe that in all cases, HT-MIMO MAC outperforms the two comparisons, and the improvements are 86% and 71% on average, respectively.

Figure. 7 and Figure. 8 demonstrate that the network saturation throughput improvement of HT-MIMO MAC protocol comes from two aspects: partial of throughput improvement is brought by exploiting every potential concurrent transmission in both uplink and downlink directions, especially by exploiting concurrent transmission with maximum spatial streams in uplink direction; the other partial is brought by exchanging control messages simultaneously as to minimize the overhead ratio.

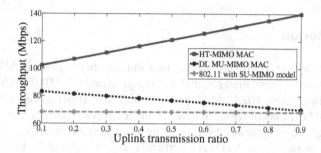

Fig. 7. Average throughput vs. uplink transmission ratio with max payload size and PDR =52Mbps

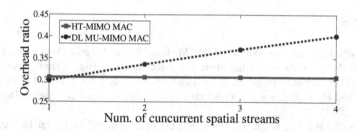

Fig. 8. Overhead ratio vs. number of spatial streams with max payload size and PDR =52Mbps

Shown in Figure 8, with the number of concurrent transmission increasing, the overhead ratio of downlink MU-MIMO MAC protocol will be a near-linear increase due to adopting the coordination method, which exchanges control messages sequentially among multiple distributed stations. And in a smaller WLAN, we can decrease the overhead ratio even more by reducing the number of subcarriers for coding control messages properly.

6   Related Work

Most of existing works related to the concurrent access control in MIMO-based networks have focused primarily on the time domain contention/scheduling schemes [6],

[9], [10], [11]. In contrast, our proposal efficiently solves this problem by exploiting diversity in the frequency domain. Besides, few existing works have taken the heterogeneity of wireless nodes into consideration and partial works consider only either uplink concurrent transmission or downlink concurrent transmission.

The similar idea of making use of OFDM subcarriers in the frequency domain to improve MAC efficiency has been adopted by [12], [13], [14]. In [12], Dutta et al. firstly introduced a signaling method based on OFDM to simultaneously transmit acknowledgments from multiple nodes; in [13], Tan et al. divided the WLAN Channel into multiple sub-channels for fine grained channel contention; in [14], Feng et al. use OFDM subcarriers to perform channel contention and piggy-backed ACKs. However, none of them implements in the scenario of multi-user MIMO networks.

7   Conclusion

In this paper, a highly efficient MAC protocol for heterogeneous MIMO-based WLAN is presented. Evaluation result shows our proposed HT-MIMO MAC protocol outperforms the existing 802.11 MAC protocol with SU-MIMO model and Downlink MU-MIMO MAC protocol remarkably. By using a novel subcarrier encoding method that uses frequency signatures to encode protocol control messages, the data-to-overhead ratio is improved. And it is an efficient way to improve the throughput performance in heterogeneous MIMO-based WLAN by making use of abundant antenna resources on the AP.

References

1. IEEE P802.11n Standard, Wireless LAN Medium Access Control (MAC) and Physical Layer (PHY) specifications: Amendment 5: Enhancements for Higher Throughput (2009)
2. IEEE P802.11ac/D0.1, Proposed TGac Draft to Wireless LAN Media Access Control (MAC) and Physical Layer (PHY) Specifications: Enhancements for Higher Throughput (January 2011)
3. Halperin, D., Hu, W., Sheth, A., Wetherall, D.: Preditable 802.11 Packet Delivery from Wireless Channel Measurements. In: Proc. ACM SIGCOMM, pp. 159–170 (2010)
4. Gast, M.S.: 802.11 Wireless Networks: The Definitive Guide. O'Reilly Press (2005)
5. Hamdaoui, B., Shin, K.G.: Characterization and Analysis of Multi-Hop Wireless MIMO Network Throughput. In: Proc. ACM MobiHoc, pp. 120–129 (2007)
6. Chu, S., Wang, X.: Adaptive and distributed scheduling in heterogeneous MIMO-based ad hoc networks. In: Proc. IEEE MASS, pp. 217–226 (2009)
7. Bianchi, G.: Performance analysis of the IEEE 802.11 Distributed Coordination Function. IEEE J. Sel. Areas Commun. 18(3), 535–547 (2000)
8. Tan, K., Zhang, J., Fang, J., Liu, H., Ye, Y., Wang, S., Zhang, Y., Wu, H., Wang, W., Voelker, G.M.: Sora: High performance software radio using general purpose multi-core processors. In: Proc. NSDI, pp. 75–90 (2009)
9. Cai, L.X., Shan, H.G., Zhuang, W.H., Shen, X.M., et al.: A Distributed Multi-User MIMO MAC protocol for Wireless Local Area Networks. In: Proc. IEEE GLOBECOM, pp. 1–5 (2008)

10. Mirkovic, J.: A MAC protocol for MIMO-based IEEE 802.11 Wireless Local Area Networks. In: Proc. IEEE WCNC, pp. 2131–2136 (2007)
11. Blough, D.M., Resta, G., Santi, P., Srinivasan, R., Cortes-Pena, L.M.: Optimal One-Shot Scheduling for Multihop MIMO Networks. In: Proc. IEEE SECON, pp. 1–9 (2011)
12. Dutta, A., Saha, D., Grunwald, D., Sicker, D.: SMACK - A Smart Acknowledgement Scheme for Broadcast Messages in Wireless Network. In: Proc. ACM SIGCOMM, pp. 15–26 (2009)
13. Tan, K., Fang, J., et al.: Fine-grained Access in Wireless LAN. In: Proc. ACM SIGCOMM, pp. 147–158 (2010)
14. Feng, X., Zhang, J., Zhang, Q., Li, B.: User Your Frequency Wisely: Explore Frequency Domain for Channel Contention and ACK. In: Proc. IEEE INFOCOM, pp. 549–557 (2012)

Investigation of Queueing System Suitable for Mathematical Modelling of TCP Short Transfer

Alexander Dudin* and Valentina Klimenok

Belarusian State University, 4, Nezavisimosti Ave., Minsk, 220030, Belarus
{dudin,klimenok}@bsu.by

Abstract. A single-server queueing system with stationary Poisson arrival process, finite buffer and impatient customers as a model of TCP Short Transfer is investigated. Service time of a customer by a server has an exponential distribution. If the server is busy and the buffer is full at a customer arrival epoch, the customer may leave the system forever or move to the orbit. Customers staying in the buffer exhibit signs of impatience: they can leave the buffer lying out of the service. Patience time of a customer has an exponential distribution. When this time expires the customer either leaves the system permanently or goes to the orbit of infinite size. Customers staying in the orbit repeat their attempts to get the service later on in a random amount of time. This time is exponentially distributed with the rate depending or independent of the current number of customers in the orbit.

Behavior of the system under study is described by two-dimensional asymptotically quasi-Toeplitz Markov chain. Stability conditions and the algorithms for calculating the stationary state distribution of the chain are obtained. Main performance measures of the system are calculated.

Keywords: Retrial queueing system, Finite buffer, Impatient customers, Stationary performance measures.

1 Mathematical Model

TCP is the reliable transport protocol used for many of the Internet's most popular applications: e-mail, news, remote login, file transfer, some streaming audio and video protocols, and the web, see, e.g. [1],[3]. Because these applications are the dominant applications on the Internet today, according to some recent studies TCP controls the vast majority of traffic on the Internet about 95 percent of the bytes and 90 percent of the packets sent over the Internet. The queueing system considered in this paper can be helpful for analytical modelling of data transmission under this protocol.

We consider a single server queueing system of capacity K, $1 \leq K < \infty$. The customers arrive to the system according to a stationary Poisson arrival process with intensity λ. Service time of a customer has exponential distribution with parameter μ.

---

* Corresponding author.

B. Bellalta et al. (Eds.): MACOM 2012, LNCS 7642, pp. 122–133, 2012.

If the server is idle at a customer arrival epoch, the service is started immediately. If the server is busy at the arrival time, the customer moves to the buffer of capacity $K - 1$. Customers staying in the buffer are picked up for the service according to the FCFS (First-Come, First-Served) discipline. If the buffer is full at the customer arrival epoch, the customer moves to some virtual area called as "orbit" with probability r, $0 \leq r \leq 1$, and leaves the system forever (is lost) with complementary probability. Customers from the orbit try their luck to get service later on. If i customers stay in the orbit, the total flow of retrials is stationary Poisson with intensity α_i, $\alpha_0 = 0$, $\alpha_i > 0$, $i \geq 1$. If the server is idle or the buffer is not full at a retrial moment, the customer from the orbit moves to the server or to the buffer respectively. Otherwise, with probability r the customer returns to the orbit and leaves the system forever with complementary probability.

The customers staying in the buffer are impatient. It means that their waiting time is bounded by random amount of time having exponential distribution with parameter γ. If a customer starts the service before this time expires he/she will leave the system as successfully served. Otherwise, with probability q, $0 \leq q \leq 1$, the customer moves to the orbit and tries his/her luck later on and with probability $1 - q$ the customer leaves the system forever.

Two possible dependencies of the total retrial rate α_i, $i \geq 1$, on the number i of customers in the orbit are considered in this paper: $\alpha_i = i\alpha$, $\alpha > 0$, and $\alpha_i = \delta > 0$, $i \geq 1$. The first one corresponds to the situation when the customers in the orbit make their retrials independently of each other with individual rate α. The second variant corresponds to the situation when retrials of the customers from the orbit are controlled in such a way as only one of the customers present in the orbit is allowed to make retrials or the individual intensities of retrials are inversely proportional to the number of customers in the orbit.

For more references to literature devoted to algorithmic analysis of retrial queues the reader may be addressed to survey paper [2].

2 Markov Chain Describing Behavior of the System under Study

Behavior of the queueing system under consideration is described by the two-dimensional continuous time Markov chain

$$\xi_t = \{i_t, k_t\}, \ t \geq 0,$$

where i_t, $i_t \geq 0$, is the number of customers staying in the orbit and k_t, $0 \leq k_t \leq K$, is the number of customers presenting in the service and in a buffer at time t.

Let us denote $q_{(i,k),(i',k')}$ the intensity of transition of the process ξ_t from the state (i,k) to the state (i',k'), $(i,k) \neq (i',k')$, and define $q_{(i,k),(i,k)}$ by

$$q_{(i,k),(i,k)} = -\sum_{i'=0, i' \neq i}^{\infty} \sum_{k'=0, k' \neq k}^{K} q_{(i,k),(i',k')}, \ i \geq 0, k = \overline{0, K}.$$

Let $Q_{i,i'}$ denote the matrix $Q_{i,i'} = (q_{(i,k),(i',k')})_{k,k'=\overline{0,K}}$, $i, i' \geq 0$. Then the block matrix $Q = (Q_{i,i'})_{i,i'\geq 0}$ is an infinitesimal generator of the Markov chain ξ_t, $t \geq 0$.

Lemma 1. The generator Q has the three block diagonal structure:

$$Q = \begin{pmatrix} Q_{0,0} & Q_{0,1} & 0 & 0 & \cdots \\ Q_{1,0} & Q_{1,1} & Q_{1,2} & 0 & \cdots \\ 0 & Q_{2,1} & Q_{2,2} & Q_{2,3} & \cdots \\ 0 & 0 & Q_{3,2} & Q_{3,3} & \cdots \\ \vdots & \vdots & \vdots & \vdots & \ddots \end{pmatrix},$$

where the blocks $Q_{i,i-1}$, $i \geq 1$; $Q_{i,i}, Q_{i,i+1}$, $i \geq 0$, are given by

$$Q_{i,i-1} = \alpha_i \begin{pmatrix} 0 & 1 & 0 & \cdots & 0 & 0 \\ 0 & 0 & 1 & \cdots & 0 & 0 \\ \vdots & \vdots & \vdots & \ddots & \vdots & \vdots \\ 0 & 0 & 0 & \cdots & 0 & 1 \\ 0 & 0 & 0 & \cdots & 0 & 1-r \end{pmatrix}, \quad Q_{i,i+1} = \begin{pmatrix} 0 & 0 & 0 & \cdots & 0 & 0 \\ 0 & 0 & 0 & \cdots & 0 & 0 \\ 0 & \gamma q & 0 & \cdots & 0 & 0 \\ 0 & 0 & 2\gamma q & \cdots & 0 & 0 \\ \vdots & \vdots & \vdots & \ddots & \vdots & \vdots \\ 0 & 0 & 0 & \cdots & (K-1)\gamma q & \lambda r \end{pmatrix},$$

$$Q_{i,i} = \begin{pmatrix} \beta_0^{(i)} & \lambda & 0 & \cdots & 0 & 0 & 0 \\ \nu_1 & \beta_1^{(i)} & \lambda & \cdots & 0 & 0 & 0 \\ 0 & \nu_2 & \beta_2^{(i)} & \cdots & 0 & 0 & 0 \\ \vdots & \vdots & \vdots & \ddots & \vdots & \vdots & \vdots \\ 0 & 0 & 0 & \cdots & \nu_{K-1} & \beta_{K-1}^{(i)} & \lambda \\ 0 & 0 & 0 & \cdots & 0 & \nu_K & \beta_K^{(i)} \end{pmatrix},$$

where

$$\beta_k^{(i)} = -(\lambda + \alpha_i + \mu + (k-1)\gamma), \ k = \overline{1, K-1},$$

$$\beta_0^{(i)} = -(\lambda + \alpha_i), \quad \beta_K^{(i)} = -(\lambda r + \alpha_i(1 - r) + \mu + (K-1)\gamma),$$

$$\nu_k = \mu + (k-1)(1-q)\gamma, \ k = \overline{1, K}.$$

Proof of the lemma consists of analysis of the Markov chain $\xi_t, t \geq 0$, transitions during the infinitesimal time interval and further combining corresponding transition intensities into the matrix blocks.   □

Behavior of the Markov chain $\xi_t, t \geq 0$, essentially depends on the form of dependence of the total retrial rate α_i on the number of customers in the orbit. We consider two forms of such a dependence.

- $\alpha_i = i\alpha$, $i \geq 1$ (classic retrial strategy). In this case the Markov chain ξ_t, $t \geq 0$, belongs to the class of asymptotically quasi-Toeplitz Markov chains, see, e.g., [4].
- $\alpha_i = \delta > 0$, $i \geq 1$ (constant retrial rate). In this case the chain under consideration is a Quasi-Birth-and-Death process, see [5]. This process can be also examined using the results of [4].

3   Stationary Distribution in the Case of Classic Retrial Strategy

The condition for existing the stationary distribution of the Markov chain ξ_t (the stationary distribution of the system states) essentially depends on the value of the probability r that a customer from the orbit comes back to the orbit after unsuccessful attempt to reach the server. The following theorem gives this condition depending of whether or not $r < 1$.

Theorem 1.
  (*i*) If $r < 1$ then the Markov chain ξ_t has the stationary distribution for any set of the system parameters;
  (*ii*) If $r = 1$ then the sufficient condition for the stationary distribution existence is the fulfillment of the inequality

$$\lambda < \mu + (K-1)(1-q)\gamma; \tag{1}$$

(*iii*) If $r = 1$ and

$$\lambda > \mu + (K-1)(1-q)\gamma$$

then the stationary distribution does not exist.

Proof. According to [4], stability condition for the Markov chain $\xi_t, t \geq 0$, is expressed in terms of the matrices Y_k, $k = 0, 1, 2$, that are defined by

$$Y_k = \lim_{i\to\infty} R_i^{-1} Q_{i,i+k-1}, \; k = 0, 2; \; Y_1 = \lim_{i\to\infty} R_i^{-1} Q_{i,i} + I$$

where the matrix R_i is a diagonal matrix whose diagonal entries are equal to absolute magnitudes of the corresponding diagonal entries of the matrix $Q_{i,i}$, $i \geq 0$.

As follows from [4], the stationary distribution of the Markov chain ξ_t exists if the following inequality holds:

$$\mathbf{x}Y_0\mathbf{e} > \mathbf{x}Y_2\mathbf{e} \tag{2}$$

where the vector $\mathbf{x}$ is the unique solution to the system

$$\mathbf{x}(Y_0 + Y_1 + Y_2) = \mathbf{x}, \; \mathbf{x}\mathbf{e} = 1, \tag{3}$$

$\mathbf{e}$ is column vector consisting of 1's.

If inequality (2) has an opposite sign (">") then the stationary distribution of the chain under consideration does not exist.

Let us prove the statement (*i*) − (*iii*) of the theorem using the general form stability condition (2)-(3).

(*i*) Assume that $r < 1$. It means that the customers from the orbit are not absolutely persistent (r-persistent). It is easily to see that in such a case the matrix Y_0 is stochastic while the matrix Y_2 is a zero one. Then inequality (2) holds for any set of the system parameters.

(*ii*) Let $r = 1$. It means that the customers from the orbit are absolutely persistent. In this case the matrices Y_k, $k = 0, 1, 2$, take the following form:

$$Y_0 = \begin{pmatrix} 0 & 1 & 0 & \dots & 0 & 0 & 0 \\ 0 & 0 & 1 & \dots & 0 & 0 & 0 \\ \vdots & \vdots & \vdots & \ddots & \vdots & \vdots & \vdots \\ 0 & 0 & 0 & \dots & 0 & 0 & 1 \\ 0 & 0 & 0 & \dots & 0 & 0 & 0 \end{pmatrix}, \quad Y_1 = \begin{pmatrix} 0 & 0 & \dots & & 0 & 0 \\ 0 & 0 & \dots & & 0 & 0 \\ \vdots & \vdots & \ddots & & \vdots & \vdots \\ 0 & 0 & \dots & & 0 & 0 \\ 0 & 0 & \dots & \frac{\mu+(K-1)(1-q)\gamma}{\lambda+\mu+(K-1)\gamma} & 0 \end{pmatrix},$$

$$Y_2 = \begin{pmatrix} 0 & 0 & \dots & & 0 & 0 \\ 0 & 0 & \dots & & 0 & 0 \\ \vdots & \vdots & \ddots & & \vdots & \vdots \\ 0 & 0 & \dots & & 0 & 0 \\ 0 & 0 & \dots & \frac{(K-1)q\gamma}{\lambda+\mu+(K-1)\gamma} & \frac{\lambda}{\lambda+\mu+(K-1)\gamma} \end{pmatrix}.$$

It can be verified by the direct substitution that the solution of system (3) is given by the vector

$$\mathbf{x} = \left(0, \dots, 0, \frac{\mu + (K-1)\gamma}{\lambda + 2(\mu + (K-1)\gamma)}, \frac{\lambda + \mu + (K-1)\gamma}{\lambda + 2(\mu + (K-1)\gamma)} \right).$$

Substituting this vector into formula (2) we easily derive inequality (1).

(*iii*) As it has been said above, the chain ξ_t does not have the stationary distribution if inequality (2) has the opposite sign, i.e.,

$$\mathbf{x}Y_0\mathbf{e} < \mathbf{x}Y_2\mathbf{e}.$$

From this the proof of statement (*iii*) of the theorem follows immediately. □

Remark 1. Inequality (1) is easily tractable. The left hand side of this inequality is an arrival rate. The right hand side is the rate of the customers departure under the condition that the system is heavy loaded. The summand μ corresponds to the rate of departure of customers that have got the service in the system. The summand $(K-1)(1-q)\gamma$ corresponds to the rate of departure of customers who leave the system due to their impatience during the staying in a buffer.

Remark 2. Inequality (1) is very important from the point of view of practical applications of the considered model. The right hand side of inequality (1) defines the limiting throughput of the system (maximal rate of arrivals for which the system is able to provide the service). Violation of this inequality implies overloading of the system (the number of customers in the system increases to infinity).

Remark 3. Stability condition (1) is valid not only for the classic retrial strategy, but for any retrial strategy such as the retrial intensities α_i satisfy condition $\lim_{i \to \infty} \alpha_i = \infty$.

Let us assume that the stability conditions are fulfilled. Then the steady state probabilities

$$p(i,k) = \lim_{t \to \infty} P\{i_t = i, k_t = k\}, \ i \geq 0, k = \overline{0, K},$$

exist.

Denote as p_i, $i \geq 0$, the row-vectors of these probabilities,

$$p_i = (p(i,0), \ p(i,1), \ldots, p(i,K)), \ i \geq 0.$$

Using results in [4] and accounting more simple block structure of the generator Q than the structure, which is allowed in [4], we get the following procedure for calculating the vectors p_i, $i \geq 0$.

Theorem 2. Numerically stable procedure for computing the stationary probabilities p_i, $i \geq 0$, consists of the following steps.

- Calculate the matrices G_i using the backward recursion

$$G_i = (-Q_{i+1,i+1} - Q_{i+1,i+2}G_{i+1})^{-1}Q_{i+1,i}, \ i \geq 0,$$

  with terminal condition

$$G_\infty = G$$

  where the matrix G is equal to the matrix Y_0 in case if $r < 1$ and is the minimal non-negative solution to the quadratic matrix equation

$$G = Y_0 + Y_1 G + Y_2 G^2$$

  in case if $r = 1$.
- Calculate the matrices $\bar{Q}_{i,i}$, $\bar{Q}_{i,i+1}$ by the formulae

$$\bar{Q}_{i,i} = Q_{i,i} + Q_{i,i+1}G_i, \ \bar{Q}_{i,i+1} = Q_{i,i+1}, \ i \geq 0.$$

- Calculate the matrices Φ_i by

$$\Phi_0 = I, \Phi_i = \prod_{l=1}^{i} \bar{Q}_{l-1,l}(I - \bar{Q}_{l,l})^{-1}, i \geq 1.$$

- Calculate the vector p_0 as the unique solution to the system of linear algebraic equations

$$p_0(-\bar{Q}_{0,0}) = 0, \ p_0 \sum_{l=0}^{\infty} \Phi_l e = 1.$$

- Calculate the vectors p_l, $l \geq 1$, by $p_l = p_0 \Phi_l$.

Derivation and details of the procedure given in this theorem are presented in [4]. This procedure is numerically stable and easily implemented on a computer.

4 Case of the Constant Retrial Rate

In this section we assume that the total retrial rate from the orbit is equal to a constant δ when the orbit is not empty. As it was mentioned above, under such a definition of the retrial rate the Markov chain ξ_t, $t \geq 0$, is a Quasi-Birth-and-Death process, see [5], which can be also considered as a special case of continuous time quasi-Toeplitz Markov chains, see, e.g., [4].

Theorem 3. The Markov chain ξ_t, $t \geq 0$, has the stationary distribution if and only if the following inequality holds good:

$$\delta \sum_{k=0}^{K-1} \psi_k + (1-r)\delta\psi_K > q\gamma \sum_{k=2}^{K}(k-1)\psi_k + \lambda r\psi_K, \qquad (4)$$

where

$$\psi_k = \frac{(\lambda + \delta)^k}{\prod\limits_{l=0}^{k-1}(\mu + l\gamma)}, \quad k = \overline{0, K}.$$

Proof. In the case under consideration the blocks $Q_{i,j}$, $j = i-1, i, i+1$, of the infinitesimal generator Q does not depend on the value of i and the generator can be represented as

$$Q = \begin{pmatrix} Q_0 & Q_1 & 0 & 0 & \cdots \\ Q_0 & Q_1 & Q_2 & 0 & \cdots \\ 0 & Q_0 & Q_1 & Q_2 & \cdots \\ \vdots & \vdots & \vdots & \vdots & \ddots \end{pmatrix}$$

where

$$Q_0 = \delta \begin{pmatrix} 0 & 1 & 0 & \cdots & 0 & 0 & 0 \\ 0 & 0 & 1 & \cdots & 0 & 0 & 0 \\ \vdots & \vdots & \vdots & \ddots & \vdots & \vdots & \vdots \\ 0 & 0 & 0 & \cdots & 0 & 1 & 0 \\ 0 & 0 & 0 & \cdots & 0 & 0 & (1-r) \end{pmatrix}, \quad Q_1 = \begin{pmatrix} \beta_0 & \lambda & 0 & \cdots & 0 & 0 & 0 \\ \nu_1 & \beta_1 & \lambda & \cdots & 0 & 0 & 0 \\ 0 & \nu_2 & \beta_2 & \cdots & 0 & 0 \\ \vdots & \vdots & \vdots & \ddots & \vdots & \vdots & \vdots \\ 0 & 0 & 0 & \cdots & \nu_{K-1} & \beta_{K-1} & \lambda \\ 0 & 0 & 0 & \cdots & 0 & \nu_K & \beta_K \end{pmatrix},$$

$$Q_2 = \begin{pmatrix} 0 & 0 & 0 & \cdots & 0 & 0 & 0 \\ 0 & 0 & 0 & \cdots & 0 & 0 & 0 \\ 0 & \gamma q & 0 & \cdots & 0 & 0 & 0 \\ 0 & 0 & 2\gamma q & \cdots & 0 & 0 & 0 \\ \vdots & \vdots & \vdots & \ddots & \vdots & \vdots & \vdots \\ 0 & 0 & 0 & \cdots & (K-2)\gamma q & 0 & 0 \\ 0 & 0 & 0 & \cdots & 0 & (K-1)\gamma q & \lambda r \end{pmatrix}.$$

Here

$$\beta_k = -(\lambda + \delta + \mu + (k-1)\gamma), \quad k = \overline{1, K-1},$$

$$\beta_0 = -(\lambda + \delta), \ \beta_K = -(\lambda r + \delta(1 - r) + \mu + (K - 1)\gamma).$$

According to [5], the necessary and sufficient stability condition for the Markov chain ξ_t, $t \geq 0$, is defined by the inequality

$$\mathbf{x}Q_0\mathbf{e} > \mathbf{x}Q_2\mathbf{e} \qquad (5)$$

where the vector $\mathbf{x} = (x_0, \dots, x_K)$ is the unique solution to the system

$$\mathbf{x}(Q_0 + Q_1 + Q_2) = \mathbf{0}, \ \mathbf{xe} = 1. \qquad (6)$$

Analyzing the structure of the matrix $Q_0 + Q_1 + Q_2$, one can easy understand that the vector $\mathbf{x}$ defines the stationary distribution of the birth-and-death process with state space $\{0, \dots, K\}$, intensity of birth equal to $\lambda + \delta$ and intensity of death in the state $k > 0$ equal to $\mu + (k - 1)\gamma$. Then the entries of this vector are defined by the well known formula

$$x_k = \frac{\psi_k}{\sum\limits_{l=0}^{K} \psi_l}, \ k = \overline{0, K}.$$

Substituting these expressions into (5) we easily get inequality (4). $\qquad \square$

Remark 4. Inequality (4) is easily tractable. The left hand side of this inequality is equal to the rate of departures of customers from the orbit. The right hand side of the inequality is equal to the rate of customers arrival to the orbit when the system is heavily loaded.

Let us assume that stability conditions are fulfilled. Then the vectors $\boldsymbol{p}_i$, $i \geq 0$, of the steady state probabilities of the chain are of the matrix geometric form and are calculated using the results by M. Neuts in [5].

Theorem 4. The vectors $\boldsymbol{p}_i$, $i \geq 0$, of the stationary probabilities are computed by

$$\boldsymbol{p}_i = \boldsymbol{p}_0 \mathcal{R}^i, \ i \geq 0,$$

where the matrix $\mathcal{R}$ is the minimal non-negative solution to the equation

$$\mathcal{R}^2 Q_0 + \mathcal{R}Q_1 + Q_2 = O,$$

and the vector $\boldsymbol{p}_0$ is the unique solution to the system of linear algebraic equations

$$\boldsymbol{p}_0(Q_1 + \mathcal{R}Q_0) = \mathbf{0}, \ \boldsymbol{p}_0(I - \mathcal{R})^{-1}\mathbf{e} = 1.$$

5   Performance Measures

With the knowledge of the steady state probability vectors, $\mathbf{p}_i$, $i \geq 0$, we can compute a variety of system performance measures to study the qualitative behavior of the model. Here we list a few measures along with formulas for their calculation.

- Mean number, L_{buf}, of customers in the buffer and in the server

$$L_{buf} = \sum_{i=0}^{\infty} \boldsymbol{p}_i diag\{0, 1, \ldots, K\}\mathbf{e}$$

where $diag\{0, 1, \ldots, K\}$ is a diagonal matrix with diagonal entries $0, 1, \ldots, K$.

- Mean number, L_{orb}, of customers in the orbit

$$L_{orb} = \sum_{i=0}^{\infty} i\boldsymbol{p}_i\mathbf{e}.$$

- Mean number, L, of customers in the system (in the buffer, in the server and in the orbit)

$$L = L_{buf} + L_{orb}.$$

- Probability, $P_{loss}^{(imm)}$, that an arbitrary arriving customer will be lost upon arrival (due to the buffer overflow)

$$P_{loss}^{(imm)} = (1 - r)\pi_K$$

where $\pi_K = \sum_{i=0}^{\infty} \boldsymbol{p}_i\mathbf{e}^{(K)}$, and $\mathbf{e}^{(K)}$ is a column vector of size $K + 1$ with all zero entries except the last entry which is equal to 1.

- Throughput, T, of the system

$$T = \mu \sum_{i=0}^{\infty} \boldsymbol{p}_i diag\{0, 1, \ldots, 1\}\mathbf{e}.$$

- Probability, $P_{loss}^{(accept)}$, that a customer accepted into the system will be further lost (due to impatience during the waiting time in a buffer)

$$P_{loss}^{(accept)} = 1 - \frac{T}{\lambda[1 - (1 - r)\pi_K]}.$$

- Probability, P_{imm}, that an arbitrary arriving customer reaches the server immediately upon arrival

$$P_{imm} = \sum_{i=0}^{\infty} \boldsymbol{p}_i diag\{1, 0, \ldots, 0\}\mathbf{e}.$$

- Utilization, U, of the server

$$U = 1 - P_{imm}.$$

- Probability, P_{buf}, that an arbitrary customer will wait in the buffer but will not visit the orbit due to impatience

$$P_{buf} = \sum_{i=0}^{\infty} \boldsymbol{p}_i diag\{0; \frac{\mu}{\mu + k\gamma}, k = \overline{1, K-1};\ 0\}\mathbf{e}.$$

- Probability, P_{orb}, that an arbitrary customer will visit the orbit

$$P_{orb} = \sum_{i=0}^{\infty} p_i diag\{0; \frac{qk\gamma}{\mu + k\gamma}, k = \overline{1, K-1}; r\}\mathbf{e}.$$

6   Numerical Example

Having the main performance measures of the system been calculated, different optimization problems, e.g., planning the system capacity K, sojourn time restriction, individual retrial rate, etc., can be formulated and solved for the queue under consideration. Here we restrict ourselves by presenting a simple numerical illustration.

Let capacity of the system be $K = 6$, intensity of arrivals be $\lambda = 4$, service rate be $\mu = 5$, the parameter γ defining impatience rate be equal to 0.5 and probabilities q and r of customer moving or returning to the orbit in case of the full system be equal to 1.

Let the retrial rate from the orbit be proportional to the current number of customers in the orbit. Figures 1-3 illustrate dependence of the average number L_{orb} of customers in the orbit, the average number L_{buf} of customers in buffer and the average number L of customers in the system on the individual intensity of retrials α.

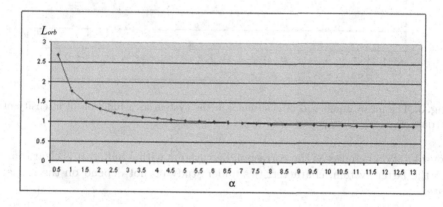

Fig. 1. The mean number L_{orb} of customers in the orbit as a function of intensity of retrials α

It can be seen that, as it can be expected, the mean number L_{orb} of customers in the orbit and the mean number L of customers in the system decrease while the mean number L_{buf} of customers in the buffer increases with grow of intensity α when α is small. In the region of large values of α ($\alpha > 7$) these performance measures become more or less invariant with respect to the value of α. This is explained by the fact that, for sufficiently large α, the retrial system under

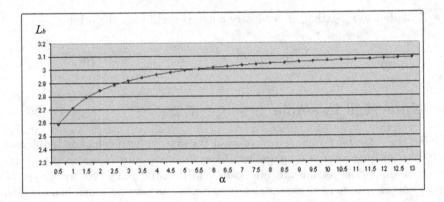

Fig. 2. The mean number L_{buf} of customers in the buffer as a function of intensity of retrials α

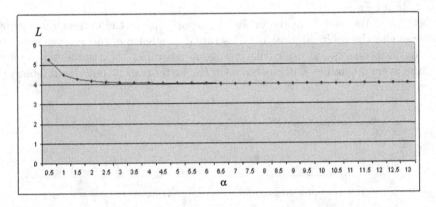

Fig. 3. The mean number L of customers in the system as a function of intensity of retrials α

consideration behaves as the corresponding system with a buffer. It is clear that, for the latter system, characteristics under study do not depend on the retrial rate.

7   Conclusion

Generalizations of the considered retrial queueing model to more complicated arrival and service process, e.g. the Batch Markov Arrival Process and the Markov Service Process or phase type service time distribution, can be done in a straightforward way.

References

1. Avrachenkov, K., Yechiali, U.: Retrial networks with finite buffers and their application to Internet data traffic. Probability in the Engineering and Informational Sciences 22, 519–536 (2008)
2. Gomez-Corral, A.: A bibliographical guide to the analysis of retrial queues through matrix analytic techniques. Annals of Operations Research 141, 163–191 (2006)
3. Hafsaoui, A., Collange, D., Urvoy-Keller, G.: Revisiting the Performance of Short TCP Transfers. In: Fratta, L., Schulzrinne, H., Takahashi, Y., Spaniol, O. (eds.) NETWORKING 2009. LNCS, vol. 5550, pp. 260–273. Springer, Heidelberg (2009)
4. Klimenok, V.I., Dudin, A.N.: Multi-dimensional asymptotically quasi-toeplitz Markov chains and their application in queueing theory. Queueing Systems 54(4), 245–259 (2006)
5. Neuts, M.F.: Matrix-geometric solutions in stochastic models. The Johns Hopkins University Press, Baltimore (1981)

Dependable MAC Layer Architecture
Based on Holographic Data Representation
Using Hyper-Dimensional Binary Spatter Codes

Denis Kleyko[1], Nikita Lyamin[1], Evgeny Osipov[2,*], and Laurynas Riliskis[2]

[1] Siberian State University of Telecommunications and Information Sciences
Novosibirsk, Russia
sibsutispds@gmail.com

[2] Department of Computer Science Electrical and Space Engineering
Luleå University of Technology, 971 87 Luleå, Sweden
{Evgeny.Osipov,Layrynas.Riliskis}@ltu.se

Abstract. In this article we propose the usage of binary spatter codes and distributed data representation for communicating loss and delay sensitive data in event-driven sensor and actuator networks. Using the proposed data representation technique along with the medium access control protocol the mission critical control information can be transmitted with assured constant delay in deployments exposing below 0 dB signal-to-noise ratio figures.

Keywords: Hyperdimensional computing, reliable communications, binary spatter codes, distributed representation.

1 Introduction

This article addresses a problem of reliable communication of information in wireless networks. We consider a special class of event-driven networks: Networks deployed in *extremely noisy* radio environments and transmitting *quanta* of information with strict requirements on the delay, reliability and security of the transmission. By *information quantum* we understand a small portion of data representing, for example, signals of occurred events, system status updates, triggers of various actions. We *explicitly exclude* from the consideration larger in size data streams, like video, audio or telemetry. Although such networks might seem as very restricted, they find their application in large variety of deployments. A typical example a communication system in this class is a network in a control loop of industrial automation process or a network in the scope of an intelligent transportation system, where the network performance is in many cases mission- and even life-critical. These installations are characterized by constant presence of uncontrollable radio interferences on the one hand and strict requirements on in-time, reliable and secure delivery of data on the other.

In this article we explore a different to the conventional packet-based way of representing and communicating structured data: Based on distributed (or holographic reduced) representation of semantically bound information. While the usage of the distributed representation is common in the domain of cognitive and neural computing, to

---

* Corresponding author.

B. Bellalta et al. (Eds.): MACOM 2012, LNCS 7642, pp. 134–145, 2012.

the best of our knowledge this is the first attempt of using the framework for communication of loss- and delay-sensitive information. Using this type of information representation an entity to be transmitted (for example, a trigger signal or a quantization level of a sensor) is associated with a *pattern* of bits of very large size (*hyper-dimensional*). Several items then can be arithmetically combined into a new pattern of the same dimension, which is called a *compositional structure* or a *holographic reduced representation* of a set of items. This structure then to some extend could be viewed as an analog of a frame to be transmitted over a wireless link. When being represented in such a way the information becomes extremely tolerant to losses. In fact, it is possible to restore an information, which was distorted up to 47%.

It is important to note that here we do not argue about replacing the traditional communication techniques and mechanisms for achieving reliability, e.g. ARQ, HARQ, coding techniques (see [8] and references therein). Rather, the suggested approach should be seen as a useful complement to the conventional architectures opening new capabilities for machine-to-machine communications, which are impossible with the current techniques. These new capabilities include extracting new contextual information from parallel transmissions, i.e. collisions, cognitive reasoning and generalization of sensing phenomena while assuring a constant upper bound on the delay of delivering information in the presence of massive errors.

Along with the adoption of the distributed representation framework for representing loss- and delay-sensitive data we also propose a medium access control protocol called HDMAC, which transmits the hyper-dimensional patterns between wireless nodes. Using the proposed communication technique the distributively represented information will be assuredly delivered in extremely harsh environments.

The article is structured as follows. Section 2 presents the main aspects of the theory for distributed data representation relevant to the scope of the article. A node architecture and the MAC protocol for transmitting hyper dimensional structures are presented in Section 3. Section 4 demonstrates the illustrative performance aspects of the proposed architecture. We discuss open issues in Section 5 before concluding the article in Section 6.

2 Distributed Representation of Structured Data: The Case of Communications

Distributed representations of data structures is an approach actively used in the area of cognitive computing for representing and reasoning upon semantically bound information [3–5, 7].

In conventional computing architectures data are presented by unique binary values. For example, character "A" has a unique ASCII code, when changing even single bit position one would obtain an ASCII representation of a completely different symbol. Considering now a structure of a protocol data unit in communication networks (i.e. frame, packet, datagram, segment) each field has a predefined offset unique in the scope of a particular protocol.

In contrast, in the domain of distributed representation a single data unit is represented by a set of bit patterns and a data structure is constructed by meshing up the fields into a bit patterns of *the same dimension* as is used for representing a single entity. In this section we present the basics of the theory of distributed representation based on hyper-dimensional vector relevant to the proposed communication approach. To assist a reader with easier matching of the networking-specific terminology with the one used in the referenced above original sources further in the text we use the following convention. We use term "role" as a synonym to concept "field in a protocol data unit" and term "role filler" as a synonym to the concept of a field's value.

Representation of Data by Noise-Tolerant Patterns. In 1988 Kanerva [2] suggested to use random vectors of high dimensionality (further on referred as hyper-dimensional random vectors or simply *HD-vectors*) for representation of information and expression of semantic relations between the represented entities. *High dimensionality* means here *several thousand* of binary positions for representing a single entity.

Randomness here means that the values on each position of an HD-vector are i.i.d. drawn from the normal distribution with mean 0 and variance $1/n$, where n is the dimension of the vector. By generating vectors in this way the number of "1" components is equal to the number of "0" components. In this article we use Hamming distance as a measure of difference between two vectors: $\Delta_H(A, B) = \sum_{i=0}^{n-1} a_i \otimes b_i$, where a_i, b_i are bits on positions i in vectors A and B^1 of dimension n and $\otimes$ denotes the bit-wise XOR operation. Note that the distances to a randomly drawn vector follow binomial distribution, hence the portion ρ of the representation space $N = 2^n$ located at distances up to d is

$$\rho = \frac{\binom{n}{0} + \binom{n}{1} + \dots + \binom{n}{d}}{2^n}. \tag{1}$$

When computing a portion of the representation space for different distances d at *high* dimensionalities one comes across a remarkable property of hyper-dimensional spaces: *Most of the representation space will be concentrated at distances* $0.5u \pm 0.03$. *Only* 10^{-9} *of the space would be closer to a randomly selected vector than* $0.47u$ *with the same fraction of the space being farther from the same point than* $0.53u^2$.

This observation means that a probability of picking at random two vectors different in *fewer* than even 45% of positions is negligibly small. If such two vectors appear the theory of hyper-dimensional distributed representation tells that *they are related (or similar)*. Using an analogy with representing character "A" used above this means that *any* bits sequence different in, say, 30% of positions from the original bit pattern representing "A" is *similar* to "A" with a very large probability.

Storing and Retrieving the Information: Autoassociative Item Memory. In HD computing an HD-vector is given a meaning when it is associated with an entity, which

---

[1] Further on we denote vectors by capital latin letters and their components by small latin letters with indices indicating the position of the component.

[2] These calculations are presented for the case of 10000-ary representation space.

it represents. Entities in the proposed communication architecture are different *roles* and their *fillers* (see terminology convention above). Examples of roles are "Destination", "Source", or "Level of a temperature sensor". Examples of fillers in our case are identifiers for nodes, broadcast address, and a specific quantization level of the temperature sensor.

The mapping between entities and HD vectors are stored in an *item memory* as illustrated in Figure 1. The item memory is autoassociative, that is it is addressed by the stored item itself. The job of the item memory is to find an associated clean version of HD vector given its noisy value as an input. The clean version is found by performing a nearest neighbor search with an objective to minimize the (Hamming) distance between the input vector and the version stored in the item memory.

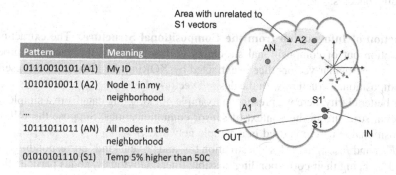

Pattern	Meaning
01110010101 (A1)	My ID
10101010011 (A2)	Node 1 in my neighborhood
...	
10111011011 (AN)	All nodes in the neighborhood
01010101110 (S1)	Temp 5% higher than 50C

Fig. 1. Illustration of an autoassociative item memory

Composition and Decomposition of Data Structures. Representing a compositional structure (i.e. composing a packet out of multiple fields with assigned values) in a distributed way involves two operations: *binding of patterns* (i.e. associating roles with fillers) and *superposition of patterns* (i.e. representing sets of bound patterns). In this article for superposition of patterns a bit-wise OR, further denoted as $\oplus$, is used. For binding of patterns we will use bitwise XOR operation.

Thus, following the line of reasoning in [5] a compositional structure is defined as in (2).

$$S = F_1 \otimes V_1 \oplus F_2 \otimes V_2 \oplus \ldots \oplus F_n \otimes V_n. \tag{2}$$

Reflecting to the case of our communication approach F_i are hyper-dimensional vectors representing semantics (role), i.e. data structure field identifiers, and V_i are the vectors representing the particular values (fillers).

The number of the role-filler pairs, which can be superimposed inside the compositional structure is limited by the properties of the $\oplus$ operation. For the correct interpretation of the received sequence by the item memory the result of the superposition should be *similar* to each involved in the compositional structure role-filler bindings, i.e. *the Hamming distance between each pair and the result of the superposition should be well below 50%.* Otherwise, with the hamming distance approaching 0.5 the HD-vector of the compositional structure will be *unrelated to its members*.

Using basic probabilities, it is straightforward to demonstrate that the probability of "1" components in the resulting HD vector is larger than 0.5. The Hamming distance between a given vector A_1 of dimension N and the result of the OR-sum of n vectors $A_1, A_2 \ldots A_n$ is $D_H(A_1, A_1 \oplus A_2 \oplus \ldots \oplus A_n) = \frac{2^{n-1}-1}{2^n} \cdot N$. An analysis of this result reveals that the Hamming distance between an arbitrary vector and the result of the OR-sum with its participation increases rapidly with the number of HD-vectors included in the OR-sum. Already with three summed vectors the Hamming distance reaches 0.4. This observation means a compositional structure constructed in form (2) may contain up to three role-filler pairs. While there are ways of scaling up the compositional structure substantially, in this article we use (2) for the sake of simplicity of presentation of the main concepts.

Extraction of Information from the Compositional Structure. The extraction of information out of compositional structures is the reverse to the encoding process. Namely, a particular vector-filler is extracted by XORing the HD-vector representing the compositional structure with the desired vector-role.

For better clarity, here we present an example of extracting data from a simple compositional structure in the context of sensor communications. Suppose the following compositional structure is used in a sample network: $S = F_{dst} \otimes V_d \oplus F_{event} \otimes V_e$. Here F_{dst} and F_{event} are roles "Destination ID" and "Event kind" correspondingly with V_d and V_e being their corresponding possible fillers. Obviously, nodes participating in the application construct own structures S independently from each other. Suppose now an arbitrary node in the network receives pattern S' (possibly noise due to transmission errors) and wants to test whether this structure is intended for it or it should be dropped. The node therefore performs the following operations:

1. XOR with HD-vector representing role "Destination ID" in order to retrieve its filler: $V_D' = S' \otimes F_{dst} = V_d \oplus NOISE$.
2. Pass noisy vector V_D' to the item memory for finding out whether it is similar to the HD-vector representing node's own ID by comparing Hamming distance between V_D' and V_{OwnID} with the predefined threshold.

3   Medium Access Control Protocol for Transmission of HD Structures

HD-Node Architecture. Figure 2(a) illustrates the HD-node architecture. The network, transport (if any[3]) and application level functionality remains unchanged. The HD approach presented above requires however a new adaptation layer, which is responsible for: a) the hyper dimensional representation of the semantic constructs and the values specific to a particular deployment; and b) the transmission and reception of the HD-represented information.

---

[3] In wireless sensor networks the functionality is not rigorously defined and an application, for example, may implement primitives of both transport and the network layers.

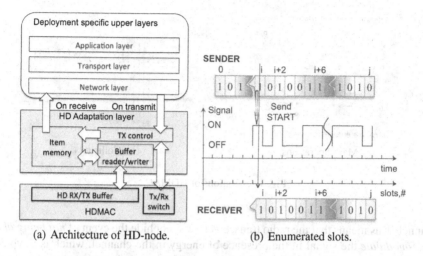

(a) Architecture of HD-node.   (b) Enumerated slots.

Fig. 2. Medium access approach using HD-represented data

The first functional block implements the item memory as described above. It is populated with the entries at the pre-deployment and the bootstrap phases, which we do not elaborate further in this paper and report elsewhere. For further discussion we, therefore, assume that all nodes have a consistent state of the item memory. The memory performs a bidirectional mapping between meanings and the associated HD vectors as well as implements the nearest neighbor search of the clean HD vectors given a pattern received by the MAC layer.

The second block interfaces the HD-processor with the MAC layer described below. This block contains a reader/writer of the receive buffer located at the MAC layer. While the protocol description is presented in the next section, we present the properties of the receive buffer here. The size of the receive buffer is equal to the dimensionality of the HD vector in bits. Therefore, if one choose to operate with vectors of dimension 1000 or even 10000 the needed buffer size is 125 bytes and 1.2kB correspondingly. We discuss the question of using reasonable dimensionality in Section 5 below.

The receive buffer starts to be filled in by the MAC layer as soon as the activity in the radio channel is detected. The rules for filling the receive buffer is described below in section presenting MAC protocol. The event (in the sense of event driven operating systems, like TinyOS) of start the filling process initiates the vector analysis function, which drowns every complete N-positions chunk of the hyper vector and passes it to the item memory. In the case the item memory block could match the received chunk of the HD vector to one or more of the clean versions, it triggers the processing at the layer above. This upper layer in its turn may interrupt the reception process and take application-specific actions.

HDMAC: PHY-Layer Considerations. Before proceeding with the description of the HDMAC functionality we formulate an important requirement to physical layer functionality: An exposure of an API for reporting the state of bit-level erasure in the

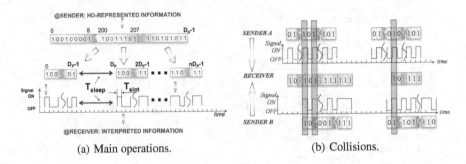

(a) Main operations.   (b) Collisions.

Fig. 3. Operations of HDMAC

channel. This means that the radio transceiver must not hide the event of *not being able to de-modulate* the signal in the presence of energy in the channel, which is a typical case for collisions. This feature is feasible to implement natively in most of the out-of-the-shelf radio platforms introducing straightforward modifications to drivers in the branch for handling the Rx interrupt.

HDMAC: Main Operations. Since in the domain of wireless sensor networks it is commonly understood that a structure of a communication protocol should be adjusted to the specifics of the particular application and the installation site, we present the operations of HDMAC in general form. The medium access control technique for transmitting the hyperdimensional data structures is a duty-cycled slotted Aloha. The uniqueness of the HDMAC is in the way how an HD-structure is mapped onto the slotted time as well as in the way of interpreting collisions as information bearers.

In HDMAC the time for all nodes is synchronized and all nodes have the same notion of the time origin. The nodes may start the transmission at any time as soon as the data to transmit is ready. The transmission starts at the beginning of the coming time slot *without* performing the clear channel assessment procedure.

In HDMAC we enumerate slots modulo the dimension of the HD-vector, the enumeration of slots coincides in all nodes. An HD-structure is transmitted serially. That is a value of "1" on position i in the resulting HD vector means the presence of transmission in time slot i, while the zero-position means absence of the transmission in the corresponding slot. This is illustrated in Figure 2(b).

Importantly, when a communication event occurs the HD-vector starts to be transmitted from the position corresponding to the number of the current time slot and *not* from the beginning of the sequence. This is to allow asynchronous reception. Although the time in HDMAC is synchronized the transmission and the reception events are not. The only requirement is that the listen schedule in nodes is appropriately dimensioned to sufficiently overlap with the ongoing transmission.

Figure 3(a) demonstrates the main operating mode of the proposed MAC protocol. Overall, HDMAC implements a duty-cycled slotted Aloha. The following tunable parameters are defined:

- T_{slot} is the duration of a single slot.
- T_{sleep} is the time when the transmitter is not active.
- D_p is the minimum size of a part of an HD-vector which a receiver may perform the decoding operation.
- D_H is the dimension of the HD patterns used to represent compositional structures. The slots are enumerated modulo this number.

The *slot time* T_{slot} is a hardware and implementation specific parameter. For example, if the proposed protocol is to be implemented on AT86RF212 transceiver from Atmel[4]) with an embedded acceleration of the IEEE802.15.4 MAC , the smallest unit to be transmitted is 48 bits, including 32 bits preamble, 8 bits Start Frame Delimiter and another 8 bits for the PHY layer header. On the other hand, standard-neutral platforms as for example a so-called byte-radio transceivers (e.g. ADF7020 from Analog Devices[5]) allows sending only 8 bits in addition to the PHY layer preamble. A smaller granularity can be natively implemented on SDR-based platforms. We also see a great potential of implementing the proposed scheme on top of low-power UWB pulse radio [10]. We, however, do not further elaborate practical aspects as they expose mainly engineering challenges with several existing solutions.

The *sleep time* parameter T_{sleep} is application- and deployment-specific. It is intended to allow enabling duty cycling operation in the presence of intermittently connected receivers or in deployments with large number of foreseen parallel transmissions of heterogeneous compositional structures. The minimum value for this parameter is zero. In this case the transmitter sends the entire HD pattern of size D_H without interruptions. The value of zero is envisioned for scenarios where the receiver (base station) is connected to an external source of energy or in general has a large energy budget.

Parameters D_P and T_{sleep} are configured depending on requirements on duty-cycling. The problem of dimensioning the listen-transmit schedule with various optimization objectives is addressed in several previous works in the domain of duty-cycled protocols for wireless sensor networks (e.g. [6,9]) and is not further discussed here.

The Mathematics of Collisions. Handling simultaneous transmission from multiple nodes, i.e. collisions, is a unique feature of HDMAC. From the above discussion on hardware considerations recall that the radio transceiver should report the state of the bit-level erasure in the presence of energy in the channel to HDMAC. Since at any moment the index of the transmitted position is the same for all nodes, simultaneous transmissions will be interpreted by the receiver as the bit-wise OR-sum of the collided vectors as illustrated in Figure 3(b). More formally, for m involved in the collisions vectors $C_{RX} = C_1 \oplus C_2 \oplus \ldots \oplus C_m$. For further discussion we reasonably suppose that all nodes in the network use the *same* compositional structure of role-filler pairs. This is equivalent to agreeing upon a common format of packet headers in the traditional communication networks.

---

[4] AT86RF212 data sheet. Online. Available:
   http://www.atmel.com/Images/doc8168.pdf
[5] ADF7020 data sheet. Online. Available:
   http://www.analog.com/static/
   imported-files/data_sheets/ADF7020.pdf

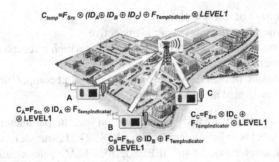

Fig. 4. An example of extracting new knowledge from "collisions. Here several parallel transmissions would allow deciding on possible false positives in the reported sensor readings.

Suppose sensors are configured to report quantized temperature level. Assume also that in this deployment compositional structure $C_{Temp} = F_{Src} \otimes V_{nodesID} \oplus F_{TempIndicator} \otimes V_{TempLevel}$ is used. Here F_{Src} and $F_{TempIndicator}$ are the HD vectors representing the roles "Source address" and "Temperature indicator" correspondingly. HD-vectors-fillers $V_{nodesID}$ and $V_{TempLevel}$ represent the particular values for the temperature levels and nodes' addresses correspondingly. Figure 4 shows the HD-vector at the receiver when all nodes transmit the signal simultaneously. While in the conventional packet based architectures this situation would lead to the loss of all involved in the collision transmissions, in the proposed architecture the receiver node not only will receive all three, but also after one transmission round may conclude that a certain temperature level is reported by more than one node. This becomes possible due to the similarity of the OR-sum to each sum member as discussed in Section 2.

Obviously, not all simultaneous transmission would lead to appearance of the new contextual information. An example of the network functionality above should however serve as an illustration of the distinct property of distributed representation of data structure based on hyper-dimensional vectors to enable cognitive in-network processing.

4   Performance Properties of HDMAC

Benchmarking the performance of the proposed technique to the performance of the traditional communication protocols is not trivial. Firstly, the difficulties come from the fundamental differences in the representation of information and operations on HD-data. There is, for example, no simple way to define the throughput metric in conventional terms, since it only makes sense when representing scalar values as in the case of traditional computing schemes. In this work we, however, do not discuss the topic of throughput definition further, since our optimization objective is reliability of information transfer subject to minimizing the delay. Also we do not discuss the performance of the architecture in the energy domain. Although energy consumption is an important performance characteristics in the consider applications it is less critical than the reliability and the delay characteristics.

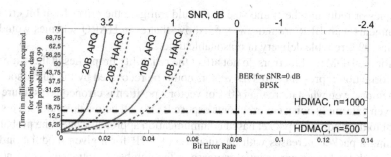

Fig. 5. Delay properties of HDMAC compared to the traditional packet based random access MAC with and without enabled forward error correction for different values of the frame size

For demonstration purposes we performed MATLAB simulations of HDMAC, ARQ packet-based MAC and HARQ packet-based MAC (with enabled forward error correction). To enable fair comparison with the traditional schemes, we simulate the case when HDMAC would be implemented on top of an out-of-the-shelf byte or packet-radio platforms. The slot length was set to the minimum possible 40 bits (in time).

We simulate the PHY-layer bit-level erasure detection procedure (see the discussion above) producing detection errors conservatively set to 50%. We experimented with HD-vectors of dimensions 500 and 1000.

In the case of packet based MACs we experimented with different sizes of transmitted frames (20 and 10 bytes). In all simulations BPSK modulation was used at the physical layer. We varied the SNR characteristic introduced by the radio channel from +4 dB (excellent channel conditions) to - 2.5 dB (extremely noisy channel), resulting in range of bit error rates for the selected modulation technique from 0 to 0.14. Without a loss of generality we assume that rate of slot errors in the case of HDMAC *is equal* to the bit error rate for BPSK[6].

Reliability vs. Delay. We define the delay metric as the time it takes to deliver an information with *99% probability*. Figure 5 demonstrates the delay properties of our approach compared to the traditional way of packet-based transmission. In operating environments with good and excellent channel conditions (i.e. with $SNR_{max} \geq +3.4dB \pm 0.1dB$) the traditional packet switching communication system would be sufficient to achieve the 99% reliability within predictably low delay bounds. In highly noisy environments, the delay for achieving the same and even lower reliability characteristics goes out of control as figure indicates. This is because at high BER values the probability of loosing a frame naturally increases. By using forward-error-correction

---

[6] A more fair way of comparison would be of course to implement HDMAC with slot length being equal to the duration of one bit transmission at the physical layer. In simulations, this would result in better delay properties for HDMAC while preserving the the same reliability figures. In order to enable this kind of benchmarking one should account for very fine grained details of implementation. In particular the quality of the bit-level erasure detection function plays an important role. The work in this direction is ongoing and will be reported elsewhere.

techniques or reducing the frame size one could mitigate the effect from bit errors in environments with BER around $4\% \pm \delta$. Above that even HARQ schemes would fail achieving 99% reliable delivery in reasonable time.

As for the HDMAC bit errors do not affect the reliability properties in the same way. The information represented by HD-vectors could be recovered by the autoassociative item memory even when more than 40% of vector's position is erroneous (as figure suggests even extremely noisy environments expose BER well below this value). This is in contrast to the traditional packet based communication approach where, the probability of loosing a packet increases with the increase of SNR for a given modulation technique, which lead to an exponential increase in the number of retransmissions needed to achieve 99% delivery probability.

5 Discussion

Security Considerations. In the envisioned application domain for the proposed architecture, security of communications is of the same importance as reliability and timing. The proposed architecture can be natively extended to implement encryption in the most native way. One important property of XOR multiplication of two HD-vectors is that the result is a vector *dissimilar, random* to all vectors included in the product [5]. Suppose that HD-pattern u is distributed in a secure way between all nodes at the bootstrap phase. Suppose also that nodes generate new version of u periodically and synchronously with a period equals to the duration of transmission of the entire HD-vector. By modifying (2) as $S = u \otimes (F_1 \otimes V_1 \oplus F_2 \otimes V_2 \oplus \ldots \oplus F_n \otimes V_n)$ the scheme implements Vernam encryption also known as a one-time pad. This feature requires, however further thorough investigation.

How Large Is "Hyper"?. Traditionally, in the context of cognitive computing the considered binary spatter codes have truly large dimensionalities - in the order of tens of thousands. This is not surprising taking into account the distance distributions in representation spaces of that dimensionalities. The key property here is the concentration of the most of the representation space around half-unit distance from an arbitrary chosen HD-vector. This is in contrast to the situation on lower dimensionalities, where most of the space is concentrated in a wider range of distances. For the purposes of communicating signals and events in mission critical applications presented in this article, the usage of very high dimensionalities is not practical with respect to the delay and energy efficiency characteristics. The proposed way of decreasing the dimensionality is to manually choose mutually dissimilar random HD-sequences of lower dimensions. The problem of finding mutually dissimilar HD-vectors is similar to finding good pseudonoise sequences (PN sequences) as for example in [1]. Our preliminary investigations in this area show feasibility of implementing the described approach using vectors with dimensions of few hundreds, which is a promising indication for applicability of the MAC in low-power communication context.

Complexity. The complexity of the proposed communication approach is deployment and implementation specific. On the encoding side it mainly depends on the number of role-filler bindings included in the compositional structure. The complexity of the decoder depends on dimension of the used HD-vectors and the implementation of the item memory search algorithms. As part of the ongoing activities, a decoder adapted to a 16-bits microcontroller was implemented indicating applicability of the proposed architecture to low-end computing architectures. This work along with the formal analysis of the computation complexity is, however, a topic for another report.

6   Conclusions

In this article we presented a packet less medium access control approach for reliable communications of status and control information in extremely noisy environments. The main motivating factor for this work is an inability of the traditional packet based communications to provide assurances on reliable delivery. To this end we presented an adapted framework of binary spatter codes and the theory of distributed representation of structured information for transmitting loss-sensitive control information. We also demonstrated the main performance benefits of the proposed approach. We conclude that the adapted framework has a great potential in the domains of industrial automation and mission critical deployments of wireless sensor and actuator networks in general.

References

1. Gold, R.: Optimal binary sequences for spread spectrum multiplexing (corresp.). IEEE Transactions on Information Theory 13(4), 619–621 (1967)
2. Kanerva, P.: Sparse distributed memory. Bradford Books (1988)
3. Kanerva, P.: A family of binary spatter codes. In: ICANN 1995: International Conference on Artificial Neural Networks, pp. 517–522 (1995)
4. Kanerva, P.: Binary Spatter-Coding of Ordered K-tuples. In: Vorbrüggen, J.C., von Seelen, W., Sendhoff, B. (eds.) ICANN 1996. LNCS, vol. 1112, pp. 869–873. Springer, Heidelberg (1996)
5. Kanerva, P.: Hyperdimensional computing: An introduction to computing in distributed representation with high-dimensional random vectors. Cognitive Computation 1(2), 139–159 (2003)
6. Lin, P., Qiao, C., Wang, X.: Medium access control with a dynamic duty cycle for sensor networks. In: 2004 IEEE Wireless Communications and Networking Conference, WCNC, vol. 3, pp. 1534–1539 (March 2004)
7. Plate, T.: A common framework for distributed representation schemes for compositional structure. In: Connectionist Systems for Knowledge Representation and Deduction, pp. 15–34 (1997)
8. Rappaport, T.: Wireless Communications: Principles and Practice, 2nd edn. Prentice Hall PTR, Upper Saddle River (2001)
9. Suarez, P., Renmarker, C.-G., Dunkels, A., Voigt, T.: Increasing zigbee network lifetime with x-mac. In: REALWSN 2008: Proceedings of the Workshop on Real-World Wireless Sensor Networks, pp. 26–30. ACM, New York (2008)
10. Tang, W., Culurciello, E.: A low-power high-speed ultra-wideband pulse radio transmission system. IEEE Transactions on Biomedical Circuits and Systems 3(5), 286–292 (2009)

Addressing Slot Drift in Decentralized Collision Free Access Schemes for WLANs

Wunan Gong and David Malone

Hamilton Institute, NUI Maynooth, Ireland

Abstract. Decentralized Collision-Free Access (DCFA) schemes are an appealing family of MAC mechanisms in WLANs due to their good system throughput and decentralized nature. In this paper we consider the problem of *slot drift* for these schemes and provide evidence that DCFA can be vulnerable to such problems. We propose two schemes to enhance DCFA in this regard: Global View Synchronization (GVS) and Smart Collision Free (SCF). GVS aims to provide slot indexing, which helps stations correct their counters after drift. SCF accelerates the convergence process to the collision-free state for WLANs, and so reduces the impact of drift. Simulation results show that both GVS and SCF improve the system performance in the presence of slot drift.

Keywords: WLAN, Decentralization, collision-free MACs, slot drift.

1 Introduction

In a WLAN, multiple stations typically share a common physical channel. The Medium Access Control (MAC) plays an important role in arbitrating accesses to the shared medium and thus influences channel utilization and system throughput. CSMA/CA (Carrier Sense Multiple Access/Collision Avoidance) and TDMA (Time Division Multiple Access) are two popular MAC mechanisms. In CSMA/CA, a station that has a packet to send has to keep sensing the wireless channel. If the channel is sensed idle, the station is permitted to start the transmission. Otherwise, it needs to defer the transmission, often using random backoff, and tries to transmit at some later time. In TDMA, time is divided into fixed or variable slots and different stations transmit in different slots. These two mechanisms have inherent drawbacks. In the former, collisions are inevitable, and in the latter, there are signaling overheads and tight synchronization requirements.

In recent years, new schemes that overcome the drawbacks and retain the good aspects of both TDMA and CSMA/CA have been proposed. Examples include L-BEB [2], ZC [3] and L-MAC [4]. In these schemes, time is divided into MAC slots and a fixed number of consecutive slots are grouped into a cycle. There are three types of MAC slots: idle slots, busy slots with successful transmissions, and busy slots with collisions. Note that these schemes allow stations to have slots of variable duration determined, say, by carrier sense.

B. Bellalta et al. (Eds.): MACOM 2012, LNCS 7642, pp. 146–157, 2012.
© Springer-Verlag Berlin Heidelberg 2012

In these schemes each station has a decentralized reservation process to reserve an exclusive slot for transmission in a cycle. This process is used when the station just joins the network or when it loses its reservation. The reservation process stops and the system converges to a collision free state when all the active stations in the system have reserved an exclusive slot. We name such schemes *Decentralized Collision Free Access* (DCFA) schemes. Obviously, for convergence to a collision-free state, the cycle length should be no smaller than the number of stations in the WLAN system.

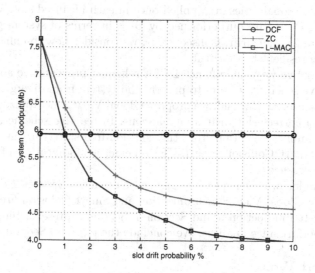

Fig. 1. The impact of Slot Drifts on ZC and L-MAC, compared with DCF

DCFAs are appealing since collision-free access can outperform 802.11's DCF. However, the collision-free state is vulnerable to perturbations caused by channel noise, new entrants and, as we will show, slot drift. In DCFAs, transmission failures are used as a signal that reservation has failed. Thus, channel errors or new stations introducing collisions may move the system from a collision-free state. However, previous studies have shown low rates of new entrants and channel noise do not significantly degrade DCFA's performance [4].

For DCFA, it is important that each station has an accurate view of where it is in the transmission cycle, and ideally all the stations in the system should follow the slot evolution process synchronously and accurately. If a station miscounts the slots we refer to this as *slot drift*, which may lead to collisions. In practice, we have identified a number of possible reasons for slot drift: 1) station sensing errors, where carrier sense leads to the misidentification of slots; 2) clock errors, where the number of slots during an idle period is miscounted; 3) hardware/software miscounting, caused by implementation details.

As examples of these: 1) the 802.11 standard [1] requires only a 90% CCA detection for 9us slots; 2) for slots involving sleep and wakeup, clock drift/synchronisation problems are well-known in sensor networks; 3) the Open-FWWF firmware for Broadcom WiFi cards highlights the challenges in correctly implementing slot counting in software.

Perhaps surprisingly, the impact of slot drift may be significant. For example, Fig. 1 shows a simulation of DCF, ZC and L-MAC in the presence of slot drift. In these simulations we adopt a simple model of slot drift: we simulate a probability p of slot drift by introducing a probability of $p/2$ that each station leads the idealized slot count by one slot and a $p/2$ that it lags the idealized slot count by one slot. These probabilities are applied once in each idealized slot. We observe that ZC and L-MAC are outperformed by DCF in terms of system goodput in the presence of 2% slot drift. Consequently, we consider how to enhance DCFA schemes to be resilient to slot drift.

We consider two ways to enhance DCFA schemes: preventative and reactive. In preventative schemes, we aim to prevent the system from diverging from the collision-free state. To this end, we propose Global View Synchronization (GVS) which aims to correct slot drift as it happens. In reactive schemes, we try to alleviate the impact deviation from the collision-free state. In this regard, we propose the Smart Collision Free (SCF) scheme, a modification of ZC which speeds reconvergence.

The remainder of this paper is organized as follows: Section 2 outlines the related works; Global View Synchronization and Smart Collision Free are separately elaborated in Section 3 and Section 4; Section 5 presents the simulation results and performance analysis; We conclude the paper in Section 6.

2   Related Work

The MAC used in 802.11 networks [1] is called DCF. A core strategy used by DCF is BEB (Binary Exponential Backoff). With DCF, each station needs to uniformly choose a backoff counter C_b in the range [0, w-1] after a packet transmission. The value w is called the contention window and it has a minimum value CW_{min} and a maximum value CW_{max}. For each MAC slot, the backoff counter decrements by one and stations start packet transmission when it reaches 0. If the last transmission was successful, w is set to CW_{min}, otherwise stations double the contention window w unless it is CW_{max}.

L-BEB[2] is an evolution of BEB. L-BEB differs from BEB in one respect: stations choose a fixed backoff counter after a successful transmission. The value of the fixed backoff counter is shared by all stations, and is the cycle length for the network. If the number of stations is less than the cycle length, L-BEB will settle into a collision-free state after an initial period.

In ZC[3], each station notes all the idle slots in a cycle. In the case of a transmission collision, the station uniformly selects one slot for transmission in its next cycle from a candidate slot set which is composed of all the idle slots and the colliding slot. In the case of successful transmission in a certain slot, stations continue to use that slot in the subsequent cycles for future transmissions.

L-MAC[4] adapts the idea of a self-managed distributed channel selection algorithm from [5] and keeps updating selection probability for each slot in a cycle. In the case of a successful transmission, the stations persist with the same slot in the following cycle and the selection probability for that slot is set to 1.

While the details of the reservation phase of each of these protocols is different, when the system converges to collision-free state, the behaviors are the same. These protocols can be implemented with a backoff counter, and do not require stations to agree on slot labeling (or indexing). However, we can still think of then as each station trying to reserve an exclusive slot in a cycle.

3   Global View Synchronization

GVS is our preventative scheme to enhance DCFA. We aim to correct slot drift on stations before their next transmissions, so the potential collisions can be avoided and the collision-free state can thus be maintained. The basic idea of GVS is that it provides a slot labeling benchmark to facilitate the correction of slot drift on stations.

As mentioned, stations in the DCFA system do not require consensus on the slot labeling. Once a station has reserved a slot, it will periodically send packets (if it has packet to send) and the period is the cycle length. We refer to the slot labeling as a station's *view*. For example, in Fig. 2 there are three stations with different views of the MAC slots. The cycle length is 4 and the highlighted square shows their reserved slots. Station 1 and station 2 both reserved slot 2, but these two "slot 2"s are different due to their staggered labelings.

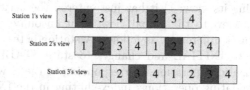

Fig. 2. Slot views of three stations

Now, we aim to make all the stations have the same view and regard this *global view* as a benchmark. If a station encounters slot drift, their slot labeling will change, and so can be corrected to match the global view. Since slot drift happen from time to time, hence it is not possible to make all the stations always have the same view. Consequently, the global view will be the stations in the view held by some large subset of stations.

Consequently, GVS deals with two issues: 1) maintaining a global view; 2) correcting drift on stations. The station performing GVS must share the common cycle length, C, with the network and maintain some slot view information which it includes in its transmissions. Stations can then observe if their view is not aligned with other stations. The details of GVS are:

1. Each station announces its view in each transmitted packet. A station's view can be represented by its current slot index, so here the announced view is actually a slot index. The announcement only uses several bits in each transmitted packet.

2. Each station maintains a "view set", S. The elements in the set correspond to views successfully sent by this station and successfully received from other stations. Since slot indices are always evolving, the stored elements indicate the difference between the current slot index of the station and the successfully sent/received slot indices:

$$d_v = (\text{index}_{rx|tx} - \text{index}_{curr} + C) \mod C.$$

3. If a station successfully transmits or receives a view, it checks whether there is already an element in its view set S which corresponds to that view (i.e. if it has seen that view before). If so, is assumes multiple stations share this view, and so it changes its view to match and then replaces S with the empty set. Otherwise it inserts that view into the set. Thus, seeing two stations with the same view results in a synchronization of views.

   if $d_v \in S$ **then**
   $\qquad$ $\text{index}_{curr} \leftarrow \text{index}_{rx|tx}$, $\ S \leftarrow \emptyset$
   else
   $\qquad$ $S \leftarrow S \cup \{d_v\}$
   end if

4. A station may have noted some important slot indices which may correspond to idle slots, reserved slot, etc. These noted slot indices need to be updated when a station updates its view. However, there are two reasons why a station may be updating its view: 1) it has just entered the network and needs to synchronize its view to the global view; 2) it encounters a slot drift. We handle these cases differently, as follows. A station enters a WLAN system with state set to INITIAL and changes to state STABLE after the first view synchronization operation. Corresponding to these, we have two types of slot index updating operations: index-shifting in the INITIAL state and index-keeping in the STABLE state. From the INITIAL state, index-shifting updates stored indices by the difference in the labeling,

$$\text{index}_{new} = (\text{index}_{old} + d_v) \mod C,$$

   because we believe the stored slots were not labeled using the global view, and so the labels must be updated. Index-keeping does not relabel the slots, because we believe the slots were correctly labeled while synchronized to the global view, and the stations view has only recently drifted.

This scheme results in all stations converging to the same view in two cycles, providing there is no slot drift or collisions in these cycles. To see this, note that if two stations share a view, then the first two to announce the same view results in the network being synchronized. If no two stations share a view, then the first station to transmit in the second cycle will synchronize the network.

There is a possibility that two stations encounter slot drift and then announce their views consecutively, or that collisions or errors may result in delays in synchronization. We evaluate GVS's practical capability to maintain a global view and improving performance in the presence of slot drift in Section 5.

4   Smart Collision Free

In this section, we look at another way to improving the performance of a collision-free MAC. We aim to speed its reconvergence to a collision-free state after being perturbed. In particular, we propose the Smart Collision Free algorithm, which is an evolution of ZC. Recall that in ZC, the candidate slot set for a station in the reservation process is composed of all the idle slots and the colliding slot in a cycle. In the case that all the stations have the same view, all the colliding stations share the same idle slot sets in a cycle for selection. If we divide the idle slots in a cycle into multiple subsets and let colliding stations with different colliding slots select from different idle slot subsets, the collision probability can be reduced and thus convergence speed can be improved. This is the basic idea of SCF: to partition the idle slot set.

The details of one possible implementation of SCF is shown in Alg.1. In each cycle, each station notes all the idle slot indices and the number of collisions. If its transmission collides, the station notes the colliding slot index and the relative position of the colliding slot in all the colliding slots in the cycle. At the end of a cycle[1], the station selects the next reserved slot by partitioning the idle slots among groups of colliding stations. Note that since stations do the selection at the end of a cycle, when a station just enters a WLAN, it should monitor the channel for one cycle.

Fig. 3 shows an example of SCF. There are 10 slots in a cycle, and in this cycle there are 3 colliding slots and 5 idle slots. Ideally, we aim to evenly split the idle slot sets into 3 subsets. However, as 5 can't be divided by 3, we allocate the first 3 idle slots (the slots are ordered by time) to 3 subsets and leave 2 slots which will be selected in a probabilistic way. Now, consider a station which collides in the second slot (the block labeled "Colliding slot" and numbered with 2). At the end of the cycle, the station needs to select the next reserved slot. Since the colliding slot position is 2, it selects the second idle slot. Meanwhile, with probability of 2/3, the station needs to select one slot from idle slots 4 and 5 and the selection is random. Then the station puts the selected slots and the colliding slot into the candidate slot set. Finally, the station randomly select one slot as the next reserved slot from the candidate slot set.

Note, the SCF scheme assumes that all the stations have the same view, so they regard the idle slots as having the same order. In the situation where not all views are synchronized, we will see that SCF may still help to speed reconvergence to a collision free schedule.

---

[1] The discussion of ZC [3] notes that decisions can be made either at the end of a cycle or after a collision, and there is no significant difference in convergence speed.

Algorithm 1. The SCF Algorithm

$slot_{curr}$: The currently reserved slot for this station.
$slot_n$: The new reserved slot for this station.
$slot_c$: The slot this station collided on.
CS : The candidate slot set.
IS : The idle slot set, with IS_i the ith idle slot.
n_c: Number of slots with a collision in the last cycle.
i_c : This station collided in the i_c^{th} slot with a collision in the last cycle.
for each cycle **do**
    if no transmission **then**
        if $slot_{curr} \in IS$ **then**
            $slot_n \leftarrow slot_{curr}$
        else
            $slot_n \leftarrow$ random element of IS
        end if
    else if successful transmission **then**
        $slot_n \leftarrow slot_{curr}$
    else   failed transmission
        Find q, r so that $|IS| = qn_c + r$.
        $CS \leftarrow \{slot_c, IS_{(i_c-1)q+1}, \ldots IS_{(i_c)q}\}$
        with probability r/n_c **do**
            $CS \leftarrow CS \cup \{$ random slot from $IS_{qn_c+1}, \ldots IS_{qn_c+r}\}$
        done
    end if
end for

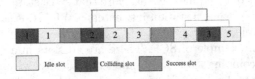

Fig. 3. An illustrative example of SCF

5   Performance Evaluation

We conducted a simulation study of GVS and SCF. We compare ZC (the scheme with the fastest convergence of the DCFA schemes) to SCF in the presence of slot drift. We also assess GVS's ability to help ZC and SCF maintain a synchronized view, and the resulting impact on performance.

As we are focused on performance of slot allocation, we work with a slot-level simulator written in C++. For the simulation, unless otherwise noted, all stations are transmitting UDP traffic with payload 1500 bytes and a PHY rate of 11 Mbps. The same channel is shared by all stations and there are no hidden node problems. For simulation of DCF, we adopted the typical 802.11b protocol and the parameters are shown in Table 1. All the results are obtained over repeated simulations.

Table 1. Network Parameters in 802.11b

Parameters	Durations(μs)
Slot time, σ	20
Propagation delay, δ	1
$CW_{min} = 32\sigma$	640
$CW_{max} = 1024\sigma$	20480
DIFS	50
SIFS	10
PLCP Header@1Mbps	192
MAC Header+CRC, 28 Bytes@11Mbps	20
UDP+IP+Payload, 1500 Bytes@11Mbps	747.6
ACK, 14 Bytes@2Mbps	56
ACK_TIMEOUT	12

5.1   Global View Synchronization

Fig. 4 shows how effective GVS is in helping stations to hold the same view when either ZC or SCF is used. We fix a cycle length of $C = 16$ and consider a system with $N = 16$ or $N = 8$ stations (Fig. 4(a) and (b) respectively). Stations always have a packet to send. We apply slot drift probability of 2%, 5% and 10% to all stations and consider the number of stations holding the majority view when GVS is applied. Specifically, let M_i be the size of the largest group of stations with a consistent slot labeling for slot i, then Fig. 4 shows the CDF of the values of M_i.

As expected, GVS performs better with smaller slot drift probability. For example, considering Fig. 4(a), we see that for 10% of the time the majority group is smaller than 14 stations for 2% slot drift, but smaller than 10 stations for

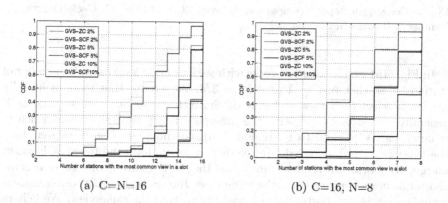

(a) C=N=16   (b) C=16, N=8

Fig. 4. CDF of number of stations with the majority view. C: Cycle Length, N: Number of stations in the system.

5% and smaller than just 6 stations if the slot drift is 10%. However, overall GVS does a reasonable job at keeping views consistent. We also see that GVS works marginally better with SCF than ZC. We attribute this to quicker convergence times. Though we have not shown results here, it is also possible to apply GVS to L-MAC and L-BEB.

5.2   Convergence Speed in Ideal Conditions

In the presence of slot drift, the collision-free state is volatile. To evaluate convergence speed, we consider a scenario with no slot drift where all stations start the slot reservation process at the same time and begin with no reserved slot. This would be representative of a situation when all stations power up at the same time. The convergence speed is measured by the average number of elapsed slots before convergence to a collision-free state.

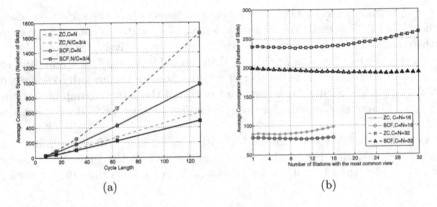

(a)   (b)

Fig. 5. Convergence speed comparison between ZC and SCF. C: Cycle Length, N: Number of stations in the system.

In Fig. 5(a) we consider networks with various cycle lengths and a number of stations N so that $N/C = 1$ or $N/C = 3/4$. We assume that stations initially randomly select their view and may not have the same view. We see that SCF generally outperforms ZC, with the difference being most significant when C is large and N is close to C. In Fig. 5(b), the number of stations that hold the "majority view" is varied. We see that under similar conditions, SCF shows marginally shorter convergence times, and that SCF's convergence times become shorter as more stations share the same view. Interestingly, ZC's convergence is actually marginally shorter when larger groups hold the same view. We believe this is because in our implementation of ZC, stations choose new slots at the end of the cycle, and there is a small advantage to stations making a decision at different times.

5.3   Long-term System Goodput

We now compare the long-term system goodput of five schemes: DCF, SCF, ZC, SCF with GVS and ZC with GVS. We fix the cycle length at $C = 16$ to allow comparison with DCF. The slot drift probability is varied from 0% to 10% and stations always have packets to send. Fig. 6 shows the goodput for $N = 16$ and $N = 8$. We see that GVS can considerably improve the system goodput in the presence of slot drift, and SCF schemes are generally better than ZC schemes. When GVS-SCF is adopted, the system can sustain up to 6% slot drift probability $N = 16$ and up to 10% with $N = 8$ before the system goodput drops below that of DCF.

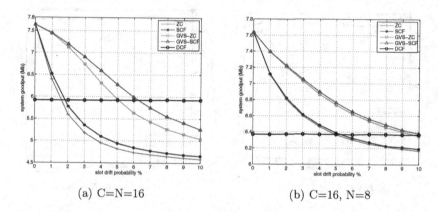

(a) C=N=16   (b) C=16, N=8

Fig. 6. System goodput vs slot drift probability, comparison of 5 schemes

It is noticeable that there seem to be no changes in system goodput for DCF when slot drift probability increases. We can explain this using Bianchi's model [7]. We know the system goodput depends on the collision probability p and transmission probabilities τ in the network. Both with and without slot drift, the network can be modeled using

$$p = 1 - (1 - \tau)^{(N-1)} \tag{1}$$

From the work of Kumar et al [6], we have

$$\tau = \frac{1 + p + p^2 + \ldots + p^K}{b_0 + pb_1 + p^2b_2 + \ldots + p^Kb_K} \tag{2}$$

where, K is the retry limit and b_k is the average number of backoff slots chosen at the kth attempt. To find p and τ we search for solutions of Eq.1 and Eq.2. We note that slot drift only has a direct impact on the b_k. Since we have modeled slot drift as a mean-zero random walk which is added to the backoff process, we expect that the b_k will be unchanged, and so DCF's performance will be unchanged by this sort of slot drift.

5.4   Fairness

Fairness is another concern in WLANs. When slot drift is applied to all stations in a system, the system remains homogeneous and fairness is not an issue. However, slot drift probabilities on different stations may vary. In this section we consider similar networks to those in Section 5.3 but here slot drift is applied to only one station. Fig. 7(a) and (b) shows Jain's index[8][9], and reveals that system fairness can be improved with Global View Synchronization. Our results indicate the station with drift can usually correct it before its transmission and thus avoid collisions.

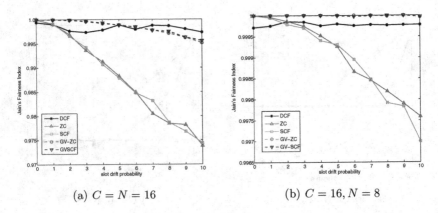

(a) $C = N = 16$ (b) $C = 16, N = 8$

Fig. 7. System fairness vs slot drift probability, comparison of 5 access schemes

6   Conclusion

In this paper, we investigated the potential problem of slot drift in Decentralized Collision Free Access systems and proposed two schemes, GVS and SCF, to deal with slot drift problems. We have shown how GVS can help the system maintain a common slot indexing and use it as a benchmark for correcting slot drift on stations. SCF speeds up the convergence process to the collision-free state and thus alleviates the impacts due to system's deviation from the collision-free state.

Acknowledgment. The authors were supported by SFI grant 08/SRC/I1403 (FAME) and 07/SK/I1216a.

References

1. IEEE 802.11: Wireless LAN Medium Access Control (MAC) and Physical Layer (PHY) Specifications

2. Barcelo, J., Bellalta, B., et al.: Learning-BEB: Avoiding Collisions in WLAN. In: 14th Eunice Open European Summer School (2008)
3. Lee, J., Walrand, J.: Design and analysis of an asynchronous zero collision MAC protocol. Tech. Rep. UCB/EECS-2007-63 (May 2007)
4. Fang, M., Malone, D., Duffy, K.R., Leith, D.J.: Decentralised learning MACs for collision-free access in WLANs. Springer Wireless Networks (May 2012)
5. Leith, D.J., Clifford, P.: A self-managed distributed channel selection algorithm for WLANs. In: Proceedings of International Symposium on Modeling and Optimization in Mobile, Ad Hoc and Wireless Networks, pp. 1–9 (2006)
6. Kumar, A., Altman, E., Miorandi, D., Goyal, M.: New insights from a fixed-point analysis of single cell IEEE 802.11 WLANs. IEEE/ACM Transaction on Networking 15(3) (June 2007)
7. Bianchi, G.: Performance analysis of the IEEE 802.11 distributed coordination function. IEEE JSAC 18(3), 535–547 (2000)
8. Jain, R., Chiu, D., Hawe, W.: A quantitative measure of fairness and discrimination for resource allocation in shared computer systems. Arxiv preprint cs/9809099 (1998)
9. Koksal, C.E., Kassab, H., Balakrishnan, H.: An analysis of short-term fairness in wireless media access protocols. In: Proceedings of the 2000 ACM SIGMETRICS International Conference on Measurement and Modeling of Computer Systems, pp. 118–119. ACM, New York (2000)

Exploiting Short MAC Superframe Cycles for Fast Bit Synchronization in IEEE 802.15.4 UWB-IR

Johannes Hund[1], Michael Bahr[1], Christian Schwingenschlögl[1],
Rolf Kraemer[2], and Sonom Olonbayar[2]

[1] Siemens Corporate Technology, Otto-Hahn-Ring 6, Munich, Germany
[2] Institute for high performance microelectronics, Im Technologiepark 25,
Frankfurt/Oder, Germany
{johannes.hund,bahr,chris.schwingenschloegl}@siemens.com,
{kraemer,sonom}@ihp-microelectronics.com

Abstract. Ultra-Wideband Impulse Radio is a promising technology for industrial automation applications due to its inherent multipath robustness and coexistence features. The ultra-wideband impulse radio PHY standardized in IEEE 802.15.4, however, is optimized for low duty cycles and not optimized for real-time communication. Especially the long preambles that are needed for synchronization cause a large overhead that might not be necessary in systems with a high duty cycle. We propose an efficient synchronization scheme, which is a cross-layer improvement and which combines this PHY layer with a MAC layer for wireless real-time communication in low latency deterministic networks based on draft IEEE 802.15.4e. This scheme splits synchronization into a network-wide frame synchronization via a broadcast beacon with a standard preamble and bit-level synchronization using just very short preambles per data frame. To achieve this, we exploit the short communication cycles and the centralized communication flow common in factory automation networks. We present and discuss simulation results of our proposed scheme that verify its higher efficiency.

1   Introduction

Industrial factory automation is a challenging application, especially for wireless networks. Multipath propagation, coexistence with other (wireless) networks, and energy efficiency are just a few examples of issues to tackle under hard realtime constrains in the order of milliseconds.

Ultra-Wideband Impulse Radio (UWB Impulse Radio) offers some inherent features to combat the above mentioned problems, as it allows non-coherent reception using slow-sampling energy detection. The slow sampling rates allow energy-efficient operation, while long integration intervals add robustness against multipath effects. As coexistence and frequency band reuse is the primary idea behind ultra-wideband radio, it is perfectly suited for application areas that are

B. Bellalta et al. (Eds.): MACOM 2012, LNCS 7642, pp. 158–169, 2012.
© Springer-Verlag Berlin Heidelberg 2012

dependent on the coexistence of multiple radio communication systems, such as in factory automation.

There are, however, downsides that require optimization. For non-coherent reception, synchronization with a precision of the integration intervals is needed upon each transmission. This synchronization is usually achieved through long preambles, which increase transmission time tremendously, thus increasing cycle-times. The combination of low cycle-time and high robustness is a vital requirement for the targeted realtime capabilities in the range of milliseconds.

An ultra-wideband impulse radio based PHY has been standardized in [1] by the IEEE 802.15.4a task group. This UWB PHY is optimized for sensor networks. We presented optimizations in [2] for using the IEEE 802.15.4 UWB PHY in industrial automation by increasing robustness and by reducing latencies. Further optimized robustness through cross-layer methods has been presented in [3]. Furthermore, we presented a communication system using the optimized UWB impulse radio PHY and discussed application layer aspects in [4].

In this paper, we present a cross-layer optimization for the system described in [4]. This system uses the UWB PHY of IEEE 802.15.4 together with a low latency MAC layer from draft standard IEEE 802.15.4e [5]. This cross-layer optimization allows it to use shorter preambles for data packets while still providing sufficient synchronization accuracy based on broadcast beacons.

The remainder of the paper is structured as follows: In section 2, we introduce our system definition, the MAC layer for low latency deterministic networks, and the state of the art prior to the improvements of this paper. In section 3, we describe the improvements. In section 4, we introduce a simulator to prove our findings section 5 finally concludes our work and wraps up.

2   State of the Art

The method presented in this paper is an enabling technology for a wireless communication system based on UWB for industrial factory automation. The system aims at usually wire-bound for sensors and actuators (also called S/A-level protocols), such as AS-Interface, and it is based on standards in both the MAC layer and the PHY layer.

2.1   MAC Layer

The draft standard IEEE 802.15.4e [5] specifies MAC extensions for Low Latency Deterministic Networks (LLDNs). The core of these extensions are a new frame type called Low Latency frames (LL-frames) or LLDN frames and a new, flexible superframe structure for low latency applications based on Low Latency frames.

Low Latency frames have a very short MAC header which is only 1 (one) byte long, plus security fields if so configured. This decreases the latency of data transmissions with very small payloads of 1 or 2 bytes enourmously when compared to the IEEE 802.15.4 data frame that has a MAC header of 7 or more bytes length. Information that is usually contained in the IEEE 802.15.4 frames but not in Low Latency frames is distributed during the configuration of the Low Latency Deterministic Network and implicitly contained in the superframe structure.

A Low Latency Deterministic Network (LLDN) is a star network with up to 254 devices connected to an LLDN PAN coordinator. The wireless devices are usually sensors and actuators that have only small data to send, but with a low and deterministic latency. Sensors send their measurements repeatedly with a high frequency to the gateway; they have only a unidirectional data communication from the sensor to the LLDN PAN coordinator (uplink communication). In contrast to this, actuators have a bidirectional data communication with the LLDN PAN coordinator. Actuators send data to the gateway and receive control instructions from the gateway.

The communication in an LLDN is organized in a superframe structure as shown in Figure 1.

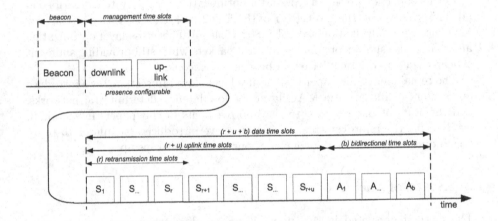

Fig. 1. Structure of LLDN superframe

The LLDN superframe is started by an LL-Beacon. The LL-Beacon contains some basic information about the structure of the superframe.

The LL-beacon is followed by two management time slots, if present. The presence and length of the management time slots is configurable and is indicated in the LL-beacon.

The remaining up to 254 base time slots are for data transmissions. They are structured into uplink time slots, that come first, followed by bidirectional time slots.

Multiple adjacent data time slots can be grouped together to larger time slots. For each data time slot, the media access can be configured to be deterministic and/or contention-based. In dedicated time slots, only the assigned device, the slot owner, is allowed to send its data.

Both, the small MAC overhead in the Low Latency frames and the efficient superframe structure of LLDNs with very precise configuration capabilities facilitate low latencies as required in industrial factory automation. The actual latency depends on the configuration of the Low Latency Deterministic Network, such as number of devices and assignment of time slots, and the used IEEE 802.15.4 physical layer (PHY).

In this paper, we use the IEEE 802.15.4 Ultra-Wideband Impuls Radio (UWB-IR) PHY and optimize it for the goals of and the use with Low Latency Deterministic Networks.

2.2 PHY Layer

The PHY layer is using Ultra-Wideband Impulse Radio (UWB-IR), based on the standard IEEE 802.15.4 [1]. This standard describes a frame structure consisting of a preamble and a data part.

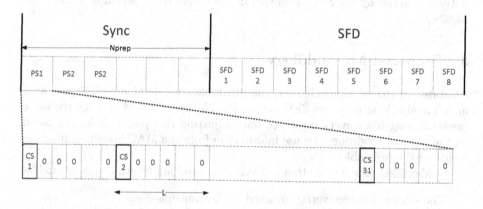

Fig. 2. UWB-IR preamble structure in IEEE 802.15.4 [6]

This paper is focused on the preamble, which is shown in Figure 2. The preamble consists of a synchronization part *SYNC* and a sequence called *Start of Frame Delimiter (SFD)*. Both parts, the SYNC and the SFD, are using one out of six different ternary sequences of 31 code symbols length, called a preamble code $\overrightarrow{C_P}$.

This preamble code $\overrightarrow{C_P}$ is then transformed into a train of pulses which is called the preamble symbol $\overrightarrow{Psym}$. Each code symbol of $\overrightarrow{C_P}$ is modulated into a pulse, where the code symbol '1' is encoded into an in-phase pulse, '-1' into a counter-phase pulse. The code symbol '0' is modulated into a pause. The resulting pulse train is then spread in time Therefore, a pause of a fixed length called the L-spreading is inserted between each code symbol.

The SYNC part of the preamble consists of $N_{Prep} = (16, 64, 1024,$ or $4096)$ repetitions of that preamble symbol. The SFD is a sequence of code 8 symbols

$$\overrightarrow{C_{SFD}} = \{0, +1, 0, -1, +1, 0, 0, +1\}$$

that is multiplied with the preamble symbol.

$$SFD_i = \overrightarrow{C_{SFD}}(i) \cdot \overrightarrow{Psym} \tag{1}$$

$$\overrightarrow{Prea} = \left(\bigsqcup_{n=1}^{N_{prep}} (\overrightarrow{Psym}) \right) \sqcup \overrightarrow{SFD} \tag{2}$$

A complete preamble is therefore between 24 and 4104 preamble symbols long. The base rate denoted in the standard IEEE 802.15.4 uses a reference pulse length of 2 ns and an L-spreading of 15 pulses. Using this base rate the shortest possible preamble length according to the standard is 16 preamble symbol repetitions followed by the SFD, resulting in the length of 24 preamble symbols or 23.808 μs.

3   Proposed Methodology

As stated in the previous chapter, the preamble consists of a SYNC part with an adjustable length and an SFD part of fixed length. Instead of using the same preamble length for every frame, or only adjusting this preamble length based on the channel conditions, we use information from the MAC layer to adjust the length of the preamble.

We identified four factors that influence the minimal length of the preamble:

- The sender and receiver(s) involved in the transmission.
- The time passed since the last transmission between this sender and receiver.
- The quality of local oscillators in both the sender and the receiver.
- The temporal variability of the radio channel.

As mentioned in section 2.1, every communication cycle or superframe is opened by an LL-Beacon, which is sent by the LLDN coordinator or controller. Subsequently, each node in the network waits for its timeslot to either send a frame to the controller (as for sensor nodes), or to send or receive a frame from the controller (as for an actuator node). In all cases the transmission involves the controller, either as sender or receiver. This means that the controller can act as a reference clock. Therefore, the LL-Beacon can be used to synchronize all nodes to the controller, which we call *frame synchronization*.

However, for the reception of a frame, a more precise synchronization than frame synchronization is needed. Such a synchronization is often called *bit synchronization* or *symbol synchronization*. In order to achieve bit or symbol synchronization efficiently, we exploit the short temporal distance between the LL-Beacon transmission and the data transmission within a superframe of a low latency deterministic network. This allows us to use a very short preamble of only one single preamble symbol for bit synchronization of data frames.

Figure 3 depicts an exemplary superframe of an LLDN with two sensors and two actuators using layered synchronization. The standard-conforming long preamble (LP) of the beacon is used to create a network-wide frame and bit synchronization, which is exploited as coarse synchronization for the data frames in order to enable the usage of short preambles (SP).

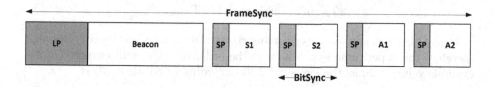

Fig. 3. Superframe using layered synchronization

3.1   Frame Synchronization

To achieve frame synchronization, the LL-Beacon will be sent with a standard preamble as described in section 2.2. Upon reception of a preamble, the receiver determines the end of the SFD sequence. Each node could use this point in time to synchronize to the controller by determining the start of the LL-Beacon frame if the length of the preamble, the guard interval of the MAC layer, and the time of flight are known. However, the time of flight of the signal is dependent on the distance between controller and node. It varies for each node and is usually unknown. Therefore, the node must use the length of the data part (which is given in the PHY header) to determine the end of the beacon frame and synchronize to the controller.

This synchronization is decaying over time. This is due to the quality of the oscillators on both node and controller. The frequency of any oscillator is deviant from the nominal frequency and therefore, each oscillator drifts over time. This so-called clock drift is measured in parts per million (ppm). In the UWB-IR PHY specification [1], a maximum drift of ± 20 ppm is acceptable.

This leads to an estimate of the maximal desynchronization due to clock drift:

$$T_{drift}(t) = (20 \text{ ppm} \cdot 2) \cdot t = 40 \cdot 10^{-6} \cdot t \qquad (3)$$

This is dependent on the time t since the last synchronization between sender and receiver.

For each subsequent base time slot (BTS) $i = 1...N_{BTS}$ for data packets of (temporal) length T_δ,

$$T_{drift}(T_\delta \cdot i) \qquad (4)$$

provides an upper bound for the desynchronization caused by clock drift. This desynchronization denotes the offset between the percieved time of the controller and the percieved time of the node that is associated with the timeslot. Taking the controller's timeframe as reference, this offset causes a deviation of the expected starting point of the transmission.

To counter this deviation, the MAC protocol allocates a guard interval in the length of 11 preamble symbols. Therefore, a deviation of transmission that is smaller than 11 preamble symbols will not harm any other transmission. Consequently, an acceptable frame synchronization is achieved through the LL-Beacon if the number of BTS N_{BTS} satisfies the condition

$$T_{drift}(T_\delta \cdot N_{BTS}) < 11 \cdot T_{Psym} \tag{5}$$

In the targeted applications in industrial control, communication cycles and therefore the superframe size will be in the order of a few milliseconds. For an example value of 2 ms, the expected drift according to equation (3) is

$$T_{drift}(2 \cdot 10^{-3}\text{s}) = 80 \cdot 10^{-9}\text{s} \tag{6}$$

which is far less than 11 preamble symbols, a single preamble symbol in IEEE 802.15.4 UWB-IR has an approximate duration of 1 μs. Therefore, a node's successful synchronization onto the beacon will provide frame synchronization for at least one superframe. Theoretically, the guard interval of 11 preamble symbols will provide frame synchronization for up to 272.8 ms according to equation (3).

However, not only the clock drift affects the difference of timeframes, but also the distance between the nodes. For an unknown spatial distribution, which is the normal case for a wireless network, the time of flight t_{TOF} can be expressed as

$$t_{TOF} = \frac{\phi_d}{c} \tag{7}$$

where c is the speed of light and ϕ_d is a random variable, that is limited by the controller's range d_{max}. Therefore the maximum t_{TOF} for an exemplaray network with a 10 m range (as used in factory cells) can be expressed as

$$t_{TOF} = \pm\frac{d_{max}}{c} = \pm\frac{10\text{ m}}{3 \cdot 10^8\text{m/s}} = \pm 33.3 \cdot 10^{-9}\text{s} \tag{8}$$

This offset is again negligible compared to the guard interval and therefore does not harm frame synchronization.

The resulting granularity Δt of the frame synchronization for the i-th BTS is

$$\Delta t = 0 \pm t_{TOF} \pm T_{drift}(T_\delta \cdot i) \tag{9}$$

Using above examples for an application with 10 m wireless range using superframes of 2 ms results to a maximum deviation of $\pm$113.3 ns.

This frame synchronization granularity could be improved further by overhearing data packets of other nodes to track synchronization, which will not be regarded in this paper.

3.2   Bit Synchronization

In order to receive a frame successfully, frame synchronization is not sufficient. A finer synchronization must be established, which we call bit synchronization. The necessary granularity of this bit synchronization is dependent on the length of the receiver's integration interval, relative to the burst length, as well as the multipath conditions.

The bit synchronization in the UWB PHY specification of IEEE 802.15.4 requires a coarse synchronization and a defined starting point. For a standard-conforming preamble the starting point is the SFD sequence, after a sequence of repetitions of the preamble symbol, which provide the coarse synchronization.

In order to use a shorter preamble, we reduce the preamble to a single preamble symbol, which will function as a singular starting point. For coarse synchronization, we exploit the aforementioned frame synchronization.

This compact preamble reduces the duration T_δ of a single base time slot, which reduces the superframe size and therefore the minimal communication cycle time. Shorter preambles therefore also reduce the granularity of the frame sync Δt.

3.3   Receiver Implementation

In an actual receiver implementation, several adaptations need to be made. Obviously, the preamble detector must be configured whether to receive a standard preamble or a compact preamble.

This preamble detector consists of a cross-correlation filter. The output of this filter is a measure for the similarity of the received signal $\overrightarrow{BB_{ADC}}$ and the expected preamble code $\overrightarrow{C_P}$.

$$Cval_n = \sum_{i=1}^{31} \overrightarrow{C_P}(i) \cdot \overrightarrow{BB_{ADC}}(i+n) \tag{10}$$

A maximum of this correlation values $Cval$ denotes a detected preamble symbol. To receive a standard preamble, the output needs to be compared (again, using a correlation filter) to the SFD sequence.

$$SCval_n = \sum_{i=1}^{8} \overrightarrow{C_{SFD}}(i) \cdot \overrightarrow{Cval}(i+n) \tag{11}$$

If this correlation value $SCval$ shows a maximum, then the SFD is found and the data part of this frame starts. For a compact preamble, a maximum of the first filter $\overrightarrow{Cval}$ (equation (10)) denotes the start of the data part.

The preamble detector needs to be reconfigured by the MAC layer in the beacon timeslot of each superframe, so it will use the filter $\overrightarrow{SCval}$ (equation (11)) for the beacon and the filter $\overrightarrow{Cval}$ (equation (10)) for data frames with a compact preamble.

$$\overrightarrow{CV} = \begin{cases} \overrightarrow{SCval} & \text{if beacon} \\ \overrightarrow{Cval} & \text{if data} \end{cases}$$

Generally, the maxima of correlation values are indicated by a sign change from positive to negative in the first derivate of the stream of correlation values $\overrightarrow{CV'}$.

However, thermal noise, interference, and other influences add noise to the received signal. This noise can cause the correlation values to resemble the sought signal. However, these maxima will always be lower than the actual maximum caused by a preamble signal.

Therefore,, a method to find a global maximum, that is implementable in hardware, must be applied. The simplest method is to use a threshold h and only accept maxima above this threshold as starting points. This threshold h must be high enough to cancel out the noise, but low enough to detect the maximum caused by the preamble.

$$\overrightarrow{CV}_{max} = CV_n \in \overrightarrow{CV} | CV_n < CV_{n-1} \vee CV_{n-1} \geq h \tag{12}$$

When assuming a stable noise level for the duration of one superframe, which is acceptable for the duration of a few milliseconds, this threshold can be assumed stable for transmission between the same sender and receiver in one superframe. That means, an actuator can store the value of the maximum $SCval_{max}$ of the $\overrightarrow{SCval}$ filter (equation (11)) during the reception of the beacon and use this value to calculate the threshold h for the data frame.

For sensor nodes, however, the transmissions are in the opposite direction. But since a deterministic MAC layer is used, the controller benefits from the configured a priori information which node will send in each transmission and can store and track a threshold for each individual node.

4   Simulation Results

We simulated the sending and reception of packets with short preambles for different artificial frame synchronization errors and different thresholds. The Saleh-Vanezuela models from the IEEE Task Group 802.15.4a [7, 8, 9] were used as channel, more precisely the industrial LOS channel (No. 7). The simulated receiver is an energy-detection receiver using a sampling interval of 16 ns, in other words an ADC clock of 62 MHz.

4.1   Synchronization Offset Caused by Faulty Frame Synchronization

Figure 4 shows the results of a simulation that was done to measure the effect of an offset to the estimated starting point, e.g. faulty frame synchronization, on the reception of the compact preambles. Therefore, packets with a single preamble symbol were received with an random offset on the receiver's wake-up time. This means that the receiver may wake up too early or too late. If a receiver wakes up too late, only part of the preamble is acquired and the correlation value is

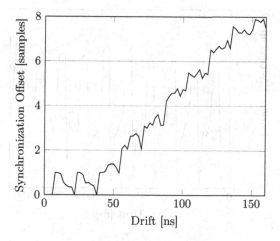

Fig. 4. Deviation of synchronization caused by clock decay

reduced, which decreases the quality of the bit synchronization. If the receiver wakes up too late to acquire the preamble at all, the packet is lost. A premature wake-up will cause the receiver to acquire noise while listening for the preamble. Decreasing frame synchronization increases the time a receiver receives random noise, thus decreasing bit synchronization quality and increasing the chance of a false positive.

An energy detection receiver as described in section 3.3 was used to synchronize onto the preamble without using a threshold. This preamble was prepended with a random offset representing the error in frame synchronization. The deviation of the resulting bit synchronization from the perfect synchronization was measured and is depicted on the y axis in the scale of samples, as the digital baseband receiver works on discrete samples of 16 ns.

It can be seen that the errors in synchronization increase with the offset. An increased offset in bit synchronization will lead to a higher error probability as a premature false positive recognition will lead to an misinterpretation of the sent signal, which is demodulated in time domain. This can be compensated to a certain extend, as shown in [2] for single packets and for repetitive transmissions in [4]. However, a larger offset in bit synchronization will statistically increase packet loss, especially in noisy environments.

4.2 Compensation through Threshold

Figure 5 shows the results of a simulation of the same experiment as in Figure 4, but uses a fixed threshold of 100. This threshold denotes a minimum correlation value for synchronization. In an actual implementation, this value is set through the reception of the beacon. This threshold suppresses most false positives caused by noise and therefore drastically reduces the offset in bit synchronization.

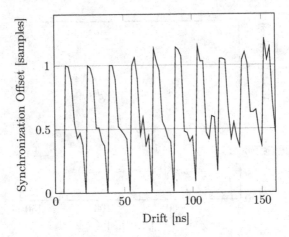

Fig. 5. Compensated offsets through threshold

It can be seen that the offset in synchronization is at most in the order of 1 sample. A target system can easily supersample bursts even with low ADC frequencies and use compensation mechanisms as presented in [2]. These measures reduce synchronization errors for the data packets to a negligible scale compared to other error sources.

5   Conclusion

We presented a novel cross-layer improvement that shortens communication cycle times for wireless industrial networks by using a layered synchronization for UWB-IR. It relies on the Low Latency Deterministic Network specification of draft standard IEEE 802.15.4e [5] and a modified UWB PHY layer of IEEE 802.15.4 [1].

The MAC layer provides an LL-Beacon that is used to establish a network-wide coarse synchronization, which allows using shorter preambles for the transmission of data frames in the superframe. Since industrial control networks use short periodic superframes to achieve short communication cycles, the clock decay between the beacon transmission and the remaining data transmissions is short enough to benefit from the coarse presynchronization. As all transmissions in IEEE 802.15.4e LLDN's are directed either to or from the controller, the preamble can be replaced by a single preamble symbol. Cycle times below 2 ms can be achieved for 32 network nodes.

An example system using this method is shown in [4], it achieves cycle times below 2 ms with 32 nodes while still using slow sampling non-coherent reception. This allows energy-efficient and robust wireless networks for industrial control applications with a hard real-time barrier below 17 ms.

References

[1] IEEE Std 802.15.4-2011: Standard for Local and metropolitan area networks - Part 15.4: Low-Rate Wireless Personal Area Networks (LR-WPANs), IEEE Std. (September 2011)

[2] Hund, J., Olonbayar, S., Schwingenschlögl, C., Kraemer, R.: Evaluation and Optimization of Robustness in the IEEE 802.15.4a Standard. In: IEEE International Conference on Ultra-Wideband, ICUWB 2010, Nanjing, China (March 2010)

[3] Hund, J., Kraemer, R., Schwingenschlögl, C.: Extension of IEEE 802.15.4a to improve Resilience for Wireless Automation using Soft-bit Combination. In: 2011 IEEE International Conference on Ultra-Wideband (ICUWB 2011), Bologna, Italy (September 2011)

[4] Hund, J., Bahr, M., Schwingenschlögl, C., Kraemer, R.: Drahtlose Adaption von AS-Interface durch Optimierung von IEEE 802.15.4a. In: Procedeedings of 2. Jahreskolloquium Kommunikation in der Automation (KommA 2011), Magdeburg, Germany (September 2011)

[5] IEEE Draft Standard 802.15.4e: Low Rate Wireless Personal Area Networks (LR-WPANs) Amendment to the MAC sub-layer, IEEE Std., Rev. D8 (October 2011)

[6] Flury, M.: Interference Robustness and Security of Impulse-Radio Ultra-Wide Band Networks. Docteur ès sciences, ecole polytechnique federale de lausanne (2010)

[7] Cassioli, D., Win, M.Z., Molisch, A.F.: The ultra-wide bandwidth indoor channel: from statistical model to simulations. IEEE J. Sel. Areas Commun. 20(6), 1247–1257 (2002)

[8] Molisch, A.F., Foerster, J.R., Pendergrass, M.: Channel Models for Ultrawideband Personal Area Networks. IEEE Wireless Communications 10(6), 14–21 (2003)

[9] Molisch, A.F., Balakrishnan, K., Cassioli, D., Chong, C.-C., Emami, S., Fort, A., Karedal, J., Kunisch, J., Schantz, H., Schuster, U., Siwiak, K.: IEEE 802.15.4a channel model - final report. IEEE P802.15 document 15-04-0662-04 (2004)

Intra-cluster Contention Resolution
in Wireless Sensor Networks

Vahid Salmani and Pai H. Chou

Center for Embedded Computer Systems
University of California, Irvine, CA, USA
{vsalmani,phchou}@uci.edu

Abstract. Contention resolution plays an important role in designing medium access control protocols. Owing to technical constraints of wireless sensor networks, the task of efficiently resolving contention poses several challenges. In clustered wireless sensor networks, many-to-one communication is the dominant pattern, which is also applicable to the star topology. This paper surveys the state-of-the-art contention-resolution techniques designed for this communication pattern with a discussion of their features and limitations. We closely examine several contention-resolution schemes, including our recently proposed BSTCR algorithm, with performance evaluation in multiple aspects.

Keywords: Contention resolution, clustered WSNs, many-to-one communication, performance evaluation.

1 Introduction

In many wireless sensing applications, sensors are grouped around specific points of interest. As a result, a wireless sensor network (WSN) can be deployed as a cluster or set of clusters. In multi-hop networks, the data-collection tree structure is naturally formed as a hierarchy of clusters, and the standard tree-routing protocols can be easily applied to the cluster-tree topology.

In a clustered WSN, nodes in a neighborhood are organized into a cluster, with one node designated as the *cluster head* (CH). A CH is typically a resource-sufficient sensor node that aggregates local traffic and forwards it to the upstream clusters or to the base station. Sensor nodes within the same cluster can communicate directly with their CH; however, they do not communicate among themselves, other than during the initial setup or the CH election phase. Therefore, the dominant communication pattern within a clustered WSN is *many-to-one*.

A medium access control (MAC) protocol coordinates the access to the wireless medium among multiple nodes. The ability to efficiently arbitrate the channel is directly affected by the efficiency of the employed contention-resolution scheme. Designing MAC protocols of WSNs, particularly the contention-resolution part thereof, is a challenging task due to the several technical limitations exposed to these networks. We review some of those challenges in Section 2.

B. Bellalta et al. (Eds.): MACOM 2012, LNCS 7642, pp. 170–181, 2012.

In Section 3, we survey the state-of-the-art contention-resolution schemes designed or suited for (but not necessarily limited to) clustered WSNs and the many-to-one communication pattern. Our focus is on *intra-cluster* contention resolution, and thus schemes such as BCCR [1] that deal with multiple contention regions and work across multiple hops are outside the scope of this work. To the best of our knowledge, this is the first survey and critical review specifically on contention resolution in WSNs.

To study the performance of some of the surveyed methods, we developed a simulator whose details are presented in Section 4. We perform a stand-alone simulation-based comparison of some recently proposed contention-resolution approaches in Section 4.1. In Section 4.2, we present a comprehensive performance evaluation of two recently proposed receiver-initiated contention resolution schemes, namely BSTCR [2] and Strawman [3] within a receiver-initiated MAC protocol. Finally, Section 5 concludes this paper.

2   WSN Constraints

Contention resolution has been a fundamental research topic for decades. However, many of the schemes designed for wired or even wireless networks are simply not applicable to WSNs due to the peculiarities of these networks. In this section, we review some of the challenges mandated by limitations and characteristics of WSNs.

a) **Limited battery life:** The scarcest resource of a wireless sensor node is its battery power. As a result, a node often cannot afford to continuously monitor the medium due to energy constraints. To address this problem, duty cycling and back-off techniques have been proposed, which may increase the risk of collisions and wasted idle slots, respectively.

b) **Transceiver delays:** In low-power transceivers, a signal cannot be detected if it has not been present for a minimum duration. For example, in case of the CC2420 transceiver, the signal is not detected if transmission is started within the last 128 μs. Moreover, a node is not able to sense the channel during the RX/TX switching phase.

c) **Imperfect collision detection:** A wireless transmitter is not able to detect collision if it cannot transmit and listen to the channel at the same time, which is often the case with most transceivers for WSNs. Receiver-side collision detection (RCD) is possible but can be prone to false positives in the presence of external interference. Moreover, the accuracy of some RCD techniques decreases as the number of colliding nodes increases [4]. Also, it is often not possible to explicitly identify the transmitters involved in the collision.

d) **Control packet overhead:** In WSNs, the packet size is typically small (less than a few hundred bytes) and even the smallest control packets can constitute large overhead. For instance, reference [5] reports that an RTS-CTS-DATA-ACK handshake series in transmitting a packet can amount to

40% overhead on their platform. Therefore, a contention-resolution scheme should minimize the number of control packets.

e) **Dynamic nature:** The number of nodes in a WSN or the number of contenders for the medium may not be known or fixed. Nodes can join or leave for several reasons. In event-driven networks, the number of contenders triggered on each event may vary. With the exception of underwater acoustic sensor networks [6], obtaining the number of contenders often requires explicitly querying the nodes in the WSN.

3   Contention Resolution Survey

Contention resolution is an integral component of contention-based and hybrid MAC protocols. Contention-based MAC protocols can be classified into sender-initiated and receiver-initiated. In the *sender-initiated* class, the most common contention-resolution technique is back-off-based collision avoidance. In *receiver-initiated* protocols, the receiver initiates a data transfer by transmitting a probe, also known as *ready-to-receive* packet.

3.1   Sender-Initiated

Optimal CSMA. CSMA/p^* [7] is non-persistent CSMA and uses the optimal non-uniform distribution p^* in determining the channel access probability. It minimizes the collision probability if the number of contenders is known but delivers suboptimal performance otherwise.

To relax the above constraint, the same authors use a truncated geometric distribution that approximates p^* with a fixed-size contention window in Sift [8]. Designed for event-driven networks, Sift takes advantage of the *spatially correlated contention* property of sensor networks and yields low latency for a subset of reports triggered by the same event while suppressing the rest.

Although Sift achieves high success probability for channel access and reduced collision probability, it assumes a minimum number of contenders are present at all times. Moreover, it might not perform well either in case of highly random data arrivals to a node or with those applications requiring timely packet delivery by the contenders.

Backoff Preamble Sequential (BPS). A limitation of low-power transceivers is a node's inability to detect an ongoing transmission if the signal has not been present for the minimum duration. To cope with the above problem, BP-MAC [9] uses a back-off preamble (BP) of a random length (and depending on a retry counter), which functions as both medium reservation and busy signals. Having sent the BP, the node senses the medium and starts transmitting data if it finds the channel to be idle. Otherwise, the node backs off before it senses the channel again.

This approach does not guarantee a successful resolution, as two or more nodes may choose the same BP duration and start data transmission simultaneously. To alleviate this problem, BPS-MAC [10] uses a sequence of short consecutive BPs to reduce the contention step by step. To improve the probability of success, nodes use a truncated geometric distribution for determining the BP length and start data transmission only after a predefined number of BPs have been successfully transmitted.

A problem with this approach is that it requires manually tuning several parameters for the best performance, and finding the best configuration may be non-trivial. Moreover, contention resolution is not guaranteed to be successful due to the same BP length chosen by more than one node, although the latter issue could be resolved using ACK messages.

Fast Collision Resolution (FCR). The main shortcoming of back-off-based collision avoidance approaches comes from collisions and wasted idle slots due to back-offs. When the number of contenders increases, many of them back off with small contention windows. Therefore, with high probability, many of the retransmission attempts will collide again in the future. Designed for wireless LANs, FCR [11] is aimed at solving the above issues by redistributing the back-off timers for all contenders to speed-up the collision resolution.

With FCR, all active nodes monitor the medium. When a deferring node detects a predefined number of consecutive idle slots, it reduces the back-off timer exponentially. On the other hand, when the start of a new busy period is detected, the node increases the contention window size and picks a new random back-off time to give the backlogged packets more time to finish.

A drawback of FCR is that it requires active nodes to constantly perform carrier sensing as long as they have data to send. Since monitoring the channel at all times is impractical in WSNs due to high energy consumption, the combination of FCR with coordinated sleeping has been proposed [12]. This adaptation comes at the cost of performance. While the algorithm performs better than IEEE 802.11 under low duty cycles, its performance under high contention has not been explored.

3.2 Receiver-Initiated

Synchronized, Shared Contention Window (SSCW). Designed for periodic data collection applications, SSCW [13] uses a fixed-size contention window based on the number of nodes. To prevent a single node from colliding more than once in the same window, SSCW uses non-overlapping contention windows. Packets collided in a given window are rescheduled at random times in the next window starting immediately after the current window.

A data-collection cycle starts with a synchronization beacon from the CH. Having successfully transmitted its packet, each node returns to RF silence and waits for the next beacon. In case of a failure, inferred by the absence of an ACK message, the node attempts a retransmission in the next window, and this process repeats until all nodes have delivered their data packet.

Authors of [14] proposed successively decreasing contention windows to improve the efficiency of SSCW based on the observation that the number of contenders will be decreasing in subsequent windows. For this purpose, the remaining nodes recalculate the windows size based on the number of current (i.e., last collided) contenders.

The main limitation of SSCW is that the number of contenders must be known in advance. Therefore, it cannot be used as a general contention-resolution technique. Moreover, it assumes that nodes always have data to transmit and that all nodes contend for the medium. Finally, the contender must keep track of the number of ACK packets from the CH, which requires a node to be listening at all times.

Flip-MAC. Designed for dense networks, Flip-MAC [15] resolves contention in two steps. First, it employs a contention-reduction technique based on a series of probe-acknowledgment cycles. In each cycle, contenders set their ID to one of two possible addresses randomly, and those that guessed correctly send simultaneous acknowledgment while the rest are out of competition. As long as the CH detects a carrier, it keeps sending the probe, which results in a logarithmic complexity.

The second step starts when a probe goes unacknowledged, at which point the CH broadcasts a confirmation message indicating that the contention level has dropped to a manageable level. Subsequently, the few remaining contenders use a common resolution technique such as back-off-based CSMA to select the winner.

Flip-MAC implements the probes as hardware-generated acknowledgments on the CC2420 transceiver to improve the efficiency. However, this feature may not be supported by all transceivers and thus have to be implemented as separate transmissions. Another consideration with Flip-MAC is that finding the best time to stop the CSMA/back-off scheme to start a new round of contention reduction may not be trivial. The receiver may have to wait for an interval of RF silence of at least as long as the maximum contention window to make sure that no node is backing off, which wastes the bandwidth.

Strawman. Designed for receiver-initiated radio duty-cycling protocols, Strawman [16] handles contention based on the analogy of drawing straws. The process starts with a probe message from the CH. The simultaneous senders then draw a random number for the length of the request signal, and the channel access is granted to the sender of the longest straw. The CH announces the winner via a decision message containing the length of the longest request signal.

A downside of Strawman is that it fails if two or more contenders share the longest request. Its enhanced version, called E-Strawman [3], solves this issue by resolving collisions in steps while keeping the average lengths of straws as short as possible. By announcing the length of the longest received signal, the receiver authorizes only the colliding winners of the current round to participate in the next round until a successful transmission occurs. The length of straw is determined randomly using a truncated decreasing geometric distribution. In a recent paper [17], Strawman uses multiple channels to further reduce contention.

For the best performance, this approach needs to be provided with the number of contenders that will be used in the first round to calculate the maximum straw length. From the second round on, the estimated average of colliding winners is used to recalculate the maximum request length, because the number of actual winners is unknown. Another consideration is that the maximum straw length cannot scale with the number of contenders as the payload length is limited. Moreover, the maximum signal length may not be estimated with 100% accuracy [17].

Tree-Splitting. The tree-splitting [18] technique is a recursive operation that randomly divides a group of colliding packets into two subgroups, each of which is subject to the same procedure as the original group. Nodes that are not involved in the collision wait until the collision is resolved. Therefore, no newly arrived packet is transmitted while the resolution of a collision is in progress. With this approach, the number of contenders or colliding nodes does not have to be known.

A combination of tree-splitting and binary exponential back-off (BEB) schemes is used in [19] to speed up the resolution in case of a small number of contenders and to maintain compatibility with random-based MAC protocols in (low-data-rate) heterogeneous networks. Having divided the collision domain and in case of a collision, inferred by the absence of an ACK, the contenders switch to the back-off-based resolution scheme. Once the first packet is successfully delivered, the CH resumes the splitting operation for the current domain. Although this approach shortens the resolution for low-data-rate networks, it may lead to a prolonged resolution under higher levels of contention.

The Binary Search Tree Collision Resolution (BSTCR) [1] scheme [2] uses a variant of tree-splitting where the collision domain is represented as a "range" of node IDs. Instead of randomly dividing the contenders, the collision domain is split exactly in half, which results in a deterministic contention resolution. Moreover, it is possible for new contenders to access the medium during the resolution process. To the best of our knowledge, BSTCR is the only non-negotiation-based technique, i.e., it does not incorporate any random component. For that reason, it is the only deterministic method in terms of the required steps for resolving contention.

3.3 Summary

Contention-resolution techniques can be classified into received-initiated and sender-initiated. Receiver-initiated schemes are triggered by probe messages from the CH and usually rely on collision detection at the CH. On the other hand, sender-initiated methods are usually back-off based. Either class may leverage

---

[1] Although we originally used the acronym BTCR, BSTCR is more accurate because we treat the collision domain as an *ordered* list of *unique* node IDs.

Table 1. Summary of the surveyed contention resolution schemes

	CSMA/p^*	Sift	BP-MAC	BPS-MAC	FCR	SSCW	Adaptive SSCW	Flip-MAC	Strawman	E-Strawman	Tree-Split+BEB	BSTCR
Reference number	[7]	[8]	[9]	[10]	[12]	[13]	[14]	[15]	[16]	[3]	[19]	[2]
Receiver initiated						✔	✔	✔	✔	✔	✔	✔
Knowledge of the number of contenders	✔					✔	✔					
Carrier sensing on contenders	✔	✔	✔	✔	✔			✔			✔	
Back-off based	✔	✔	✔	✔	✔	✔	✔	✔			✔	
Receiver-side collision detection based								✔	✔	✔	✔	✔
Preamble based			✔	✔					✔	✔		
ACK messages required		✔				✔	✔				✔	

preambles of random length in combination with back-off or RCD methods. The most common component of contention resolution is carrier sensing, which is used in all surveyed methods except SSCW. In receiver-side collision resolution, the CH performs carrier sensing to accomplish the RCD operation. ACK messages are mandatory in some cases, but can help the resolution operation in general. Table 1 compares the surveyed approaches from different aspects.

4   Performance Evaluation

Since conducting real experiments is costly and time-consuming, especially with a large number of nodes, we essentially use simulations for performance evaluation. We have developed a simulator [2] in Java, which runs at symbol-period-level granularity to conduct our evaluations in a more controlled environment than existing simulators can provide. The standard models of the existing network simulators such as ns-2 or OPNET assume that a transceiver does not need any time to sense the channel or to switch between TX and RX modes [10]. The widely used TOSSIM simulator fixes this issue, but it simulates only nodes running TinyOS [20].

We have simulated the Telos platform, which incorporates a TI CC2420 radio transceiver. CC2420 is popular and is used by the majority of the surveyed techniques in Section 3. Moreover, the timings of CC2420 has been widely studied and well understood. We have taken the timer values such as RX/TX switching,

---

[2] Source code is available at
http://newport.eecs.uci.edu/~vsalmani/download/mac_sim.tar.gz

CCA sampling, radio on/off transition, etc., from the data sheet [3]. Other processing times such as RX/TX buffering times are also taken into account using the measurements presented in [21]. The physical layer is defined according to the IEEE 802.15.4 standard. In addition, we have implemented the automatic acknowledgment feature of the CC2420 radio transceiver.

The rest of this section is dedicated to evaluation of some of the surveyed methods, which will be fulfilled in two parts. First, we perform a stand-alone and abstract comparison to see how the algorithms perform regardless of the underlying MAC protocol. Next, we assess the performance of the compared algorithms in the context of a light-weight MAC protocol in a more realistic scenario.

4.1 Stand-Alone Evaluation

We select the evaluation candidates among the surveyed approaches in Section 3.2 because the majority of the recently proposed contention-resolution schemes have been receiver-initiated. Moreover, the presented results in this section will be complementary to our previous experiments in [2]. We choose Flip-MAC [15], (Enhanced) Strawman [3], and BSTCR [2] for further analysis. Because they are general-purpose and fairly robust approaches, they can be used as the contention-based component of the majority of MAC protocols and wireless-sensing applications. Since the selected algorithms are based on receiver-side collision detection, we assume that the CH can successfully detect all collisions. Also, we assume perfect straw length estimation on the CH as the best case for Strawman.

In this section, we compare the three approaches as independent and stand-alone modules. In this scenario, each contender successfully transmits an "ADD" message to the CH and then quits the competition. In case of Flip-MAC and Strawman, new rounds are started immediately after completion of the current round until all contenders successfully transmit their message. We simulated a cluster composed of 5 to 105 sensor nodes and a CH. The experiment was repeated 100 times, and the results were averaged out.

Fig. 1a shows the *total resolution time*, i.e., the time that the last contender takes to deliver its "ADD" packet. The completion time grows linearly with the number of contenders for all three algorithms. However, BSTCR outperforms the others, because unlike Strawman, it reduces the contention in half, and unlike Flip-MAC, it keeps splitting until one contender is left. The reason for Flip-MAC's longer time is that in each round, it has to start splitting for *all* remaining contenders, whereas BSTCR does not split the same collision domain more than once but just backtracks to the already reduced contention for subsequent splitting. Moreover, Flip-MAC has to wait for an interval of RF silence before starting the next round (see Section 3.2).

We define *control message exchange rate* as the total number of exchanged control packets divided by the total number of contenders. In other words, this parameter shows how many messages are required on average for each contender

---

[3] CC2420 data sheet – 2.4 GHz IEEE 802.15. 4/ZigBee-ready RF Transceiver:
   http://www.ti.com/lit/ds/symlink/cc2420.pdf

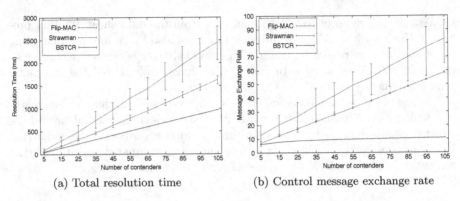

(a) Total resolution time   (b) Control message exchange rate

Fig. 1. Total resolution time (a) and control message exchange rate (b) as functions of number of contenders

prior to being granted access to the medium. As depicted in Fig. 1b, BSTCR is far superior to others, because the number of exchanged messages it requires is logarithmically proportional to the number of contenders, whereas in Flip-MAC and Strawman, the message overhead scales linearly. As a result, BSTCR would impose much less overhead on the MAC protocol.

Scalability has been a challenge in MAC design. Contention resolution as a key component of any hybrid MAC can greatly influence the overall scalability of the protocol. It can be inferred from Fig. 1 that BSTCR is better-suited for handling larger scales and in particular can lead to better scalability in terms of the overhead imposed by control packets.

It is worth mentioning that completion times of Flip-MAC and Strawman fluctuate across different runs, because they incorporate a random component. In contrast, BSTCR is deterministic and always demonstrates the same performance. The determinism of BSTCR makes it more suitable for applications with real-time constraints.

4.2   Holistic Evaluation

Based on the results from the previous section, we decided to continue the evaluations with BSTCR and Strawman only. In [17], Strawman and Sift were compared as the contention-based component of the RI-MAC [22] protocol, and the results indicated the superiority of Strawman. In this section, we evaluate BSTCR and Strawman as the contention-based component of a lightweight hybrid MAC protocol.

A hybrid MAC protocol is usually composed of schedule-based and contention-based parts. Contention resolution is used as the contention-based component. We choose Bin-MAC [2] to serve as the MAC protocol. Bin-MAC is a receiver-initiated protocol and belongs to the scheduled-contention category. It works in a round-robin style and supports duty cycling, which makes it a good match for Strawman. BSTCR is the default contention resolution scheme for Bin-MAC. Bin-MAC represents each slot as a range of node IDs. In case of a collision, the

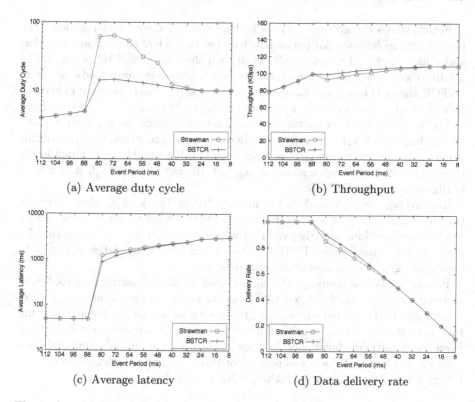

Fig. 2. Average duty cycle (a), throughput (b), average latency (c), and data delivery rate (d) as functions of number of contenders

contention-resolution method is triggered and the colliding nodes can acquire their own time slot. A distinguishing feature of Bin-MAC is that it retains the results of the already resolved contention across rounds and deals with only newly occurring contention.

In our implementation of Strawman on Bin-MAC, when a collision occurs in a time slot, we repeatedly run Strawman round by round and keep track of the winners. Once all collisions are resolved, the winners list is sorted and the time slot is split so that each contender acquires its own time slot.

In our simulations, we model a cluster composed of 20 sensor nodes and a CH. Simulation time is 2×10^7 symbol periods. We vary the event period from 112 ms to 8 ms to evaluate the performance under very low to very high contention. Each event is assumed to require 10 successful transmissions (1100 bytes) to be reported completely. We assume the data buffer on each sensor node to be 2 KB.

In WSNs, the *duty cycle* and communication-related energy consumption are directly related. Contention resolution has an impact on duty cycling, because the contenders cannot keep their usual sleep/wake-up schedule while they are involved in the resolution process. Duty cycle is defined as the percentage of time the radio is on, including the time the radio is sending, receiving, or listening. These three modes of operation consume roughly the same energy [21].

Fig. 2a shows the average duty cycle. Under very low and very high load, the two algorithms have similar performance due to the lack of contention. Note that under high loads, all nodes acquire their own slot and Bin-MAC performs like a fully reservation-based round-robin protocol. Under medium loads, however, BSTCR shows better performance, because it resolves the contention faster and thus the nodes can switch back to duty cycling earlier compared to Strawman.

Fig. 2b shows the average throughput. Under low loads, both algorithms utilize the bandwidth as much as possible. In overloaded conditions, both algorithms reach the maximum throughput as a pure round robin can. Under medium loads, both algorithms experience some throughput degradation, though it is almost negligible in case of BSTCR.

The average latency is depicted in Fig. 2c. As the load reaches a certain threshold and collisions start to happen at event period 80 ms, the contention resolution-algorithms are triggered and we see a sudden increase in average latency in reporting events. BSTCR shows a slightly better latency, but both algorithms gradually converge in performance.

Finally, we define *delivery ratio* as the number of successfully reported messages to the total number of generated messages. Fig. 2d shows the observed delivery ratio. BSTCR's performance degrades with an almost fixed slope, meaning that it is able to deliver nearly as many messages as a pure round robin can. However, Strawman shows slightly worse performance under medium loads. We refer the reader to [2] for a comparison of Bin-MAC, which utilizes BSTCR as the contention mechanism, with three other protocols.

5   Conclusions

Contention resolution has been a challenge to medium access control protocol designers. We provide reasons why MAC design is even more challenging in WSNs. We present a survey of the state-of-the-art techniques for resolving many-to-one contention in clustered WSNs. We review the categorization, essential components, use-cases, and pros and cons of the surveyed methods.

Using extensive simulations, some of the recently proposed approaches of contention resolution is evaluated. To assess the algorithms more comprehensively, we break the evaluation process into the stand-alone and holistic (i.e., part of a MAC) steps. More specifically, our evaluation is focused on Strawman and BSTCR techniques. The results show the superiority of BSTCR, as it resolves contention faster while requiring less control-packet exchange. It also leads to better scalability and determinism.

References

1. Yuan, Z., Xue, C., Wang, L., Chen, Y., Sun, W., Shu, L.: A backoff copying scheme for contention resolution in wireless sensor networks. In: ACM WINTECH, pp. 81–82 (2009)
2. Salmani, V., Chou, P.H.: Bin-MAC: A hybrid MAC for ultra-compact wireless sensor nodes. In: IEEE DCOSS, pp. 158–165 (2012)

3. Ghadimi, E., Soldati, P., Osterlind, F., Zhang, H., Johansson, M.: Hidden terminal-aware contention resolution with an optimal distribution. In: IEEE MASS, pp. 182–191 (2011)
4. Demirbas, M., Soysal, O., Hussain, M.: A singlehop collaborative feedback primitive for wireless sensor networks. In: IEEE INFOCOM, pp. 126–130 (2008)
5. Woo, A., Culler, D.E.: A transmission control scheme for media access in sensor networks. In: ACM MobiCom, pp. 221–235 (2001)
6. Syed, A.A., Heidemann, J.: Contention analysis of MAC protocols that count. In: ACM WUWNet, pp. 2:1–2:8 (2010)
7. Tay, Y.C., Jamieson, K., Balakrishnan, H.: Collision-minimizing CSMA and its applications to wireless sensor networks. IEEE Journal on Selected Areas in Communications 22(6), 1048–1057 (2004)
8. Jamieson, K., Balakrishnan, H., Tay, Y.C.: Sift: A MAC Protocol for Event-Driven Wireless Sensor Networks. In: Römer, K., Karl, H., Mattern, F. (eds.) EWSN 2006. LNCS, vol. 3868, pp. 260–275. Springer, Heidelberg (2006)
9. Klein, A., Klaue, J., Schalk, J.: BP-MAC: A high reliable backoff preamble MAC protocol for wireless sensor networks. Electronic Journal of Structural Engineering (EJSE), 35–45 (December 2009)
10. Klein, A.: BPS-MAC: Backoff Preamble Based MAC Protocol with Sequential Contention Resolution. In: Sacchi, C., Bellalta, B., Vinel, A., Schlegel, C., Granelli, F., Zhang, Y. (eds.) MACOM 2011. LNCS, vol. 6886, pp. 39–50. Springer, Heidelberg (2011)
11. Kwon, Y., Fang, Y., Latchman, H.: Design of MAC protocols with fast collision resolution for wireless local area networks. IEEE Transactions on Wireless Communications 3(3), 793–807 (2004)
12. Kwon, Y.: Fast Collision Resolution MAC with Coordinated Sleeping for WSNs. In: Shen, H.T., Li, J., Li, M., Ni, J., Wang, W. (eds.) APWeb Workshops 2006. LNCS, vol. 3842, pp. 368–372. Springer, Heidelberg (2006)
13. Tian, Q., Coyle, E.J.: A MAC-layer retransmission algorithm designed for the physical-layer characteristics of clustered sensor networks. IEEE Transactions on Wireless Communications 5(11), 3153–3164 (2006)
14. Haque, A., Murshed, M., Ali, M.: Efficient contention resolution in MAC protocol for periodic data collection in WSNs. In: ACM IWCMC, pp. 437–441 (2010)
15. Carlson, D., Terzis, A.: Flip-MAC: A density-adaptive contention-reduction protocol for efficient any-to-one communication. In: IEEE DCOSS, pp. 1–8 (2011)
16. Österlind, F., Wirström, N., Tsiftes, N., Finne, N., Voigt, T., Dunkels, A.: Strawman: making sudden traffic surges graceful in low-power wireless networks. In: ACM HotEmNets, pp. 14:1–14:5 (2010)
17. Österlind, F., Mottola, L., Voigt, T., Tsiftes, N., Dunkels, A.: Strawman: resolving collisions in bursty low-power wireless networks. In: ACM IPSN, pp. 161–172 (2012)
18. Janssen, A.J.E.M., de Jong, M.J.M.: Analysis of contention tree algorithms. IEEE Transactions on Information Theory 46(6), 2163–2172 (2000)
19. Kim, D.S., Kanury, S.R.: Collision reduction for heterogeneous wireless sensor networks. In: ICACT, pp. 464–469. IEEE Press (2010)
20. Eriksson, J., Österlind, F., Finne, N., Tsiftes, N., Dunkels, A., Voigt, T., Sauter, R., Marrón, P.J.: Cooja/mspsim: interoperability testing for wireless sensor networks. In: Simutools, ICST, pp. 27:1–27:7 (2009)
21. Suriyachai, P., Roedig, U., Scott, A.: Implementation of a MAC protocol for QoS support in wireless sensor networks. In: IEEE PerCom, pp. 1–6 (2009)
22. Sun, Y., Gurewitz, O., Johnson, D.B.: RI-MAC: a receiver-initiated asynchronous duty cycle MAC protocol for dynamic traffic loads in wireless sensor networks. In: ACM SenSys, pp. 1–14 (2008)

Author Index